3

The NORFOLK
ALMANAC
of DISASTERS

For the heroes of Norfolk

The NORFOLK ALMANAC of DISASTERS

Pamela Brooks

breedon **books**
PUBLISHING

First published in Great Britain in 2007 by

The Breedon Books Publishing Company Limited

Breedon House, 3 The Parker Centre, Derby, DE21 4SZ.

ISBN   978-1-85983-560-9

Printed and bound by Antony Rowe Ltd. Chippenham, Wiltshire.

CONTENTS

Introduction 6

January 8
February 30
March 47
April 61
May 71
June 81
July 96
August 109
September 129
October 146
November 160
December 177

Bibliography 190

Introduction

The idea for this book came to me some years ago, when I was working on *Norwich: Stories of a City*. I found the sheer heroism of the people involved in the rescues of the 1912 floods and the fires and World War Two really inspiring, and that inspiration grew stronger when I delved more deeply into the history of Norwich with *Norwich: Street by Street*.

When I started to research the rescues over the county as a whole, there was one theme that came out time and time again. The emergency services and lifeboat crews involved in the rescues all had the same modest attitude: 'I'm not a hero: I was just doing my job.' The same was true of bystanders who'd gone in to help; their view was that 'anyone would have done the same'. This, for me, is the true spirit of Norfolk – and makes me very, very proud to be from this part of the world.

Obviously this is not a comprehensive account – a book covering over a thousand years of the county's history would need to be volumes and volumes long if all the details of every single disaster in the county were included! And because of the way I've organised the book, on a 'dip in and look at a day' basis, some things are missing because I couldn't pin them down as far as the month, let alone the day – particularly for events from before 1600. Some days have seen more than one major disaster over the years, whereas other days seem to have escaped pretty much unscathed and therefore don't have an entry.

I've concentrated on fires, floods, storms and shipwrecks rather than accidents (with a couple of exceptions, such as the Thorpe rail disaster of 1878, which had such a huge impact that it made the national newspapers for weeks). I have included some of the major rebellions in the county (such as the 1272 Norwich riot, the 1381 uprising, Kett's Rebellion and the 'Great Blowe' from the civil war) as well as events from the two World Wars, but I've avoided recent disasters of a more political nature involving agriculture and livestock.

I hope that the book will stir memories for you – memories of people pulling together and helping in times of crisis. While I was researching, I came across events that made me remember my childhood – such as the (literally) blazing summer of 1976 and being snowed in during the winter of 1978. My dad told me his memories of the winter of 1947, my stepmum talked about 1963, my husband remembered the roof of his school blowing off in 1976, and even my children can remember the snow of January 2003, which nearly made them miss being a bridesmaid and pageboy at my cousin's wedding in Essex. And as for the gales of 1987, 2002 and 2007... when you read within, I think you'll agree we've seen even worse, in the past.

This is also the place where I would like to say thank you. First of all to my husband Gerard and my children Christopher and Chloe, who never complain when they have to fish me out of the library or come on field research trips with me (or when I ask them to stand next to flood markers to put what happened into pictorial perspective). To the staff of Norfolk County Library and Information Services, particularly Clare Agate and the staff at the Heritage Centre, for help with photographs and locating some of the more obscure material. To Dot Lumley, my agent, for her unstinting patience and encouragement. To family and friends who didn't mind me running on about my latest discovery from the archives, and who chipped in with suggestions of their own (Jo Hamilton and Victoria Allen in particular for the latter). To Michelle Grainger, my editor, for giving me the chance to tell these stories. And last, but most definitely not least, to the heroes and heroines of Norfolk, who've made our county a better place – and without whom this book could never have been written.

Pamela Brooks,
March 2007

January

January has always been a month of snow, gales and floods. Two of the worst ever floods in the county occurred in January during the 20th century; both the 1978 floods and the 1953 floods were used as benchmarks for all subsequent floods, and there are flood markers recording incredible levels of water all along the coast. It was also a month of extreme cold: January 1963 was the coldest month of the century, and the fifth-coldest month since records began.

However, it's also been a month of rescues – Henry Blogg, possibly the greatest lifeboatman ever, was awarded his first gold medal from the RNLI for a rescue he and his crew performed in January.

January has also seen medical disasters in the county. In 1819 a smallpox epidemic started in Norwich, and despite surgeon Edward Rigby's vaccination programme over 500 children fell victim to the disease and died between then and September.

1 January

New Year's Day was often a difficult one across the county. In 1779 there was a severe flood at King's Lynn, which the *Norfolk Chronicle* described as being caused by the 'highest tide known at Lynn', 15in above the mark at the pilot house. In Norwich, there was a bad storm at 2am which, according to *White's Directory* of 1845, rolled up the lead of St Andrew's Church 'and blew it a considerable distance', as well as damaging other churches and houses. The *Norfolk Chronicle* added that the lead weighed 456lb and broke down the wall for between 10 and 12 yards on the south side of the church. The storm also caused £20 of damage to the Norfolk and Norwich Hospital (equivalent to nearly £2,000 in today's money). Seven hundred sheep were drowned at West Newton. The windmill at Trowse was blown down; Mulbarton Church was badly damaged; 12 buildings were blown down at Coltishall and the school was damaged; a house at Sloley burned down; and at Bramerton a chimney was blown down.

The coast suffered really badly. Snettisham and Woolferton Point were described as 'all a sea', with cattle swimming and haystacks floating away on the tide; the damage was estimated at thousands of pounds. Six barns were blown down in Snettisham and Ingoldisthorpe, and Brancaster quay was damaged. At Holme and Titchwell the sea flooded houses and there was much damage to dyke banks and houses in Marshland. The jetty was washed away at Great Yarmouth, and a house on the seafront was blown down and its contents washed into the sea; the flood went up to the first floor in other houses. There was much damage at Cley, Blakeney and Salthouse; at Wells two sloops and two brigs were blown out of the sea. Many ships were blown ashore – including nine at Mundesley, several at Eccles and more at Sheringham and Weyborne. The storm raged outside Norfolk, too – and the *Norfolk Chronicle* reported that the tide in London ebbed and flowed three times in the space of three hours.

In 1855 there was a major flood in the east of the county; at Great Yarmouth the water rose over the quay, and the railway from Great Yarmouth to Reedham was under water. Three years later, Great Yarmouth was hit by fire; it started at Colby's the fish merchant in St James's Place, and several houses were lost.

JANUARY

1963 saw Norfolk in the middle of blizzards in the worst winter since 1739. The following day, ships had to break a channel in the ice on the River Yare before they could sail down it. January 1963 was the third coldest winter ever recorded (the others were 1683–84 and 1739–40). Later in the month, on 23 January, the coldest temperature was measured at -19°C at Santon Downham.

2 January
1976 saw a severe gale across the county that lasted for the whole weekend. Winds were measured at 105mph at Cromer and 103mph at Norwich, and RAF Coltishall measured its strongest wind since 1968, at 86mph. Many roads in Norwich were blocked by fallen trees. King's Lynn was cut off, and a woman was blown across Regent Road in Great Yarmouth. At Poringland a man was injured when his greenhouse fell on him.

There was a red alert flood warning on the coast the following night, and the sea tore a 30ft gap in the sea wall at Walcott, which had been rebuilt after the 1953 floods; concrete from the wall smashed holiday chalets, and shops and houses were flooded up to a depth of 5ft. On the Sunday the RAF provided warm air blowers to help people dry out. Police and firemen evacuated 150 people with rowing boats, but 74-year-old Alfred Grimes refused – he said he'd sat out the 1953 floods and would sit out these ones too! People at Cley, Blakeney and Salthouse were also evacuated when the marshes went under water.

Cromer Pier was closed after its concrete supports washed away, and 200 beach huts were wrecked. The coast road from Cromer to Great Yarmouth was unrecognisable, littered with sand, concrete and wood. A quarter of a million homes lost power, and live power cables were brought down on to the road at Thetford. The roof of Toftwood School at Dereham was ripped off; among the other 200 schools damaged at the weekend was the Avenues School in Norwich, where a gable was blown in. A corner of the roof at Loddon library was blown in and a Tudor barn at Shelfanger was blown down. A chimneystack crashed through the roof at Wormegay, and a roof blew off at North Wootton.

On the Sunday, the Queen was at Sandringham Church; it wasn't lit or heated due to the power lines being down. As the Bishop of Norwich (the Right Reverend Maurice Wood) announced the last hymn of the service, 'The people that in darkness sat a glorious light have seen', it turned out to be very appropriate – power was restored for the first time since the gale on the Friday night and the church was lit up!

3 January
In 1841 there was a severe gale with thunder, lightning and hail.

1978 saw a storm across the county that blew down trees and blocked roads. Clippesby Mill, near Acle, caught fire in the storm and holidaymakers on a cruiser raised the alarm when they got to the lock at Acle. The mill was a mile and a half from the road, and the Acle fire crew was already fighting a blaze at Fishley Manor Hotel; the Martham fire engine couldn't get across the marsh due to the mud, so an army Landrover ferried a portable pump and firemen across, and they used water from the river. The fire was confined to the stock of the mill and nobody was hurt. Meanwhile, the Fishley Manor hotel had been hit by lightning; the owners were having breakfast when the lights went out and then back on again. They saw smoke and realised the roof was on fire, but they couldn't raise the alarm because the phones were dead, so they drove a mile to Acle to get help. The fire was fought by 30 firemen from four brigades.

In the same storm, Long Stratton School was badly damaged, to the tune of £5,000. There was £3,000 worth of damage at the mill in Long Stratton, with tiles blown off the roof; the sliding doors also collapsed and the wind blew them across a meadow 100 yards away.

4 January

1857 saw a violent gale, which *The Times* described as 'very destructive at Norfolk' – the report went on to list eight ships that had been driven on to the beach at Great Yarmouth, but fortunately all the crews were saved. The *Norfolk Chronicle* added that there was a great deal of wreckage strewn on the beaches. The *Thomas and Elizabeth* of Seaham was driven on to the shore, but the master and crew were rescued in heavy surf by the lifeboat.

There was another gale in 1922, with the addition of a blinding snowstorm that left 6ft drifts at East Dereham. The sea wall came down at Cley, and there was much flooding at Mundesley at high tide – the water was already storming against the promenade wall three hours before high tide came in at 10.30am and scooped out a huge section of the cliff. The *Eastern Daily Press* noted that the ancient forest bed was laid bare at Bacton and houses along the Bacton coastline were demolished.

1939 saw a £1,500 fire in the Lamb Inn in the centre of Norwich. Licensee Lilian Louise Hubbard and her grandson John cleared up and went to bed at 12.30am, when all was well – but Lilian woke at 4.45am smelling smoke. She called to her grandson, who jumped out of his bedroom window to give the alarm – clad only in his pyjamas! He also saved Jimmy the cat, but the canary in the kitchen was killed by smoke.

1952 saw a major fire at the Michelin Tyre depot on Lady's Lane, Norwich. The manager left at 5.30pm, when all was well, and the fire was raging two hours later. Twenty thousand motor tyres and tubes went up, worth £25,000 (the equivalent of nearly £500,000 in today's money), and it took 30 firemen an hour to control the blaze – by which time the roof had collapsed, but the firemen prevented it from spreading. Opposite, the Theatre Royal was playing *Aladdin* to a packed house, and the audience knew nothing about the blaze until they came out!

1978 saw Hill House at Northrepps gutted by fire. The tenant had gone out to dinner, leaving his dogs asleep in front of the fire; although he'd put a guard over the fire, he returned to find the house ablaze. Luckily, the dogs had managed to escape. Fifty men and eight engines from seven fire brigades fought the blaze.

1998 saw a 60mph gale across the region; trees came down, roads were blocked, roofs were torn off and there were power cuts.

5 January

1858 saw a disastrous run of fires in Norwich. It started at Butcher's paper mills in St Martin's; a watchman saw flames at 1.30am and raised the alarm, but a strong south-easterly gale set the mill ablaze before the fire engines could get there. The fire brigade worked on stopping the fire spreading to the neighbouring buildings; when the roof fell in, a policeman was on it at the time, and Mr English and Constable Williams burst through the door in an attempt to rescue their colleague. However, the heat drove them back. They were delighted to see their colleague reappear from the flames; although he suffered burns to his arms and legs, the paper reported that at the time of printing (four days later) he was recovering. The fire was out by 4am, and it's thought that the fire started when cinders fell from the boiler grate on to a wooden partition. The damage was estimated at around £1,000 (equivalent to nearly £71,000 in today's money).

Later that morning, fragments from the fire ignited sawdust at Orfeur's timber yard in Fishgate Street. The section along the river was a mass of flames; the 70 firefighters managed to contain the fire to the yard but saved only some of the machinery.

Following the huge snowstorm of the previous day in 1922, a workman had a lucky escape in Dereham. A workman was just unlocking the door to the garage for buses at Balding Bros agricultural and motor engineers, in a building that was formerly a skating rink, when the sheer weight of the snow made the roof collapse.

1977 saw a huge blaze in a barn at Taverham – the second barn on the farm to go up in flames in the course of two months. The previous barn was gutted and hay was bought to replace its contents – but this one went up too. A tank with 5,000 gallons of diesel was only 5ft away from the blaze, but the three fire crews managed to save it. The 95 tons of hay burned itself out, and the damage was estimated at £10,000.

6 January

The day after the fires at Butcher's and Orfeur's in 1858, at 3 o'clock in the morning Constable Hazell was patrolling Fishgate Street when he smelled burning around the area of Andrews and French's soap factory. He raised the alarm, but as with the paper mills the fire took hold before the brigade could get to it. Horses were moved from the stables and men and women helped form a human chain with buckets; luckily, the fire was stopped before it reached the tallow vats, but the *Norfolk Chronicle* reported that the whole area was in a state of ruin. They were also very impressed by the way the brigade had handled things, offering their 'unqualified commendation of all the arrangements, of the chief constable's presence of mind, tact, skill and cool judgement, and the very high state of efficiency of the fire brigade'.

1861 saw heavy snow across the county, with falls of up to a foot recorded.

1867 saw a severe storm at Great Yarmouth. In turbulent seas and a heavy downpour, the brigs *Ark* and *Sarah* collided and were lost with all 16 crew.

1881 saw a gale overnight; the brig *Alert* was going from Sunderland to Dartmouth with coal when she was caught in the gale and lost her mainmast. The Sheringham lifeboat rescued the seven crew at Blakeney just before the ship grounded at Cley and took them to Wells; within half an hour of the rescue, the ship was a complete wreck. When the lifeboat arrived, the ship was so low in the water that the crew of the *Alert* dared not go below for their money or clothes; all they managed to save was the opera glass the captain was using to watch for the lifeboat. The Sheringham crew reacted with typical modesty: 'We do not want to praise ourselves but we should like our old boat, the *Augusta*, to get some praise this time.' The *Norfolk Chronicle* added that the boat was good in low water as it was lighter and broader in the beam than the national lifeboats were – and if there had been five minutes more delay in the rescue, the seven crew would have been lost.

1977 saw the mill at Fakenham damaged by fire. The office accommodation was the worst hit, but the fire crew stopped the blaze spreading by using water from the River Wensum.

7 January

1839 saw a major gale across the county. At Great Yarmouth, 13 ships and a hundred or so crew went missing in a gale. The post of the windmill at Diss snapped in the middle and the mill was blown down; although much of the wheat was saved, the damage was estimated at £500 (equivalent to nearly £32,500 in today's money).

Two years later, there was a severe cold snap, which froze fish to death in the streams and even poultry under cover froze to death at night. During a storm that night at Shouldham, a cottage was hit by lightning that the *Norfolk Chronicle* reported was 'of uncommon brilliancy and seemed to cover the very air with a light blue'. The lightning set fire to the shed, and the blaze rapidly spread to the cottage roof. An unnamed hero was the 'rural policeman' who risked his life rescuing an elderly woman from the cottage – the roof fell in just as he got her out.

1930 saw the wireless shop of Messrs West in Regent Street, Great Yarmouth, gutted. The fire was discovered at 12.30am by PC Sutton; by the time the fire brigade arrived, the heat was so intense that the front plate-glass window shattered. The shop was gutted within three hours, but the fire brigade managed to contain the blaze to the building.

1971 saw a huge hole opening up near the edge of the old Fishwharf at Great Yarmouth – it was four yards across and a yard deep, containing a foot of water. Another area nearby, 12 yards by 6 yards, also started to sink. The area was shut off until repairs could be made.

1973 saw an £8,000 blaze which closed the El Piana nightclub on Timberhill in Norwich for a month. The club had recently been revamped at a cost of £5,000, and luckily the work had included fireproofing to the kitchen, where the fire started. The three fire crews attending were able to confine the blaze to the kitchen.

8 January

1922 saw major floods around the Broads. Flood tides burst the banks of the river, and the water became brackish 20 miles upstream. St Benet's Abbey at Horning was surrounded by water, and the low road was inches deep in water; schoolchildren going to a dance rehearsal had to be carried to school on their parents' backs. The quay was swamped, grazing lands at the mouth of the River Ant were submerged, and at Hoveton the water was up to the bridge.

1974 saw a huge storm across the county with 70mph winds. On the Acle road, a heavyweight lorry acted as a windbreak for a pantechnicon (large furniture van) which had been blown over by a 52-knot wind; police sealed off the road and they drove side by side along the Acle Straight to Great Yarmouth. Many trees were blown down at Thetford, and there were power cuts across the county. The entire roof of a barn was blown off at Little Cressingham and smashed on to the corner of the village hall 100 yards away; fortunately, nobody attending a party there was hurt, but cars outside were badly damaged.

9 January

The Cromer lifeboat team made two dramatic rescues in 1917, in a day when the wind was at 50mph and the seas were heavy. A Greek steamer was in trouble two miles from Cromer; 40 people had to wade into the sea up to their armpits to launch the lifeboat, due to the heavy seas, but the lifeboat reached the steamer at 2pm and rescued the 16 crew. They also noticed the Swedish steamer *Fernebo* in trouble four miles out; although the lifeboatmen were exhausted from the previous rescue, as soon as they heard that the crews at Sea Palling and Sheringham couldn't launch their lifeboats, they decided to try to help. For half an hour, the lifeboat was constantly beaten back to shore by the gale; a

A bust of Henry Blogg, the most decorated lifeboatman ever. (Photograph by author)

small boat from the ship with six of the crew left the *Fernebo* but was hit by a huge wave that filled the boat and threw the men into the water. The men of Cromer rushed on to the beach and made a human chain, wading into the sea up to their necks, and saved the crew. Then the *Fernebo* struck a mine and broke in two. The Cromer lifeboat crew won 14 medals between them for the rescue of the steamer; coxswain Henry Blogg was awarded his first gold medal, William Davies was awarded a silver medal, and the remaining 12 crew members won a bronze – the first time that the RNLI had awarded a bronze medal.

There was a terrible tragedy on Timberhill, Norwich, in 1928 when three women died in a fire at Leveridge Bros sweet manufacturers and general warehouse. The fire started in the matchbox room on the top storey; the fire brigade couldn't open the door, but when they forced it down they found three badly burned bodies. The women had died from suffocating in the smoke.

1973 saw a fire just round the corner from the 7 January fire when Julee's Hair Salon in Orford Hill, Norwich, caught fire. Again, the damage was £8,000 worth. Police carried guns and ammunition from the shop below to safety, and the fire crews managed to stop the blaze spreading to Timberhill. The stag on Orford Hill was damaged by the fire and had to be brought down. When workers went up on a platform, they discovered that not only was a metal tie keeping it in place, there were also metal bars from the stag's leg going into a concrete plinth. Eventually the stag, which weighed ¾ tonne, was cut down. It was later restored.

10 January

In 1756 an earthquake was felt in Norwich.

Bad weather was seen across the county in 1806; the *Norfolk Chronicle* reported 'one of the most tremendous and awful tempests' hitting Bradwell at 5 o'clock in the morning. The devastation covered a quarter of a mile; trees were torn up by the roots, a large three-bay barn was blown down, seven haystacks were torn into shreds, and tiles were ripped off the roof of Mr Sangster's farmhouse. Next door, Mr Babbs's farm sustained almost £400 worth of damage (equivalent to nearly £40,000 in today's money). The dock didn't escape, either – three of the four granaries by it were destroyed and a wagon was carried over the edge of the dock. A gunboat in the creek was dismasted; one vessel was torn out of the dock and another was pushed in, and both of their riggings were torn to shreds.

In 1830 there was a flood at Cley, after a high tide, and the residents had to move their belongings to the upper floor of their houses. The road between Cley and Salthouse was impassable, due to a flood 6–8ft deep; one elderly couple had to be rescued from the top floor of their house. The brig *Ocean* was wrecked at Cley, though all the crew were saved. At Blakeney, the brig *William and Mary* was wrecked; five of the 12 crew were rescued, but the others got into a boat and drowned after being struck by a heavy sea. There was much coastal erosion in Norfolk, especially at Mundesley.

1894 saw a gale that lasted for two days. At Sea Palling, the 130-tonne Danish schooner *Sophia* of Frederisia let its anchor down to ride out the snow and hail – but the anchor didn't hold in the heavy seas. The crew cut off the main mast and fore top mast and set them adrift, and this time the anchor held, but the crew spent the night exposed to a strong gale. The anchor chain parted and the ship drifted; a steamer nearby saw what had happened but was unable to get close enough to help, because of the huge waves. The Sea Palling lifeboat crew sent rockets with lines, but when the line broke they decided to launch the lifeboat. The crew of six – their clothes crusted with ice – were all saved. That night, the German barque *Wallis and Sohn* of Barth grounded on Scroby Sands and was dashed to pieces, but the crew managed to reach the safety of the Cockle lightship.

2007 saw floods throughout the county, with water over a foot deep in some places; some roads had to be closed. At Wymondham, two lorries became stuck in deep water on the A11 and a third crashed into them; fortunately, nobody was hurt, though the road was blocked.

11 January

In 1616 there was a major fire at Thetford, and much property was destroyed.

1866 saw a huge gale in Great Yarmouth. The *Theodore* from Sunderland was beached by Wellington Pier, and the eight crew, in danger of being washed overboard, had to secure themselves to the rigging, but the lifeboat managed to rescued them all with lines.

1912 saw a dramatic rescue by the Caister lifeboat crew. The German ship schooner *Fulke* was bringing rice to Great Yarmouth to be transported to Colman's in Norwich when it became stuck on the Cross Sands and sent up distress flares. The sea was too heavy for the lifeboat to reach the ship, so it dropped anchor about 15 yards away and threw a line to the ship. The first crew member tied the rope round his waist and was thrown into the sea and pulled across to the lifeboat. Another crew member was about to jump in when a huge wave knocked the lifeboat away from its anchor and pushed it next to the ship, near enough for the rest of the crew to jump in. All seven crew were taken to safety.

In 1976 there were high winds and a greater tidal surge even than 1953. Boats were thrown on to the quay at Wells, and people were evacuated from the floods at King's Lynn, Hunstanton, Burnham Overy and Blakeney.

12 January

In 1290, according to the 18th-century historian Blomefield, there was a great flood in Norwich; water overflowed St Martin's bridge and the gates of St Giles' Hospital and knocked down many houses. (These were clearly fairly flimsy, of wooden construction; stone buildings were not knocked down as easily.)

1930 saw a huge fire in Loddon, when the warehouses and granaries of Woods, Sadd & Moore Ltd caught fire around 3pm. The wooden buildings formed two separate ranges; the one nearest the River Chet caught light first, and then high winds carried the fire across the road to the second range. The villagers rallied round to help save the books from the offices, and also the council records that were in the top floor of the same building. Men took ropes to drag a lorry to safety. The glare could be seen for miles around, but the heat was too much for people to approach the buildings. Loddon fire brigade couldn't cope with it; they were joined at 7pm by the brigades from Bungay and Beccles, and shortly

Flood markers at the quay at Blakeney. The lower one (just above my husband Gerard's head) shows the level of the 1978 flood; the upper marker shows the level of the 1953 floods (see 31 January). (Photograph by author)

Flood markers at the quay at Wells. The lower one (at Chloe's eye level) shows the level of the 1978 flood; the upper marker (at Chris's eye level) shows the level of the 1953 floods (see 31 January). (Photograph by author)

after by the Norwich brigade, which brought a big motor pump. It took 'many hours' to subdue the blaze, and the damage ran into thousands of pounds.

1972 saw an 80ft petrol slick on the river at Great Yarmouth burst into flames, which leapt 20ft into the air. The petrol was carried downstream by the ebbing tide – but a 250ft barge was in the way, stopping it going towards the harbour mouth. There was a tiny gap, only a few inches wide, between the side of the barge and the quay, and the blazing petrol seeped through. The mooring ropes of the barge caught fire, but the blaze was quickly extinguished and the petrol burned itself out before it could do any more damage.

1973 saw the worst fire for years in Diss, at the Omar Mobile Homes stores. The explosion shattered windows in shops 30 yards away, and at the height of the blaze the flames were 20ft through the roof. The corrugated iron walls glowed red, and the flames spread so quickly that the fire brigade couldn't save it; they were, however, able to confine the blaze to the buildings.

1978 saw the worst floods since 1953 at King's Lynn after a bad tidal surge; 400 homes were flooded and 22 children had to be moved from their ward in hospital. A thousand people were evacuated from their homes in the Wisbech area. There were floods at Hunstanton, although they weren't quite as severe as 1953, and most of Hunstanton pier was washed away. At Heacham and Snettisham the bank was breached, and hundreds of caravans and beach huts were swept away. The shingle bank was breached at Salthouse, and the Blakeney was severely hit by floods. At Wells, there were breaches in the sea wall and the 300-tonne Medway coaster *Function* was washed up on to the quay.

1993 saw torrential rain, which lasted well into the next day, together with gale force 8 winds; weather experts said that the amount of rain falling in some places in the 48 hours from 10am on 12 January was almost double the amount of rainfall usually expected for the whole of October! Coltishall had 95.8mm of rain, Norwich had 75.2mm and Marham had 50.8mm. Unsurprisingly, hundreds of homes were swamped and dozens of schools were closed. The rail line between Holt and Sheringham was closed after a landslip, and there was also a landslip at Bungay. The Dereham to Fakenham road was closed and cars were abandoned along it; there was flooding at Dereham, and the A47 was closed for over five hours at Scarning. At Swaffham the emergency services received 250 calls for help in an hour. Saham Toney was cut off, and streets and homes were flooded in Carbrooke and Watton. There was a 4ft flood at Stalham, and the police diving team rescued an elderly couple at Little Hale from 5ft of water. The Association of British Insurers estimated that the damage ran into hundreds of thousands of pounds.

13 January

1776 saw Norfolk in the middle of a cold snap, with snow drifts of up to 12ft. Two weeks later the *Norwich Mercury* reported that the winter was the worst since 1740, and a gale on the 27th saw four ships ashore at Great Yarmouth. Two days after that, the thermometer was sitting one degree below the temperature of the 1740 winter.

1866 saw a rescue go very badly wrong, when the *Rescuer* lifeboat from the Ranger company in Gorleston went to the assistance of a ship in Yarmouth in rough water and capsized; 12 out of the 16 crew drowned, leaving eight widows and 30 children. At the inquest, survivor Edward Woods said the rescuers didn't have their lifebelts on because they weren't much use. The coroner was well aware of the problem: at the time, all the lifeboat companies were private and competed for salvage rights, so they would run risks and try to race each other to a wreck. The coroner said that the ship in question was showing a 'waif' (i.e. a flag which signalled that they were not in trouble but needed something non-urgent on board), and that the lifeboat crews should not risk their lives and take risks unless a ship was really in trouble.

1913 saw a huge gale and a flood at Great Yarmouth; at 3pm the river overflowed its banks and all the roads from Haven Bridge to Gordon Road were under water. Shops opposite the tramway terminus were flooded, and the water was knee deep at Southtown station. The marshes were also flooded. Cromer was hit badly; it was difficult for people to walk in the wind, and at 6pm the high tide washed up to the gangway at Cromer – the *Eastern Daily Press* said it was the worst sea for 30 years. The 860-tonne collier *Hayfru* was seen in difficulties, but the sea was so bad that the Cromer lifeboat couldn't get out to it until the following day. Even at 8am there were heavy breakers and the lifeboat was grounded, but helpers waded waist deep in the waters to refloat the lifeboat. It returned at 5pm with the sole survivor of the 14-strong crew, 23-year-old Niels Nielson from Copenhagen, who was the ship's donkeyman. He told the story of two terrible nights at sea: they'd got stuck at 10pm on the 12th, and they launched their lifeboat with three men in it, but it was dashed to pieces. Two of the men were brought back on board, but the third drowned. During the night, the waves washed more of the crew overboard and they couldn't be saved. In the morning, the second engineer managed to get a boat out, but they could see it sinking as he moved off. Shortly afterwards, the collier broke in half, and there were only two sailors left clinging on to the rigging. On the 14th, at around 9am, the other sailor couldn't hold on any more; only Nielson was left by the time the Cromer lifeboat arrived a couple of hours later.

1977 saw Norwich grind to a halt in a blizzard. Three inches of snow fell in three hours during the rush hour and brought city traffic to a standstill; the snowploughs and gritters were trapped in traffic jams. Some areas over the county lost power, and there were traffic jams elsewhere when snow drifted and blocked roads.

14 January

1808 saw a heavy gale at sea; the village of Cley was badly flooded.

In 1931 a cat caused a house – part of which dated back to Domesday – to burn down. Great Yarmouth doctor Edward Crosby Peers discovered a small fire by the back staircase in Hopton Hall early that evening, which he thought was caused by the family cat upsetting a lamp. He and two gardeners extinguished the flames; thinking all was well, Dr Peers, his wife and daughter spent the evening 'listening to the broadcast programme'. At 9.30pm his daughter decided to go to bed – and discovered that the staircase was alight. They raised the alarm but the fire spread rapidly. Villagers helped to get the furniture out, but by this time the fire had taken hold in the roof. The roof fell in near a small group of firemen, who had a narrow escape. By midnight, the top floor had burned out, and, although the fire brigade was still working two hours later, they couldn't save the house.

1959 saw thick fog in the region, in addition to heavy snow – the *Eastern Daily Press* reported 'scores and scores of accidents'.

1987 saw Norfolk in the middle of a cold snap with a great deal of snow. Two days before, it had been London's coldest day since 1940. The River Wensum froze in Norwich, and the following day 320 snowploughs were out across the county.

15 January

1806 saw another rough day in the county, when the vane and spindle of St Gregory's Church in Norwich was blown off.

In 1827 there was so much snow that rabbits around Thetford and Brandon perished when they went out for food and couldn't find their burrows again.

16 January

1740 saw what the *Norwich Remembrancer* called the 'coldest day in the memory of man', adding that the cold was 'more intense than 1708 and 1715'. When the frost finally thawed, there was a major flood.

1841 saw a thaw after a cold snap, resulting in widespread flooding across the county.

1867 saw a severe frost, heavy snows and a gale; there were 7ft drifts on railway lines and roads were impassable. At 9.10pm the Lowestoft train from Norwich was trapped in a cutting until the following afternoon; a train from King's Lynn was also stuck at a cutting near Heacham. There were 4ft drifts at Dereham, 5ft drifts at Harling, and the *Norfolk Chronicle* reported that 'huge banks of snow line the pavements'. The North Walsham mail took an hour and a half to travel four miles, and the Reepham mail cart had to be dug out three times near Drayton.

1913 saw Sexton's shoe factory in Fishergate, Norwich, destroyed. Fire broke out shortly after midnight, and the *Eastern Daily Press* called it an 'acre of flame'. Harry Sexton, the head of the firm, said that a large quantity of valuable machinery and the factory covering an acre were completely destroyed; £100,000 worth of damage (equivalent to over £6 million of today's money) was caused, and 1,000 people were put out of work.

17 January

1932 saw a fire at a cooperage in Great Yarmouth; the alarm was raised at around 4.30 in the morning, and despite the fact that the store for barrels and staves was in one of the most densely built-up areas in Great Yarmouth, the fire brigade managed to contain the blaze within four hours and nobody was hurt, although some nearby houses were scorched.

1967 saw a huge blaze in a Great Yarmouth cannery, which started in an office on the ground floor. It was brought under control by 2am, but the labelling machines, cartons and hundreds of tins were destroyed, putting the factory out of action for a week.

18 January

1881 saw a terrible snowstorm and gale on the coast; at sea, 13 ships were lost and almost 50 lives. There were plenty of rescues – and also desperate tragedy.

GREAT FIRE IN NORWICH. JAN. 16ᵗʰ 1913.
SEXTON'S FACTORY DESTROYED. DAMAGE $100.0

Fire at Sexton's boot factory, Norwich. (Picture courtesy of Norfolk County Council Library and Information Service)

The previous night, the River Yare had frozen; during the day, there was a hurricane (though the reported 'velocity of 548 miles recorded' might have been a bit of an exaggeration). Between six and eight inches of snow fell and the gale blew it into drifts of more than 10ft. Train lines were blocked, and a mixture of sand and snow blocked roads.

The French ketch *Charles Redow* was lost with six or seven crew. Then the schooner *Rhoda* from Middlesbrough was driven ashore between Wellington Pier and jetty; three men and the captain's wife were rescued with lines. The lifeboat then rescued three men and a nine-year-old from the French ketch *Mamma de Ciel*; then four more from the schooner *Sarah Ann*, which had a cargo of stone for Great Yarmouth's new town hall, but sadly the mate was lost in the 'raging surf'. The brig *Battle of Corunna* from Whitby was the next one in trouble; the crew lashed themselves to the rigging to avoid being washed overboard. Two rockets failed to get lines to the crew – and one sailor fell trying to reach the third. The lifeboat tried for two hours to get out to the ship, but the waves kept driving them back and the crew of the *Battle of Corunna* died.

The next ship to need rescue was the *Guiding Star*; in the thick snow, the lifeboat crew couldn't get lines to the ship via the mortars, so they had to send the lifeboat out. A few yards from the shore, the lifeboat gave the signal to be pulled in – but the beachmen were not banking on the enthusiastic help they got. The lifeboat overturned, only a few yards from the shore, and six of the crew got tangled up in the tackle and drowned. The men they'd rescued also drowned, and the boat washed up on the shore, still capsized.

But despite their loss, the rescuers were still needed because the barque *Edith Mary* was in trouble. Two of the crew managed to swim to safety and three more were rescued, but the ship broke up before the lifeboat could get to them. Then an unnamed brig beached near Wellington Pier; ropes were thrown, but the crew were just too numb with cold to handle them. Sadly, again, the ship broke up and the crew was lost before they could be saved.

At the inquest following the disaster, coxswain William Haylett explained that the boat capsized when it was hauled in too fast – the rope was like a 'bar of iron', bringing the boat down. Then the heavy sea capsized the boat. The coroner agreed, saying that he had been on the boat himself a few times and thought there was no problem with the boat – the problem was the rope being pulled in too fast by people eager to help but not really knowing what they were doing.

The six crew left four widows and 22 children behind. George Abram of Middle Temple Lane paid tribute in a letter in *The Times*, saying 'they were all steady, honest, hardworking men, ready, as the Yarmouth boatmen always are, night or day to risk their lives to save others'.

2007 saw the worst storm in the county for 17 years, with 78mph winds that left thousands without power, roads flooded and trees felled across the county. One woman lost her antiques centre a month before it was due to open. One man had a very narrow escape in Norwich – a tree fell on his car, but he'd leaned over to pick up a book from the passenger footwell so he only suffered severe bruising.

King's Lynn, Bentinck Street, after a Zeppelin raid in 1915. (Picture courtesy of Norfolk County Council Library and Information Service)

19 January

1915 saw bombs dropped over Norfolk in the first of the Zeppelin raids in World War One. Three German airships were seen off the Dutch coast at 1.30pm. Great Yarmouth was the first place that the bombs fells, at 8.20pm; *The Times* reported an eyewitness account that there was 'a report as if a big gun had been fired in the main street of the town', and authorities extinguished the electric lights. Another resident said 'The uproar was deafening, and at the same time there were flashes in the clouds, rather suggesting a searchlight.' The raid saw the first house in Britain damaged during an air raid, in St Peter's Plain. There were also the first casualties, as three people were injured and 72-year-old Martha Taylor and 55-year-old shoemaker Samuel Smith were killed. Yarmouth borough records said that the damage caused during the raid amounted to £2,500, including £550 for the fish wharf (equivalent to just over £130,000 and just over £30,000 respectively in today's money).

Cromer was bombed at 8.30pm and Sheringham a quarter of an hour later; bricklayer Robert Smith had a narrow escape when the bomb crashed through his roof, fell into his tiny kitchen and landed in the space between the copper and the stool on which his youngest child was sitting before bursting out of the wall. Luckily the bomb didn't explode, though it did set the roof on fire. Heacham was next in line, but the bomb didn't explode; at Snettisham, a bomb blasted out the east window over the chancel and two windows behind the organ. Finally, at 11pm, eight bombs landed at King's Lynn, killing 14-year-old Percy Goate in his bed and 26-year-old widow Alice Gazeley, who had just had supper with a neighbour in Bentinck Street and was buried by falling rubble as she went back to her house.

1942 saw an air raid over Sheringham which left four dead.

1969 saw a huge blaze at A. Ford & Son sack merchant's factory in Diss. Forty firemen from three stations managed to confine the fire to the upper floor, and sprayed nearby buildings containing more sacks with water to stop it spreading.

In 1973 employees came to the rescue when a fire started in a chemical warehouse of marine engineers Jack Powles Ltd in Mountergate, Norwich. They used dry powder extinguishers and the blaze was out by the time the three fire engines arrived; nobody was hurt.

1978 saw the 17th-century Gapton Hall at Burgh Castle gutted by fire. It had been smouldering for a while but nobody noticed because of the fog. The fire brigade was called but couldn't save the roof; they could only damp the fire down. Afterwards it was thought that 60 percent of the living quarters had been destroyed and 40 percent of the roof.

20 January

1607 saw a major flood in Marshland. A contemporary pamphlet explained that after a bad winter with sheeprot, when the animals 'dyed in such aboundaunce, that even Dogges grewe wearie of them', two horse thieves tried to steal some cattle in the area and drove them on to the marsh. They managed to escape the hue and cry – and then the sea breached the banks and overflowed the marsh, drowning the cattle. The thieves decided to turn over a new leaf and went to see the sexton, who rang the church bells to raise the alarm. Even so, houses were up to their middle in water and 12 miles of fen were inundated. Walsoken, Cross Keys and Stow

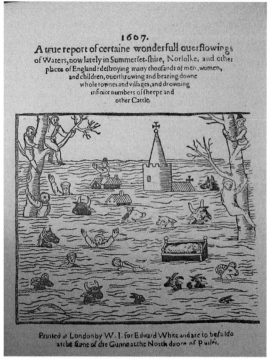

1607.

A true report of certaine wonderfull ouerflowings of Waters, now lately in Summerset-shire, Norfolke, and other places of England: destroying many thousands of men, women, and children, ouerthrowing and bearing downe whole townes and villages, and drowning infinite numbers of sheepe and other Cattle.

Printed at London by W. I. for Edward White and are to be solde at the signe of the Gunne at the North doore of Paules.

Frontispiece of a pamphlet from 1607: *A true report of certaine wonderfull overflowings of waters*, held in the Norfolk Heritage Centre at the Millennium library. (Photograph by author, courtesy of Norfolk County Council Library and Information Service)

Brink were all flooded; Great Yarmouth bridge was carried away and Haven House (still occupied by Nicholas Josselin, the haven man, and his son) was carried six miles into the marshes from the harbour – amazingly, the house 'stood upright' throughout. The 18th-century historian Mackerell added in his *History of King's Lynn* that the flood went right up to the cross in the Tuesday Market Place in King's Lynn.

In 1838 the temperature hit rock bottom – after a period of snow, the thermometer was at 2°F (30°F below freezing!). The river at King's Lynn froze, and although there was a temporary thaw frost hit again later in the week. It was so cold that, in the middle of the following month, water indoors was frozen solid.

1961 saw Cromer's covered tennis courts burned to the ground. Pre-war, it was one of the most popular tournament venues in the country and many top stars played there – it had the reputation of being the premier tennis courts in the country before Queens in London. The alarm was raised at 3am by the caretaker of the Newhaven Court hotel, but the flames spread very quickly, and by the time the fire brigade got there a 150ft length of the roof was ablaze and the glow was visible from Sheringham and other villages miles away. Despite problems with low water pressure, the fire brigade stopped the fire spreading, but the courts were lost.

22 January

1947 saw a memorable winter – the big freeze started on this day and lasted for 50 days. Riverside pubs were even able to put tables on the ice for people to enjoy a very cold pint!

In 1963, almost two years after the tennis courts behind them burned down, the Newhaven Court hotel in Cromer caught fire. The hotel was so badly damaged that it was pulled down and the land redeveloped. Forty firemen from six brigades arrived to discover the whole roof ablaze, and they were fighting flames that were 50ft from the ground; it was so cold that water froze when it reached the ground, making conditions icy underfoot.

The guildhall at King's Lynn, built in 1422–28 to replace the one that was burned down. (Photograph by author)

23 January

1362 saw the St Mary's Wind, also known as 'the great drowning' or 'grote mandrenke' – one of the most devastating storms in English history. It started with a hurricane and ended with a week of flooding. Holinshed calls it 'such a passing wind that the like hadn't been heard of in many years before'. The spire of Norwich Cathedral was blown down, and the hurricane also blew houses down in King's Lynn. It's thought that 30,000 people on the North Sea coast died.

In 1421 there was a severe fire at King's Lynn; the Trinity Guildhall burned down before the snow could put the fire out.

1868 saw a tragic fire at Frederick Pigg (the hosier, boot and shoe manufacturer) in Market Row, Norwich. Neighbour Mr Waters raised the alarm when he heard crackling; meanwhile, Mr Pigg was woken by the smell of smoke. The nanny managed to bring out Edith, aged two and a half, but Sarah Pigg went back into the house to rescue her two youngest children, 13-month-old Mabel and two-month-old Fanny Eliza. Tragically, the three of them were buried by the falling roof. Barrels of petrol stored at the rear of the premises were moved, and although the fire was out at 3am it wrecked three shops and damaged neighbouring houses. A little over six hours later, Mrs Pigg's and the children's remains were found in the rubble; the inquest showed much humanity by not expecting Mr Pigg to give evidence, as he was 'much distracted', clearly grief stricken.

1894 saw more gales, snow and floods. There was a storm at Great Yarmouth and the tide was at an 'alarming height', enough to make townsfolk think that the flooding would be even worse than that of the month before (see 21 December). They barricaded what they could, but Hall Quay was flooded, as was the beach, and the Beach Gardens narrowly escaped destruction. It was even worse in the area by St Andrew's Church because the sewer outlets were blocked and raw sewage joined the flood waters. At Roughton, the sails of a windmill were blown off and knocked a horse and cart over; the horse was injured slightly and its harness was broken. At Acle, the river came over the wall, and at Brundall the River Yare burst its banks.

1897 saw a ship wrecked on the shore at Sheringham and a daring rescue by the crew. Snow, driven by a strong gale, had been falling for the previous two days and the seas were tumultuous. The 236-tonne Norwegian brig *Ispolen*, which was heading for Gravesend with a cargo of ice, started to leak and was driven towards the coast. Because the lifeboat slipway had been washed away the previous day, the lifeboat had trouble launching, but managed to get to the *Ispolen* when it grounded. The crew didn't understand English, so didn't respond to the lifeboatmen's call for ropes; the sea drove the lifeboat away, and it had to paddle back again – this time two oars short as they'd broken at the first approach. The lifeboat men threw grappling hooks into the ship's rigging and were able to haul alongside so the eight crew could jump in. They landed at Sheringham and were given dry clothes. Later that evening, the *Ispolen* broke up.

In 1915 the Sheringham lifeboat rescued a crew of 21, when the *Empress* of Sutherland hit a wreck on the Sheringham Shoal and sank.

In 1963 Horstead watermill caught fire because of an electrical fault, and three engines came to put out the blaze. However, firefighters had to cut holes in 12in-thick ice in the river so they could get access for their hoses, and despite the blaze the water froze on the ends of the pipes. Although the fire brigade had the fire under control in an hour, the mill was gutted.

25 January

1443 saw Gladman's Insurrection in Norwich. William Hempstead, the mayor, was charged on 28 February 1443 with 'having in purpose to make common insurrection and commotion' – in other words, their actions had been so violent that they'd forced the bishop of Norwich, abbot of St Benet of Hulme and the prior of the cathedral to give up their legal actions against the city.

What seems to have happened is that Hempstead persuaded John Gladman, a merchant in the city, to wear a paper crown and carry a sceptre and sword, and ride to the gates of the cathedral with a troop of 3,000 men. Gladman apparently usually rode through the city dressed as the 'King of Christmas' on Shrove Tuesday, 'in token that all mirth should end with the 12 months of the year,' and before him in the procession another 12 figures were dressed up to represent the 12 months of the year (including Lent 'clad in white with red herring skins and his horse decorated with oyster shells'). However, Shrove Tuesday most definitely wasn't in January. Like the 1272 revolts, this was a row over the jurisdiction of the city, and the city complaining that the priory was interfering with their rights.

Gladman allegedly threatened to burn the priory and kill the prior and monks, then the men dug under the gates and placed wood against the priory, ready to burn it down. The priory responded by giving Gladman papers relating to the meadows and mills by the river. The city men kept the gates shut for a week and wouldn't allow any of the king's ministers to enter, and, as a result, the king seized the city liberties until 1447, when Hempstead pleaded guilty and asked for the king's mercy. The city paid a fine of 1,000 marks and the liberties were restored.

1975 saw a mini tornado which caused chaos in the Saturday Market Place in King's Lynn. Stalls, fruit and wooden planks were thrown into the air and hundreds of pounds' worth of fruit and vegetables were damaged. Stallholders and customers had to hold on to stalls to stop them, and themselves, being blown over. There were gale force winds for three and a half hours across the county; winds of 70mph were registered at RAF Marham and hoardings blew down in Great Yarmouth. A shop window 20ft high by 10ft wide shattered in the first floor showroom of Fifth Avenue in Norwich, blowing 1.2 tons of glass on to shoppers below. Luckily, nobody was hurt.

1990 saw major storms across England and Wales which caused damage estimated at over £2 billion; although the winds were not quite as strong as in the October 1987 gale, they were over a wider area and even more trees were damaged. There were gale force 12 winds (80mph) on the coast, and even inland the wind was blowing at gale force 9 (50–60mph). Trains were up to six hours late and hundreds of trees came down. At Norwich Airport, cars were put in front of light aircraft to stop them blowing away; a 40ft shop front at Magdalen Street was torn off. In Great Yarmouth, the roof of a portable building was blown off and hit a man, and sadly a man at Swaffham was killed.

26 January

In 1165 there was an earthquake across East Anglia; according to the monastic chronicler Matthew of Westminster, it was severe enough to ring church bells and throw people to the ground.

Cromer was hit by a high tide in 1845, which washed away the jetty and damaged sea walls. According to the 19th-century historian Charles Palmer, there was a heavy gale at Great Yarmouth – and a real tragedy after a daring rescue. Five ships had been beached; the yawl *Phoenix* landed the crew of one ship safely, then went to a second ship to help but smashed against its side and was wrecked. The 13 crew of the *Phoenix* clung to the wreck; seven were drowned and six were rescued by the lifeboat crew.

1884 saw a major gale at Norwich, with thunder and lightning between 8 and 9pm and much damage to roofs and chimneys. The fan or 'fliers' at Lakenham mill was also blown off that evening and landed 200 yards away.

1939 saw major floods across Norfolk, which the *Eastern Daily Press* described as the worst since 1912. Bungay was cut off, and thousands of acres in the Waveney valley were flooded. Around Diss, the water rose at 6in per hour; in some places the floods were 10ft deep and half a mile wide. Two houses were flooded badly at Needham and Edward Stapleton carried women and children out; he said later that the water came over the top of his thigh boots.

In 1962 a lorry driver tried to drive his blazing tanker into a heap of sand at Longwater Gravel Pits in Costessey to stop the flames spreading, but the heat was so intense that he was forced to jump from the cab. Mr Boyce was delivering petrol when the side of the tank hit a feed hopper and split. The leaking petrol caught fire, and the blaze spread to the asphalt works that produced 300 of tons asphalt a day, causing £40,000 of damage. The heat was so intense that a mechanical shovel 15 yards away was badly damaged, and the three fire engines couldn't get near the tanker at first. Luckily, nobody was hurt.

27 January

In 1207 the monastic chronicler Matthew of Westminster says there was a major storm about midnight; it blew houses down across the region, uprooted trees and killed many sheep and cattle.

1884 saw a serious fire at the draper's shop of E. Bostock in King Street, Great Yarmouth. The alarm was raised at 12.30am, and when the fire brigade got there, very quickly, they discovered the shop was full of fire. The shutters fell, sending flames into the street and high into the air. Although the blaze was under control within three hours, the draper's shop was gutted, as was the Rose Tavern next door. The cause of the fire was unknown.

1939 saw more subsidence in Norwich – this time in Merton Road. Eighteen-year-old Joan Ramsey was cycling down a passage at the side of her house when she fell into a hole that turned out to be 4–5ft deep, 9ft long and 3–4ft wide. She was not badly injured, and, although the city engineers reassured the family that they were safe, the family spent the night with friends.

In 1972 a storm developed overnight and tore down scores of trees. Power lines went down, leaving hundreds of homes without electricity. Nearly an inch of rain fell, and roads were flooded to a depth of more than 12in of water. At breakfast-time, RAF Coltishall recorded gale force 10 gusts of wind (60mph).

28 January

1809 saw a huge flood in Norwich, after a rapid thaw. The river overflowed Fyebridge Quay and Bishopgate. During that weekend, some of the houses were 6–7ft under water, and people were actually able to row boats in St Martin at Oak Street. One young boy tried to rescue his hat when it blew into the water overflowing in Duke's Palace Yard; when he reached for it, he fell in. He couldn't swim, and the river was running so rapidly he was carried through Blackfriar's and Fye bridges; he was rescued just as he sank, on the point of drowning, but the *Norfolk Chronicle* reported that the boy would do well. The marshes flooded, so it was impossible to trace the course of the river – the barge from Norwich to Great Yarmouth had to turn back.

Following the floods in 1809, the gales hit Norwich. Shopkeeper Mr Graham of Little Cockey Lane died when the chimney of his next door neighbour fell on his garret. The neighbours tried to rescue him, but his ceiling was lead, weighing over a quarter of a tonne, so it took two hours to reach him. Mr Graham was found dead by the rescuers, and sadly his wife also perished, a few minutes after the rescue. At Sprowston Hall, a tree was blown down. Coincidentally, it had been planted on exactly the same day, 160 years before – the day that Charles I was beheaded.

1837 saw a countywide epidemic of flu – according to the newspapers, 'cases occurred in almost every family'.

29 January

1917 saw a rescue involving a very famous boat – explorer Ernest Shackleton's ship *Nimrod*. It was going from Blyth to Calais with cargo of coal when it struck the Barber Shoals near Great Yarmouth, water filled the engine room and the ship began to break up. The starboard lifeboat was washed away; the crew of 12 got on to the port lifeboat but a huge wave capsized it. Three men managed to get clear, but one just couldn't hold on. Mate James Truelson and boatswain Russell Gregory put their feet in the lifelines and shouted for help but couldn't be heard. It was bitterly cold and waves swept over them, but after five hours the tide turned and they were thrown on to the beach between Caister and Great Yarmouth. *The Times* reported that they were recovering from their ordeal in Great Yarmouth Sailor's Home.

30 January

1877 saw a major gale along the coast and 112 fishermen died. At Great Yarmouth, the sea broke over Marine Parade and many houses on the New Quay were flooded; at Eccles, the sea wall was breached. There was a daring rescue when the barque *Constantine* was struck by a squall near the St Nicholas lightship at around 10am; the crew clung to the masts until the lifeboat came out and threw a line across. One by one, the 12 crew were brought to safety.

2001 saw signalman Alec Thompson averting a major disaster when a Landrover towing a trailer with half a tonne of concrete crashed through the gates at the railway crossing in Spooner Row on icy roads during the fog. Alec threw the levers to switch the signals to red, and every second counted because a train was due to travel through the crossing en route from Wymondham at 75mph within the next 30 seconds. Alec also got the emergency signal out and alerted signal boxes on either side of his crossing, and his quick thinking saved the train and 75 passengers. His comment afterwards was typical of a Norfolk hero: 'I really don't think I'm a hero... I was just doing my job.'

31 January

There was a bad fire in Cromer in 1949 when the Royal Links Hotel caught light, and vehicles from five fire brigades attended the blaze. The hotel hadn't been open since army occupation during the war; the fire started in a paint store and the workmen tried to deal with it, but the flames were soon out of hand and the wing was fully alight by midnight. The fire brigade's work was hampered by low water pressure and falling slates, and the building was gutted by 2.30am.

1953 saw the worst peacetime disaster that Britain has ever known – a storm in which 307 people were killed, 32,000 people were evacuated and thousands of livestock were drowned. It was the greatest storm surge ever recorded in the North Sea – reaching 2.97 metres at King's Lynn – and over a fifth of the town was flooded. Thirteen people died at King's Lynn, and 65 more between King's Lynn and Hunstanton. The damage to property was incredible; the sea broke over the sand hills at Sea Palling and caused houses to collapse; Cromer Pier was battered, the sea wall was damaged and there was a large cliff fall at the east end; at Salthouse the sea defences gave way and many buildings were in ruins; at Hunstanton houses were smashed and sea water got into the mains. At Great Yarmouth, 2,500 homes were flooded when

A door is the only remains of flood-damaged property at Heacham after the 1953 floods. (Picture courtesy of Norfolk County Council Library and Information Service)

6ft of water came pouring down the streets. There was much damage to the sea front; huts and railings were torn to bits, and the jetty and part of the sea wall were wrecked.

Headlines from the local papers included:

Eighty foot waves at Mundesley: buildings swept away over promenade

'Very grim' in West Norfolk – thousands of acres under sea water

Bacton house now at cliff edge: previously stood 50 to 60ft away

In 30 minutes much of Salthouse was ravaged: woman killed and at least 30 houses destroyed

Norfolk coast disaster: from Palling to Salthouse

Many help with evacuation: stories of tragedy and bravery

Seas' wild rush into towns and villages

Floods affected over 3,000 houses at Lynn: about one fifth of town's area under water

Water supply failure at Hunstanton: over 30 people missing, believed drowned

As well as tales of tragedy, there were tales of heroism – of people making incredible rescues. American serviceman Reis Leming from Washington State saved 27 lives in Hunstanton and was awarded the George Medal for his bravery. He pushed a six-man rubber dinghy for several hours to rescue women and children off a ¾-mile stretch of wrecked bungalows before he collapsed with exhaustion. When asked about the rescue his response was worthy of the Norfolk lifeboat crews: 'Shucks, it wasn't much.'

Fireman Fred Sadd in Gorleston was also awarded the George Medal; he spent hours that night in the icy water, alternately pulling and pushing a boat and getting trapped people to safety.

2003 saw snow across the region and Norfolk was cut off – the A14 and A11 were blocked, and the M11 was gridlocked after two days of snow. 180 out of 450 schools were shut across the county.

February

February is one of the coldest months of the year, and 1374 was no exception – the records of Norwich Cathedral refer to 'a deep snow in February that laid upon the ground seven weeks, and on thawing occasioned a great flood.' February 1929 was also bitterly cold – so much so that the seas froze around the pier at Hunstanton. February 1947 was actually the coldest February on record, and snow fell every day at some part in the UK from 22 January to 17 March. 1963 was also a severe winter – the coldest since 1740, and at Santon Downham near Thetford they had 64 consecutive days with snow lying on the ground.

February is also a month of storms and floods; some of the worst erosion along the Norfolk coastline has taken place during February storms.

1 February

1876 saw a large fire at Riches & Watts, the agricultural engineers in Duke Street, Norwich, causing £3–4,000 of damage (equivalent to between £194,000 and £258,000 in today's money). There was a wood yard between the foundry and Bullard's maltings, and the fire crews were worried that the whole lot would go up. The fire started around 9pm in the pattern rooms above the brass foundry, and flames could be seen high above the buildings; it lit up the district, so many people watched from the street and climbed on to walls and bridges to see the fire. Luckily there was no wind, so, although it was 20 minutes before the firefighters got the water supply going, they were helped by Bullards' workers and the flames were out in two hours. The fire destroyed many patterns and 20 engine sets; the cause of the blaze was unknown.

1941 saw an air raid on Great Yarmouth which damaged Grout's silk mill.

1954 saw a major cold snap everywhere. Eighteen degrees of frost was measured at West Raynham, and the River Yare was covered with ice several inches thick at Berney Arms, meaning that even the tugs couldn't get through between Norwich and Great Yarmouth. The thaw started three days later.

In 1972 there was a huge drama on Kett's Hill, Norwich, which saw men lassoing a blazing gas cylinder. It was thought that gas leaked from the cylinder and came into contact with a coal fire burning in the shed at J. Thurston and Son, entertainment contractors; the blast shattered windows, blew the door off its hinges and caused £300 damage to funfair equipment. One man was hurt by the flying glass. Staff lassoed the burning cylinder and dragged it clear, then doused the fire in the shed while firemen tackled the cylinder.

1974 saw a warehouse gutted in King's Lynn; £12,000 of furniture and office equipment was lost in the blaze, and dozens of firemen fought the blaze in Tower Street.

1986 saw a storm on the coast with major winds; high seas came over the sea walls. The coast road at Walcott was flooded, and a home for elderly people was evacuated.

2 February

1570 saw the 'Candlemas day' flood in Norwich. *White's Directory* of 1845 says that the flood affected the north side of the city, and Fye Bridge was washed down. (See photograph on 26 August.) The Elizabethan historian Henry Manship referred to it as a 'great rage of water' which did much damage at Great Yarmouth, Dunwich, Wisbech and King's Lynn.

1791 saw part of the Jetty at Great Yarmouth carried away by a destructive high tide, and the Denes were under water. On the Southtown Road the water was deep enough for boats to ply; the *Norwich Remembrancer* adds that there were breaches in the defences at Waxham and many cattle were lost.

1823 saw a shocking event for a congregation of 120 'ranters', who were in a 15ft-square room in the City of Norwich Pub in St Stephen's Street. The floor gave way and they were thrown into a cellar 9ft below – the *Norfolk Chronicle* reported that they were 'with considerable difficulty extricated'. The barmaid had an extremely lucky escape – she'd gone into the cellars to draw beer and left only seconds before the floor fell in. Twenty-five of the congregation (including some children) suffered serious injuries. Four had fractures: Samuel Bell of Norwich and Thomas Simmons of Witchingham both broke a leg, William Suffle of Norwich had a fractured shoulder, and poor William Gardner of Great Yarmouth had a compound fracture of his leg, which had to be amputated immediately.

1954 saw five fire brigades fighting a blaze at Snetterton Hall Farm. The roof of the house was gutted and the first floor badly damaged; one fireman had a lucky escape when the staircase collapsed and buried him in debris. It was so cold that the snaps to pumps and nozzles froze, hampering the rescue efforts.

3 February

There was a major fire in Norwich in 1768, when the buildings of Ward and Company's workrooms were burned, together with a large quantity of wool.

1854 saw a heavy snowstorm and gale which blocked roads across the county. The railway between Great Yarmouth and London was blocked, and it took the Fakenham train nearly 12 hours to get to Norwich. Telegraph poles were blown down, and the port at King's Lynn was frozen up.

4 February

Great Yarmouth had quite a shock at 5am in 1947 when a mine exploded on the beach. Luckily, nobody was hurt, but windows were broken and ceilings were cracked by the blast around Wellesley Road, Sandown Road and North Drive.

5 February

1947 saw Norfolk in the grip of blizzards which left drifts of up to 10ft. Bacton was virtually cut off, and a week later people were marooned at Mundesley – food and supplies could only be delivered to the village by sledge.

6 February

In 1847 there was a major fire at Mr Kitton's warehouse in Rose Lane. The warehouse and its contents – barrels of grease and resin – were completely destroyed.

1897 saw a sudden thaw and heavy rain, leading to floods around the county. *The Times* reported that 'many parts of Norfolk are under water'. As often in Norwich, the River Wensum flooded the Heigham area.

In 1920 the water and steam mills at Weybread, plus wheat, flour and machinery, were destroyed by fire. The fire started at 5.30am and half an hour later the flames licked above the top of the mill and could be seen for miles around. When Harleston fire brigade arrived, they were on the wrong side of the river and couldn't cross the bridge; the mill couldn't be saved.

1975 saw a daring rescue in King's Lynn when firemen saved two seamen from a Dutch ship. The men had been inspecting a pump in the bilges when they were overcome with carbon monoxide poisoning. The rescuers gave them oxygen, lashed them to an aluminium ladder and carried them over yet more ladders connecting the ship to the quay, where they were taken to hospital by ambulance.

7 February

1795 saw a huge flood in Norwich after a rapid thaw; the River Wensum overflowed due to the melting snow. According to the *Norfolk Chronicle*, the floods were 6–8ft in some places; the worst affected areas were Heigham and the parishes of St Miles, St Mary, St Clement and St George.

1860 saw a fire at pastry cook W. Aberdein's in Dove Street, Norwich. It was not that serious, but Cubitt's ironmonger's shop was next door – and there were over 400lb of gunpowder stored in the shop! The *Norfolk Chronicle* reported that the gunpowder was removed safely in wet blankets.

1969 saw a blizzard across the county, with winds up to 40 knots. There were stranded vehicles on most of the roads in Norfolk.

1972 saw a blaze at the depot of the Esso Petroleum Co. in King's Lynn, when fuel oil in a storage tank caught fire. The fire started when an oxy-acetylene cutter was used to dismantle three 12,000-gallon tanks. A company spokesperson said there were 20 gallons of oil in the tanks at most, and the blaze was put out before three fire engines arrived; however, employees were evacuated using full emergency procedures, and the company praised the staff for the calm efficiency in which they carried out the evacuation.

8 February

In 1946 there was major flooding around the county. Norwich had almost 1.2in of rain in 13 hours, and the wind was over 50mph.

9 February

1894 saw a huge storm across the east coast. The Cardiff steamer *Resolven*, with a cargo of 2,300 tons of coal, ran ashore on the Cockle Sand near Caister at midday during severe wind squalls. The captain decided to jettison the cargo to lighten the vessel in an attempt to get it off the sandbank; 70 beachmen and boatmen helped with the task, but two days later the seas were still so heavy that they couldn't get it off. The lifeboatmen brought the crew to safety, and two days later the steamer was a total wreck.

In Acle there was much damage to roofs, followed by severe weather over the weekend. The earth was dry, so dense clouds of dust were blown about in the countryside – storms known as 'February fill dyke' (presumably because that's exactly what the dust did). At Sheringham, the lifeboat crew saw a schooner in distress and went to rescue it, but they could find no sign of it; they assumed that either it had sunk or it had blown away faster than they could travel. It was hard to get the lifeboat home in the heavy seas, so they had to put the lifeboat to anchor for a while; when they tried again, it took them four hours to travel the four miles from Cromer to Sheringham.

1899 saw a freak storm which the *Eastern Daily Press* reported as 'a February squall in the early hours'. At Great Yarmouth, the seas were tumultuous and the spray rose in the air 'like big clouds', mingled with blizzards. At high tide, the North Quay was flooded and several lives were lost at sea.

1925 saw a huge gale which cut off all telecommunications with Norwich; the windows of Bloomfield's fruiterers on Dereham Road were blown out. The wind speed was measured at 64mph in Great Yarmouth and cables snapped on the tramway. At Thetford the shaft of the 65ft high chimney at the waterworks was blown down on to the roof of the boiler room; luckily nobody was hurt. Across the county, there was damage to roofs and trees, including many uprooted at the Salhouse plantation. And at Kenninghall the banqueting room used by Elizabeth I was demolished; the ruins had been used as a granary by farmer Mr Spence. Nobody was hurt, but two pigs died and several farm implements were ruined.

In 1958 an earthquake was felt in North Norfolk. People heard a bang at 11.30pm at Sandringham, Fakenham, Cromer, Dereham and North Walsham; the vibrations lasted for two seconds and were felt in King's Lynn, and also as far north as Spurn Head in Yorkshire and as far inland as Nottinghamshire.

10 February

1825 saw the highest tide in Great Yarmouth for 35 years. At 8 o'clock in the evening, the river overflowed, flooding nearby cellars, granaries and stables. Many people gathered on the quay; there were worries that the bridge would collapse, but luckily it held. Wherry Quay was flooded halfway across; at North Quay the water came right up to the houses; Southtown was 3–4ft under water and could only be reached by boat; the gasworks was on an island, and the marshes were inundated. Gorleston was also 3ft under water, and at Cromer there was major damage to the cliffs.

1871 saw a major storm, with much snow; the *Norfolk Chronicle* described the heavy seas rolling over the pier and jetty at Great Yarmouth 'in towering masses'. Between Great Yarmouth and the Humber, 60 ships were wrecked.

The bad weather from 8 February 1946 continued, and the *Eastern Daily Press* said that the floods were the worst for 34 years. The east end of Aylsham was cut off from the centre when the Bure overflowed its banks, and scores of acres were flooded. The Drayton to Costessey road was 4–5ft deep in water.

11 February

1774 saw a fire at Bridgeham, where John Worley's house was destroyed.

1807 saw major snowfall in the county, and the mail coaches reached Norwich late because they overturned on the way.

The snow was even worse the following year – the *Norfolk Chronicle* reported that there were drifts up to 10ft deep, and it was the first time there was complete obstruction to communications since the winter of 1797. Coaches were delayed by four days, and people had to go in post-chaises and fours instead. Labourers clearing the roads had to cut through three miles of snow and ice, and the mail guards carried sacks on their shoulders and waded breast-deep through the snow to get the mail through. It was nearly eight weeks before the snow had completely melted.

12 February

1938 saw major floods at Horsey, due to a gale and high tide; 7,500 acres of grazing marsh were flooded and half a mile of sand hills were breached. It took three months to repair the sand hills and five years to restore the worst affected marshes. Salthouse's salt marshes turned into a lake and the sea lapped against village walls; the direction posts sticking up were the only things showing where the roads were. The *Eastern Daily Press* said that it was the worst gale for 40 years, with 75 to 80mph winds at Cromer. The flood continued over the next couple of days so 15 square miles of lands were underwater and the Great Yarmouth to Horsey road was flooded to a depth of 6ft.

1962 saw major gales; RAF Marham measured the wind speed of gusts at 60mph, and there were 50ft sheets of spray over the sea wall at Hunstanton.

1977 saw the River Wensum flooding at Sculthorpe. Thirty sheep and lambs were rescued by boat in a two-hour operation involving a dinghy and a punt with only one rowlock.

13 February

1870 saw a major storm which had lasted for four days; during the day, the barque *Victoria* was lost, along with its cargo of coals and nine out of the 16 crew. William Sharp, one of the five survivors, gave a dramatic account of what happened. They sailed on 10 February and a gale the following morning put out the galley fires, so the crew had nothing to eat. The ship had sprung a leak, so all hands went to the pumps; however, in the storm, the ship broke away from its anchor. The crew tried to get the second anchor out, but the cable fouled; then the second mate fell overboard and drowned. The ship drifted towards the beach at Great Yarmouth, and waves broke it into three. At that point, the water tank fell on the captain and killed him; several other crew members were washed away and drowned. The survivors clung to the fore of the ship, and four of them got on to the foremast. One of them saw Sharp's hair and pulled him out of the water by it; at that point, he lost consciousness. The first mate was killed when a plank was thrown at him by a wave; his body fell on top of the cabin boy and drowned him. Sharp and four others were finally rescued by the boatmen, who waded in to the surf with lines and cork belts, and Sharp was nursed back to recovery at Yarmouth Sailors' Home.

1990 saw Burleigh House in King's Lynn damaged by fire. The flames were spotted at 5am by a security guard, who raised the alarm; when the fire brigade arrived, the roof and top floor were ablaze. The fire crews extinguished the blaze, but around a quarter of the top floor was ruined.

2001 saw 200 residents evacuated from the 92 flats at Normandie Tower in Norwich. The tower was Norwich's first high-rise tower block, built in 1965–66; a water pipe had leaked for days and the city surveyors were concerned about subsidence in nearby chalk pits. Fortunately, the flats could be shored up.

14 February

1922 saw a tragic accident in King's Lynn. Amelia Barber, in her 70s, lived in Norfolk Street above the shop she'd sublet to Miss White. She usually went to bed at 5.30pm with a candle; later that night her neighbour Ruth Mitchell saw signs of fire and raised the alarm. Miss White opened the door and flames burst through, so it was impossible to enter the shop. It was impossible to get into the back of the house, too, because of the flames on the ground floor and lack of access to windows on the first floor, despite a ladder. Four men held a second ladder in their hands so one of them could smash the attic window to get in. Finally, fireman Samuel Holmes gained entry and searched through the smoke; he couldn't find anyone on the bed, but later found Amelia Barber under the bed, sadly deceased. The jury at the inquest commended the 'four unknown men' who'd tried so hard to rescue her.

The following year, there was a huge blaze in Norwich at Bullen Son & Kemp in Lothian Street, a cabinet maker and antique dealer. The fire – cause unknown – broke out at 2am; the *Eastern Daily Press* noted that there were hundreds of spectators watching the firemen fight big tongues of flame, which reached into the sky and lit the whole area. Although the building was gutted, the fire brigade contained it so it didn't spread next door to Cushion's timber yard.

2001 saw a stormy night on the coast, with the county on flood alert. Blakeney had flooding in the car park and on the roads, and only the sand barriers stopped businesses and houses flooding; when the flood water drained away, it left lots of seaweed on the roads. The cliffs at Happisburgh retreated by a shocking six metres overnight.

The cliffs at Happisburgh, showing remains of former properties that were once metres away from the clifftop. (Photograph by author)

The slipway at Happisburgh, which once led from the clifftop down to the beach and now ends in mid-air. (Photograph by author)

15 February

The Mayor's Book in Norwich records flooding after snow thawed in 1571; it was 'a handful' higher than the St Leonard's flood of 1519. According to the 18th-century historian Francis Blomefield, the snow started 10 days before Christmas and continued to Candlemas day (2 February); the whole of the north of the city was flooded on 5 February, and the waters continued rising. Blomefield says that the mayor and aldermen had to give 'relyfe of bread, drynke and herrying, to be given to the pore on the further side of the water, who are now kept in their houses by a great rage of water', and adds that the flood was 'so violent that it threw down walls and buildings' and 'removed the stools in all the churches' except St Augustine's. The flood also did much damage at Great Yarmouth, King's Lynn and Marshland.

In 1580, according to the 18th-century historian Francis Blomefield, on the Wednesday of Easter Week there was an earthquake in the city. He says there was 'a violent noise like the running of many carriages, and made all the joints of the timber work in the chamber crack and shake'.

In 1773 there was a fire at the County Gaol in Norwich Castle. John Hunt was ill and the keeper had put him in St Nicholas Chapel, where his son Edmund could look after him more comfortably. However, that night the castle bell rang and the keeper saw smoke: sadly, some straw had caught fire and the smoke suffocated the Hunts.

In 1735 there was a bad flood at the coast when a huge storm at high tide made the sea overflow the defences at Cley. Rector Robert Thomlinson of Cley described 'an inundation of the sea, which drowned all Cley and Blakeney Marshes, destroyed 80 acres of wheat then growing in

Cley Marshes. It broke down the banks very much… in many houses the water stood two or three feet deep.' Many of the inhabitants had to be rescued by boat from the upper floor of their houses, and according to Thomlinson the marshes didn't recover for several years.

In 1979 Gimingham watermill was destroyed by fire. The same day saw the Wells lifeboat crew launching a rescue in a blizzard – when the waves, at 40ft, were bigger than the 37ft lifeboat. The Romanian cargo ship *Savinesti* had lost its anchors and had engine failure. Despite the fact that the lifeboat kept filling up with water and had lost its radar, MF radio and echo sounder, the crew searched for three hours to find the ship. While the storm hit gale force 12, the lifeboat stood by the cargo ship until it was relieved by the Humber lifeboat two hours later. It took the Wells crew two hours to make the last seven miles home; by that time, most of the crew were too cold to walk and had to be helped ashore and into dry clothes. Two of them got frostbite, and one crewman said that the cold North Sea was actually warmer than the blizzard. Wells was cut off by snow for three days after the rescue.

1994 saw the biggest earthquake in the UK for 100 years, measuring 4 on the Richter scale. The epicentre was approximately five miles south of Swaffham, but the tremor at 10.16am was felt 100 miles away at Kettering. There was a second tremor an hour after the first, although it was milder, measuring 2.6 on the Richter scale. UEA expert Dr Paul Burton said that it was probably 10 to 15km below the surface, and might be on an old fault. Eyewitness reports included: 'like a massive explosion' and 'like a train going past'. Fortunately there was no damage, except for some broken crockery.

16 February

King's Lynn was hit by a flood in 1816, after a high tide which was several feet higher than the usual spring tides. The town was flooded and the Corn and Malt building on the ground floor sustained much damage. The same evening, a boat was forced on to the quay at Wells, and houses and warehouses were flooded; for the first time in 25 years, the Denes and west side of the haven at Great Yarmouth were also flooded due to the high tide.

1845 saw a major cliff fall near Cromer lighthouse – nobody was reported hurt, but the debris was spread across six acres of beach.

17 February

The coast took a battering in 1836; the *Norfolk Chronicle* reported a 'terrific tide', along with snow, hail and a gale. At Great Yarmouth, the tide overflowed the quay; even after the tide ebbed, houses remained flooded in the south of the town. People north of the quay were evacuated, but the front of the Norfolk Tavern fell and it was destroyed, along with two other houses. Several other houses had their foundations undermined to a depth of 8ft, and the beach was strewn with masonry. The paper reported that it was 14 years or so since the tide was last that high and estimated the damage at £2,000 (equivalent to nearly £145,000 in today's money). John Berney Crome (son of 'Old' John Crome) painted a picture called *Great Gale at Yarmouth on Ash Wednesday 1836*, which actually shows water lapping at the front doors of houses.

Cley was also affected; the streets and houses were flooded to a depth of 4ft, and the following day the water was 2ft higher. Hundreds of acres of marshland were under water and the sluice at Cley was wrecked. Damage was estimated at several thousand pounds.

1837 saw a high tide at Cromer, which washed away the Subscription Room, Bath House (with one poor man still in it) and other buildings on the beach and side of the cliff at Cromer. The cliff itself fell the following day, bringing down a house with it.

In 1876 a fire started in the carpenter's shop in Upper Hellesdon and spread to the mill, which was completely gutted. The machinery, plant and flour were also destroyed.

In 1950 the tower mill at Wymondham – one of the last in Norfolk to grind corn – was destroyed by fire in just half an hour. The fire was thought to start in the engine room and flames quickly went up the five timber storeys. The mill fell on to the granary next to it, which held hundreds of tons of corn; it too quickly caught light and was gutted. Five fire engines arrived and the flames were under control by 10am, but the fire brigade were there overnight to damp down. The Baptist Church House, 10ft away, was saved, although its windows were cracked and paint blistered.

1963 saw a Norwich café collapse; the previous day, the owners of Warren's Transport Café on Golden Ball Street realised there was a problem when they couldn't open the back door easily. Cracks appeared in the kitchen walls on 17 February, and they realised the café might collapse at any minute, so they managed to rescue their furniture and belongings shortly before two square yards of the cellar floor caved in. The same weekend, Spitalfields Road subsided and the floor of several buildings collapsed; city engineers believed it was caused by the frost. Three days later, a confectioner's and horticulturist's had to be abandoned in Golden Ball Street because of the subsidence. *The Times* reported that since frosts began seven houses and three shops had to be evacuated.

1966 saw a major fire at RAF Neatishead, which broke out in the underground radar station (now the RAF Air Defence Radar Museum). A divisional fire officer died and two firemen were missing, believed dead; the fire was still burning 24 hours after the alarm was raised. It broke out in an unoccupied technical room 60ft underground – the only room not in use in the bunker. Six fire brigades from Norfolk and Suffolk were called in, and they had a mile-long length of hose from the River Bure to the RAF station. However, the heat was so intense that they had to evacuate the bunker then flood it when they realised that the missing men had no chance of survival. On the following day, a second fire broke out; because the concrete walls retained heat, it was hard for the firemen to get in. The building was gutted. A week later 21-year-old Leading Aircraftman John Cheesman was charged with setting fire to the bunker. Later in March, the court heard that he left a lit cigarette on a table-tennis table while he went to get some white hardboard; then, when he smelled the smoke, he realised he might have started a fire and was too scared to raise the alarm. However, in another statement he said he lit some brown paper near the table-tennis table with matches. In April, *The Times* reported that he was sent to prison for seven years. In July, the British Empire Medal was awarded to James William Todd of the fire service 'for gallantry' – he worked continuously for seven hours in the smoke-filled room, where lights simply couldn't penetrate the smoke and he had to use guidelines to find his way. He had considerable burns to his face and neck and was the last one to come out of the bunker.

18 February

The bad weather from the previous week in 1807 continued; there was a hurricane with sleet and snow which tore into the shipping. The Yarmouth Revenue cutter *Hunter* was patrolling the coast as usual, keeping an eye out for smugglers, when it was caught in a storm which smashed it on to Haisbro Sand before bringing it on to the shore near Cart Gap.

A plaque from the memorial that Manby originally put up in his garden in Great Yarmouth, showing how the mortar worked. (Photograph by author)

There were more than 40 men on board; all lives were lost. According to the 19th-century historian Charles Palmer, 144 dead bodies were washed on to the shore near Great Yarmouth.

Twelve other ships were wrecked between Cromer and Gorleston in the same north-north-east gale that night – including the gunbrig *Snipe*. The ship was wrecked within 50 yards of the shore; more than 60 people died through drowning or exposure, including 30 of the French prisoners on board, women and some of the crew. Although people on the shore were desperate to help, they couldn't save the crew. But the events that night encouraged William Manby (better known as 'George') to invent his 'Manby Mortar', which could fire rescue lines out to ships. As a result, over 1,000 lives were saved over the next few years, starting with the crew of the brig *Elizabeth;* the brig was wrecked 150 yards from the shore on 12 February 1808, but everyone on board was saved.

The 'Manby Mortar', which fired a rescue line to a ship. (Photograph by author)

1932 saw a major fire at the music emporium of Wolsey & Wolsey in King Street, Great Yarmouth. A passer-by saw smoke around 9.35pm and raised the alarm; the fire brigade couldn't find the source of the fire at first but finally tracked it to the basement. It was also one of the first times the brigade used the water tower, raising a fireman above the level of the roof to direct a jet into the middle of the flames – as well as a searchlight with what the *Eastern Daily Press* called an 'incandescent flame'. It was thought at one point that the whole corner block would go up; however, firemen pumped water at the rate of 700 gallons a minute into the flames and extinguished the blaze. Several thousands of pounds' worth of stock was ruined, and onlookers were fascinated to see 'skeletonised pianos' the next day – whereas some of the radio speakers remained intact!

1941 saw an air raid over Norwich. A single bomb dropped on the Vauxhall Street, Horace Street, Walpole Street and Coach & Horses Street area damaged almost 50 houses, leaving 140 people homeless.

1955 saw the worst blizzard across the county since 1947. Cromer and Sheringham had 16in of snow between that afternoon and the following night, and over 100 snowploughs were out across the region to clear blocked roads.

19 February

1938 saw heavy cliff falls at Sidestrand; it was estimated that 20,000 tons of cliff fell, and residents watched a piece of cliff 120 yards long fall halfway to the beach before the piece of ground they were standing on began to crumble.

Children at Swaffham Boys' School had a lucky escape in 1947 when there was an explosion in the boiler room just before they were due to go in to lessons. A wall was blown down, the boiler was wrecked and most of the windows were shattered; it was thought that the explosion was caused by frost.

1996 saw the worst storm of the winter across the county. Four inches of snow fell, during a high wind, and many rows were impassable. The snowplough bill for the county topped £120,000, and police said that 999 calls were coming in at the rate of one a minute as lorries jack-knifed and cars slid all over the road. Police closed the A47 to the west of Norwich. High winds and high seas caused flooding over the coast; the floods swept away a bank at Salthouse and the resulting 4ft flood in the village was reckoned to be the worst since 1853. Thirty houses were evacuated at Walcott – and the occupants were put up at the village pub. The quay flooded at Wells; Cley marshes were flooded, putting the nature reserve at risk. There was damage to the shingle bank at Weybourne, and two breakwaters were smashed at Happisburgh – which was battered again two nights later. The *Eastern Daily Press* reported on 21 February that some puffins had been blown off course; one ended up in a garden at Lakenham but sadly didn't survive.

20 February

In 1932 there was a major fire in Norwich at the shoe factory of Barfield & Richardson in Botolph Street. The caretaker, who lived nearby, heard a noise; when he investigated, he saw flames and raised the alarm. The *Eastern Daily Press* reported 'flames 30ft above the roof, a raging furnace below'; the roof fell in a piece at a time and firemen had a narrow escape when part of the wall collapsed. The building was gutted, and 300 people were laid off.

21 February

1890 saw two large granaries at Cubitt & Walker's in North Walsham destroyed by fire, causing £4,000 worth of damage (equivalent to over £260,000 in today's money); the blaze was caused by a spark from an oil lamp. At 2.40am a workman who had been fitting machinery at Brig Gate Mill saw a light in the sheds and looked through the windows to see if someone was there with a candle. He realised that the sacks were ablaze and raised the alarm – but sadly a huge mistake was made when the doors were opened, because the fire spread rapidly and flames lept through the roof. North Walsham fire brigade were quickly on the spot, but the roof of the three-storey high granaries fell in. They were able to save the mill, even though the top of it caught fire at around 6.15am, and the fire was quenched later that morning.

In 1948 two pairs of thatched cottages near Brundall were burnt out; 91-year-old Mrs Rose lost her home of 60 years, and the Goodwin family of 10 lost everything. The fire started in the roof of another cottage and spread so quickly that although Mr Goodwin got his wife and four of the youngest children out he was unable to rescue the furniture. Neighbour Mrs Brown lost her cottage, but her dog was safe – and in a drawer in her rescued furniture she kept her fire insurance policy. The weather was so cold that, despite the heat of the blaze, ice formed in the lane from water pumped from the dyke.

1993 saw a high spring tide and a gale lasting two days, with some of the worst flooding across the coast since 1953. Hundreds of people were evacuated and scores of homes were flooded. Bungalows at Hemsby and Walcott were washed away; there were breaches in the shingle banks at Salthouse and Weybourne and a quarter of a mile of the bank was washed away at Cley. The sea tore open the flood barrier at Sea Palling and crashed into a police car – nobody was hurt but the car was severely damaged. One man was swept for a distance of 50 yards when the floodgate broke. Four thousand people were evacuated at Gorleston, and the jetty car park at Great Yarmouth was under water. There was a break of 30 to 50ft in the wall of the River Bure at Acle, and the Acle Straight was closed. At Walcott, the waves were 20ft over the sea wall; the seafront at Cromer was a mass of debris, and 387 oil rig workers had to be lifted to safety when their rig broke free of the platform. There was a two-metre surge tide into the River Yare, causing serious floods at Brundall and Surlingham; the broads flooded on 22 February and, as happened in March 1988, water rushed up the River Thurne and forced tens of thousands of fish upstream. A hundred thousand fish were still at risk of dying in the salt water.

22 February

1898 saw a dreadful disaster at Wells, when five of the coastguards drowned after their boat capsized – along with six of the crew of HMS torpedo boat *Alarm*.

The *Alarm* was making a routine visit to bring stores for the coastguard, and signalled they were ready for the Wells crew to come and fetch the stores – a replacement Morse signalling lamp and a mounting post. Chief Boatman John Devlin signalled back that the conditions were too bad to get a boat out – they only had a four-oared gig (a small boat), which couldn't cope with the bad weather. But he was told to go anyway. So when the tide brought enough water into the channel to launch the boat, Devlin set off at the helm, aided by 38-year-old George Bearman, 42-year-old Henry Perry, 33-year-old George Jordan and 31-year-old Patrick Driscoll. They had to row against the wind; two hours later they were exhausted and couldn't keep the boat on course when they rounded the point at the end of the channel.

Another coastguard, Williams, had gone to the point to signal to the *Alarm* that the coastguards were on their way. But he heard a noise and saw the capsized boat with a single person clinging to it – John Devlin. Williams sent a signal to the men on the quay at Wells, a mile away, and waded into the sea to drag Devlin to safety. Two men came to the end of the bank and found Williams and Devlin just above the shoreline, exhausted. Devlin died that night, although Williams recovered, but the other four men were still missing. A search party scoured the beaches for hours and finally found the bodies of George Bearman and George Jordan.

But the disaster didn't end there. The following morning, another search party came across the bodies of Henry Perry and Patrick Driscoll – but they also found the wreck of the gig from the *Alarm*. It seemed that when the Wells coastguard hadn't arrived to collect the stores, the *Alarm* decided to send six of its men to shore in a gig with the stores. The captain had no idea they were missing until they received the signals from the shore telling them what had happened.

Williams was too weak to attend the inquest, but told his story to the coroner. He'd heard a yell and shouted 'Is that the gig?' When an affirmative answer reached him, he told them they were 'right for the harbour,' and he'd show them a light round the Point. He went to the Point with a light, but the boat didn't arrive. He called out again, and the men called back that they were all right. Then he heard the call 'lifeboat ahoy' and realised something was wrong. He went into the water – which he said made him feel numb – and saw the boat 20 yards from the shore and someone clinging to her. He swam out and saw Devlin, who seemed to be on the point of letting go of the boat. He told Devlin, 'Don't let go, we are near shore.' Williams too gripped the drifting boat and discovered that he could touch the bottom. So he pulled the boat to the shore, got Devlin off the boat, and asked the two men from the quay to strip him down and rub him. They refused and instead carried Devlin the 1½ miles to town, even though both Williams and Devlin were freezing. 'Had he been rubbed at once, I believe he might have been saved,' was Williams's sad tale.

The jury reached a verdict of accidental death and asked the coroner to say 'they didn't think any fisherman well acquainted with the coast would have put to sea in such weather as the Coastguardsmen did'. They added that 'when the wind blows from a northerly direction... the flood tide makes with great rapidity and a very dangerous current runs in the channel and breakers of tremendous force roll over the sandbank beyond the Point'. The tide was often five or six knots in spring. They added that they thought Williams 'behaved in a most excellent way in getting his officer out of the sea'.

The Wells coastguard left five widows and 17 children, and a monument was erected in the cemetery near their graves.

1908 saw a severe storm across the county. The gale started at 4.30 in the afternoon, and although it only lasted for 15 minutes it did a huge amount of damage. Tiles, gables and chimneys fell across the county. Miller Isaac Stacey was killed when his mill was blown over at Terrington Fen End; the market in the Tuesday Market Place in King's Lynn was wrecked. Forncett station was partly wrecked; Dereham was battered by hail and most of Whitbread's maltings in Neatherd Road was wrecked. In Norwich, several roofs were stripped; there were floods in the streets at Great Yarmouth, and at Gorleston a hoarding was blown on to the tram tracks and had to be removed before the trams could continue.

1967 saw 60mph winds at Great Yarmouth which caused £2,000 of damage at the caravan park. Over 2,000 homes were without power, and roads were blocked. On the same day, subsidence hit Norwich in the Ber Street area yet again; this time, a hole 5 yards square and 6ft deep opened up very close to the new housing development, and Horn's Lane had to be sealed off until the hole was filled.

23 February

1796 saw a tragic accident at King's Lynn, when the ferry boat was crossing the river from the Common Staithe Quay to Old Lynn at about 7pm with 40 passengers on board. According to the 19th-century historian William Richards, at 6pm 40 people got into the ferry to cross the river. The boatmen said that there were too many people to go over at once, but they refused to listen. Although it was a calm evening, there was a strong tide; the journey went well until they neared the opposite shore. The boat collided with the cable of a barge and was overturned; over 20 people died. One of the passengers, John Price, was a sailor, and he rescued four other passengers; he tried to save a fifth, but the woman was torn from his arms by the rapid tide and he very nearly followed her. Richards added that two of the victims were about to get married; they were found clasped in each other's arms.

In 1853 there were major floods at King's Lynn after a large tide and heavy snowfall. The previous day, the *Norfolk Chronicle* reported that the thermometer read 19°F below freezing, and one poor man actually froze to death.

24 February

Deep snow fell in Norwich in 1673 and 'it laid on the ground for seven weeks', according to the 18th-century historian Francis Blomefield. When it thawed, there was a major flood and the bridges at Hellesdon and Trowse were badly damaged.

Norfolk's version of 'Whisky Galore' happened in 1837, when the steamer *Raby Castle* was wrecked at Salthouse in a severe gale with lashings of snow. Thankfully, the seven crew and two passengers managed to get to safety, despite the high seas. The cargo included wine, oranges, nuts, tea, toys and hampers – as well as lots of spirits. The cargo was actually worth £5,000 (equivalent to nearly £350,000 in today's money) but only £800 of it was recovered. The *Norfolk Chronicle* reported that by 7am there were about 300 people on beach. An hour later, the ship broke up, and the crowd on the beach had more than doubled in number. And then 'the most outrageous and beastly conduct was exhibited' – the people on the beach buried some barrels of spirits in the sands, to get them later; others broached casks and collected the spirits in oilskin hats. It was impossible to guard the cargo because there was so much of it. The paper concluded their report by saying that 'many men were conveyed from off the beach dead drunk, and it is with disgust, we add many women were in the same state'.

1965 saw a major fire in a two-storey warehouse behind Roy's Surplus Stores on Magdalen Street, Norwich. Five engines fought the blaze, and the smoke could be seen all over the city. A wall collapsed and a fireman was taken to hospital with cuts and shock, but he was allowed home later that day. The warehouse was gutted, but the fire brigade stopped the fire spreading to the flats next door.

25 February

1958 saw arctic blizzards across the country. The frost was 9°F below zero, and there were snowdrifts up to 15ft deep, which stranded children in schools.

26 February

1773 saw a major storm that lasted two days; 30 ships were lost off Great Yarmouth.

In 1778 there was a major fire in Pump Street, Norwich, which destroyed the house of the baker Mr Smith and four other houses. The *Norwich Mercury* reported that one man managed to save his sheets and bed – but then they were stolen from the poor chap!

1916 saw the Sheringham lifeboat coming to the aid of the SS *Uller* of Bergen; the ship was travelling from Sunderland with a cargo of coal when she hit a sandbank on 24 February. She drifted, seriously damaged, for the next day and a half, then hit the Blakeney Overfalls bank in a storm. The crew signalled for help in thick snow and gale force winds; the Cromer and Wells lifeboats couldn't launch because of the weather, so the Sheringham crew braved the trenched and barbed-wire cliffs to get to the lifeboat house and launched their open boat. Waves crashed over the boat and the crew was soaked long before it reached the *Uller*. The damaged ship still had steam and the Sheringham crew stood by all night in snow; the following day, the *Uller* was able to travel towards Grimsby, despite the fact the water in the damaged bow had tipped the ship so the propeller was half out of the sea.

1971 saw a dramatic double rescue when there was an explosion on the Arpet A oil rig platform, 22 miles off Cromer. The flames could be seen from 20 miles away, and the blaze wrecked the galley, food store and the crew's quarters, as well as hurling the jib of a crane into the sea. The operating company, Phillips Petroleum, said it was caused by mechanical failure. Two of the 17 men on board, Keith Bailey and Ronald Ley, were hurt and flown to Great Yarmouth for treatment.

1972 saw a huge blaze at the Haymarket in Norwich when Ratners jeweller's shop caught fire. The alarm was raised at 7pm, although onlookers couldn't see the flames, just lots of smoke. Six engines came to fight the blaze; the fire crews were worried that the gas board and Lamberts might catch light and the resulting fire would be like the disastrous fire at Garlands the previous year [see 1 August]. There was also a threat to St Peter Mancroft Church, which was only 10ft away! The fire was in a false ceiling between the ground and first floor, and the fire crews had to fight it from below; they did, however, manage to confine the blaze to the jeweller's.

27 February

In 1840 there was a major fire at Thorrold's, the engineer and iron foundry near Foundry Bridge in Norwich. It started in the furnace room at about 10.30pm, and the *Norfolk Chronicle* described 'a vast and vivid body of flame, culminating from the roofs towards the lofty chimney which stands in the centre, cast its red light on surrounding houses and on the countless faces of the multitude who crowded the approaches to the bridge'. Mr Thorrold lived at Hethersett and didn't reach the city until 1 o'clock in the morning, so the paper noted that there was no real direction to stop the fire. Although there were two engines in attendance, their leather pipes were defective – as often seemed to happen in the 19th century, the firefighters were reliant on a human chain armed with buckets. However, it was not enough to save the foundry: the fire gutted the new buildings and everything was lost, including the steam engine, models, patterns, tools and materials.

1972 saw gale force winds with gusts of 52–60mph, which raised dust storms. In Beccles, one man had a lucky escape – a willow tree was uprooted and crashed on to his car, just minutes before he was going to drive home for lunch.

1990 saw a storm with gale force 10–11 winds. Sea defences were battered at Heacham and Hunstanton, and chalets and caravans were damaged.

28 February

In 1860 there was a huge gale across the county, causing major damage to buildings and many shipwrecks. In Norwich, St Augustine's Street and Magdalen Street were 'reddened with tiles', according to the *Norfolk Chronicle*. There were many narrow escapes from the falling chimney pots and tiles. The 18ft chimney shaft of Mr Ketton's oil-cake mills near Foundry Bridge was blown down through the roof of the boiler house; two Norfolk hotels suffered major damage when their chimneys crashed through the roofs. Eight bedrooms and furniture were damaged at the Norfolk hotel, and the *Norfolk Chronicle* reported the damage as £50,000 – this was probably a typographical error, however, as that would be the equivalent of three and a quarter million pounds in today's money! Six bedrooms were damaged at the Castle Hotel. In Adelaide Street a row of 20 terraced houses all lost their chimney pots; 75 yards of wall at the new workhouse were blown down. Although the newspaper reported that it was not quite as bad out at sea as it was inland, 'masses of spray rose like pillars of snow' on Scroby Sands. The ship *Zephyr* was grounded on Scroby and the sea washed over her; the lifeboats rescued the entire crew, but the 15-year-old passenger, William Strange, was lost. He had been seasick throughout the journey and was lashed to rigging to keep him safe in the squall, but he died in the water.

In 1907 there was a huge fire at Hobbies engineering works, Dereham, which caused £25,000 of damage (equivalent to over £1.8 million in today's money) and put 150 people out of work. The fire started at 7pm when Dennis Brooks knocked over a can of gaseous oil near a naked flame. Mr Walker, the clerk doing the payroll, came to investigate the noise, saw the fire, and managed to escape from the flames. Oil and paint stored on the top floor fed the fire; the neighbouring cottages were evacuated and the fire brigade tried to save them. The fire continued to spread over a quarter of an acre and threatened Crane and Smith's wood yard; luckily, it was contained, but all the machinery was lost, including patterns for the casting of fretsaw blades. Some of the buildings were saved, and all the horses were rescued.

March

March is meant to come in like a lion and out like a lamb – but some of the most severe gales have taken place towards the end of the month. March winds have caused some of the worst shipping disasters, including that of the *Invincible* (see 16 March).

March has also seen some huge fires in the county. In addition to the ones mentioned below, in 1973 a blaze ravaged three-quarters of Redgrave Fen, near Diss, and it was feared that Britain's biggest and rarest spider, the raft spider, was extinct because the fen was its only known habitat. The spider got its name because it floats on water with its back legs on a leaf and its front legs on the surface tension of water; it's reportedly very shy and can dive underwater and remain submerged for 10 minutes. When the spider was spotted again in October 1974, experts thought that the ability to remain submerged probably saved it.

March has also seen epidemics in the county; in 1872 smallpox was rife in Norwich, and at the height of the epidemic 30 people a week were killed by the disease. The previous year, the Royal College of Physicians had advised people to get re-vaccinated, saying that 35 percent of people who hadn't been vaccinated died from smallpox, but the mortality rate was less than one percent in people who had been vaccinated.

1 March

In 1463 there was a fire in Norwich, and the roof of the cathedral was destroyed.

1794 saw a major fire when the hot press shop belonging to Mr Winn in St George's Colegate in Norwich went up at 5am, destroying the premises and goods. Luckily, a brick wall separated oil from the premises or there would have been a catastrophe. The fire – which was caused by a chimney fire – was out in two hours but did an incredible £1,500 worth of damage (the equivalent of over £127,000 in today's money).

In 1820 there was a severe storm and a deep flood in King's Lynn.

1938 saw Horsey hit by floods again; the high tide was 3ft over its normal level and poured through a gap in the sea defences – one villager said the sea was moving at around 20mph. Sixty-year-old Tom Fuller was nearly drowned as he tried to get home, but he was pulled to safety.

1949 saw gales and floods across the county, which the *Eastern Daily Press* reported as the worst storm for 50 years, with thousands of pounds' worth of damage to sea walls and hundreds of acres flooded. Squalls of 80mph were measured at Great Yarmouth. People were marooned at Salthouse, and at Cley the flood was 4ft deep. At Wells the tide overflowed the quay to 3ft in depth, and Blakeney saw its worst flood since 1895. At Snettisham the flood was 4ft – 30 families had to be rescued by boat, and one woman and her two-day-old baby were made homeless. At King's Lynn, the floods reached the Church of St Margaret. (See 11 March for photograph.)

2 March

In 1839 the newspapers reported that smallpox was prevalent in Norwich; around 100 people died from the disease.

1952 saw an avalanche at Sheringham, when mud slid down a 100ft cliff at the east end of the promenade, tore down wire netting and went straight across the concrete wall on to the promenade.

3 March

In 1949 there was a huge explosion at Besthorpe, which led to the three-storey flour mill being gutted. Francis Leman had just lit a blow-lamp to heat a hot-bulb type engine and was oiling the engine when the lamp exploded. Luckily, he was protected by the engine, but the main paraffin tank caught fire in seconds. He carried quite a few 16-stone sacks of barley to safety but lost several coombs of oats and barley (a coomb is a measure equivalent to four bushels or a little under 8,900cu in) plus the mill's grinding machinery. Attleborough fire brigade had a new 500-gallon tender, so they were able to get the fire under control in half an hour – but they were unable to save the mill.

1988 saw the road swallow the Number 26 double-decker bus in Earlham Road, Norwich. Neither the driver Jim Pightling nor any of the passengers had seen the hole – and when the bus started to pull away from Paragon Place a large section of the road collapsed beneath the rear wheels of the vehicle. The hole was 26ft deep, caused by chalk pit subsidence. A gas main ruptured and people were evacuated from nearby houses until the gas board managed to cap the pipe at 2am.

4 March

In 1818 there was a severe gale that affected the whole of the county. *The Times* said that the March winds were known as St Winnold's storms in Norfolk, and quoted a rhyme:

> First comes David, then comes Chad
> Then comes Winnold, as if he were mad.

Several ships were driven ashore, and the new mill at Hempnall lost its top. In the church at Pulham St Mary, the enormous chancel window – 20ft by 11ft – was demolished. Chimneys blew down across Norwich, including the whole of the chimney at Thompson's brewery in King Street; the gales also demolished the steps leading to the coppers – luckily before the stoker was due to light the furnace!

1938 saw Horsey hit yet again; the sea went over the wall again at both tides, adding millions of gallons of water to the flood. The *Eastern Daily Press* commented that it was lucky the breeze was light or the temporary sea defences would have been swept away.

5 March

There was a major fire in Peacock Street, Norwich, which destroyed the factory of Williams Ltd and four cottages. The *Eastern Daily Press* reported that the glare in the sky could be seen for miles, and even 200 yards from the factory the heat was too intense to bear. Due to the inflammable material in the factory – furniture, timber and machinery – the fire burned rapidly, and the roof fell in within half an hour of the fire being reported at 9.40pm.

1969 saw a £30,000 blaze at the workshop of boatbuilders Norfolk Knights at Horning. It started in the resin bay around 5pm and flames shot across the room. Workers tried to put out the fire with extinguishers, but within 30 seconds the room was well alight. Luckily the 12 employees were safe and the diesel tank didn't explode, but the workshop itself was gutted in the blaze, along with the loss of four boats, a dozen engines, fibreglass moulds and raw materials.

6 March

1880 saw a bad fire in New Buckenham, which caused £2,000 of damage to houses and shops. Mr Ball's shop sold 'fancy goods' and was also a pharmacy. He was going to bed at about 12.30am after friends had been over for the evening when he saw a light in his shop; when he investigated he realised the shop was on fire. He woke the others in the house, but the fire spread so fast that they barely had time to get dressed before fleeing the house. PC Read rescued valuable books and furniture from the house, despite the suffocating smoke. A human chain was formed with buckets from the village pump to the shop, but then the fire spread up from the fancy goods to the pharmacy and the whole interior was on fire, punctuated with loud explosions as the various chemicals caught light. Calls for help were sent to the fire brigades from Banham, Attleborough, Wymondham and Norwich; they were unable to save the shop, but concentrated on trying to stop it spreading to the neighbours. Benjamin Lawrence's house and butcher's shop was also gutted. At 3am the Attleborough engine arrived; they used up 80 gallons per minute, which soon drained all the wells and pumps dry, so they were forced to use water from the river, putting their hoses across Mr Palmer's garden. By 6am the fire was out, but fire crews kept watch for the next 24 hours. When Mr Bell was finally able to retrieve his cashbox, all the silver in it had melted into a lump.

1883 saw a strong gale and a high tide with hail and snow; houses on Marine Parade in Great Yarmouth were in danger of being flooded, and the jetty was damaged. Thousands of fish were killed in the River Yare when the salt water came in.

1969 saw major gales and a dramatic rescue from a North Sea oil rig. Heavy seas meant that spray covered the 80ft high platform of the Oil Prince drilling rig, and it started to break up. Although the oil rig workers put rope ladders down, they couldn't get to the trawler by the rig. A 190ft derrick crashed down, but luckily landed in the opposite direction to the helipad, and a helicopter airlifted the men to safety at Lowestoft. RAF Watton recorded gusts of 86mph and both power and phone lines were down across the county in the afternoon, thanks to a combination of wind and a snowstorm. At Great Yarmouth, the beaches were flooded to the sea wall, and in Norwich a 10ft-square window at the showrooms of James Woodhouse & Sons in Orford Street was blown out.

7 March

Great Yarmouth had a hurricane in 1839; the streets and rows were strewn with bricks and debris from the roofs of houses.

1931 saw a blaze cause £2,000 worth of damage at Savage's saw mill in King's Lynn.

1976 saw a six-year-old saving his family from a fire at Gorleston. Robert Jackson woke in the night and, smelling smoke, called his mum. The fire broke out in an airing cupboard where his toys were kept; his dad was fishing at sea, so his mum got Robert and his 11-month-old baby sister out. The smoke was so thick that she had to feel her way down the stairs. Firemen soon had the blaze under control, but the maisonette was badly damaged by smoke.

8 March

1942 saw an air raid over Sheringham which left one person dead.

1977 saw a fire in a barn at West Beckham containing 350 tons of corn. The blaze started in a drying machine; two fire brigades attended and got the flames under control, but the drying machine and part of the roof were ruined at a cost of several thousands of pounds.

9 March

There was a whirlwind at Kilverstone in 1735 which blew the lead off the tops of nearby churches and tiles off houses, flattened a piece of ground and apparently blew water out of the river, carrying it 1½ furlongs away.

1854 saw a huge fire in Castle Street, Norwich, when the *Norwich Mercury* building went up in flames. The roof fell in, and the compositors' room – along with most of the cases of type – was destroyed.

10 March

1977 saw a fire cause £200,000 worth of damage in the meat store of United Kingdom Cold Storage Ltd in Thetford. The polystyrene insulation caught light, and the crew of two fire engines managed to put out the blaze.

11 March

1883 saw a huge flood in King's Lynn across 400 acres of reclaimed land. That evening, there was a high tide – some 4–5ft higher than usual – and a storm. The quays and river banks broke; and, as the *Norfolk Chronicle* commented, the old marshfolk wouldn't have done what the Norfolk Estuary Company did, allowing people to cut away part of the bank at the base so they could fill various hollows with the material. The bank collapsed, allowing the water in. A family in the farmhouse were rescued from the top floor by boat the next morning, but 900 sheep drowned. A plaque in the porch of St Margaret's Church shows the level of the flood.

1958 saw a major fire at the Samson & Hercules in Norwich; the new snack bar in the basement was destroyed, and the Queen Anne Room on the right of the main entrance was badly damaged. The fire started among tins of paint; the alarm was raised just past 4am, and then firemen discovered that the intense heat had melted a gas main, which then fed the fire. They finally managed to subdue it three hours later.

1976 saw a load of matches go up in flames, and lorry driver Edgar Wallace had a lucky escape. He was transporting 900 cartons of matches when he saw smoke in his mirrors. He pulled into a layby on the A47 at Scarning and unhitched his lorry, which burst into flames – aided by the matches. Firemen were able to save 200 cartons of matches, but there was much damage to the trailer, plus the canvas cover was lost at a cost of £200.

Three fire brigades were called out to Bacton later the same evening when there was an explosion at the Shell gas production terminal, which blew down walls and started a fire in the building. The automatic fire extinguishers sensed the escape of gas and put out the blaze; when firefighters with breathing apparatus went in, they found a 'white haze'. Fortunately, nobody was hurt.

1986 saw a flood in King's Lynn. Also at Watlingham Plant Hire workshop several thousands of pounds' worth of equipment was destroyed by a fire which started under a welding bench. The blaze could be seen two miles away; 115,000 gallons of oil was on fire and gas tanks exploded, and 30 firemen were needed to fight the blaze. None of the 15 employees were hurt.

The flood markers in the porch at St Margaret's Church in King's Lynn. The depth of the 1883 floods is just about Christopher's waist; there are also marks for 1 March 1949 (at the level of the shelf), 31 January 1953 (Chloe's eye level) and 12 January 1978 (just above Chloe's head). (Photograph by author)

12 March

1928 saw a disastrous fire at King's Lynn; three men died in an explosion at the Distillers Company Ltd factory in Alexandra Dock. The building was 160ft long, 100ft wide and four-storeys high and used for making acetone and butanol alcohol. Jack Fenn was in charge of the cookers on the ground floor, John Aldridge and Ernest John Green were in charge of the stills on the upper floor of the building, and there were six other men in the building at the time of the explosion. The survivors said that it all went dark; there was a terrific explosion and the doors were blown out – they made a rush for the open spaces but several of them were scorched before they made it outside. Mr Shaw, the captain of the fire brigade, was shaken out of bed by the explosion; he thought perhaps a ship had blown up, looked out of his window and saw the fire.

The survivors tried to rescue Fenn, Aldridge and Green, but they were forced to abandon their attempt just before the roof and walls collapsed. The steamship *Poldiep* was discharging at the quay next to the factory and pumped water on to the burning building; even so, the fire lasted five hours and thousands of townspeople watched it. The damage was estimated at

£50,000 (equivalent to over £2 million in today's money); although the distillery was flattened, the offices survived without much damage.

The inquest was adjourned for a report from the Inspector of Factories, who examined the ruins with the works manager. They found a split in the well at the bend of a pipe that led to the still which was being charged, and concluded that it was probable liquid seeped through the split and came into contact with an electric light globe, breaking the glass and then igniting. The verdict was accidental death, and the King and Queen sent their sympathy via the coroner.

13 March

1866 saw an explosion in the brewery of Arnold & Wyatt at St Mary's Plain, Norwich. The boiler was lit as usual at 5am and the brewer Edward Le Mills levelled the 'mash ton' at around 11am. He stood on the steps, and then the boiler exploded; 26-year-old engine driver William Whitworth was killed when his body was 'hurled into the beck containing six quarters of boiling wort'. He left a wife and child, and there was £2,000 of damage to the boiler and buildings (equivalent to £126,000 in today's money), which were all uninsured. The cause of the explosion was a mystery, because the boiler had recently been overhauled; it had two safety valves and was only at two-thirds of the maximum pressure at the time of the explosion.

14 March

1947 saw huge floods following a combination of heavy rain and a rapid thaw after the snowiest winter of the 20th century. Over the next week there were gales – including one where a 100mph gale blew down an air raid siren that was used as a fire alarm. It was the worst flood for years in Thetford and the worst ever seen in the Fens, with thousands of acres flooded and hundreds made homeless – despite the fact that on 20 March over 1,000 men sandbagged the King's Lynn to Ely road to stop the Fen flood joining the Thetford flood. The spring tides made it worse, and, despite the fact that a dam was built at Southery to keep the waters back, a culvert burst over the weekend. On 25 March *The Times* reported that Mr Williams, the Minister of Agriculture, called it a 'disaster of the first magnitude', which would have a serious effect on food production – winter wheat and potatoes had been lost, and farmers weren't going to be able to sow grain in the spring. The following day, *The Times* reported that the government was giving £1 million for the relief of distress caused by floods.

15 March

1865 saw Frazer's Sawmills in St Martin's, Norwich, gutted by fire; £4,000 worth of damage was caused (the equivalent of nearly £270,000 in today's money).

Following the floods of 1 March 1949, Cley and Salthouse were flooded again to a depth of 3ft.

1971 saw a huge blaze when 50 tons of paper were destroyed at Great Yarmouth. The paper was stacked near to a warehouse, waiting to be exported; the fire damaged the building next to it and the smoke ruined meat products in the building. The cause was unknown, but bystanders told the *Eastern Daily Press* that it just suddenly caught fire.

16 March

16 March 1801 saw the great tragedy of HMS *Invincible*, which had sailed from Great Yarmouth intending to join the Baltic Fleet under Admiral Nelson just before the Battle of Copenhagen. The ship, commanded by Captain John Rennie, carried 600 men and plenty of ammunition and stores. The ship's pilots were familiar with the passage through Haisbro Gap, but a strong tide and a fresh wind forced the ship off course. At 2.30 in the afternoon she struck a sandbank called Hammond's Knoll, just east of Haisbro Sand. The crew cut away all the masts and manned the pumps all night to try to save the ship.

The ship's crest from the memorial stone at Happisburgh Church, commemorating the men of the *Invincible*. (Photograph by author)

The *Nancy*, a smack who was out fishing for cod, came to the rescue. Rear Admiral Thomas Totty boarded her, together with the youngest crew members. The boats from the *Invincible* were launched, but were driven out to sea. At daybreak, the *Nancy* tried to save the rest of the crew, but the ship went down. A collier picked up some of the men in the boats, but around 400 of the men who'd set out in the *Invincible* perished – including poor Captain Rennie.

Over the next few days, bodies were washed up along the coastline. At Happisburgh, literally cartloads of bodies were collected and taken up to the church; 119 men were buried in a mass grave on its north side. However, there was no memorial, until Mary Cator, a resident of the village, started a county-wide collection in 1913 to raise funds for a stone. Because there was not a written record of the burials, she couldn't prove the men were buried there and had to return all the donations. But in 1988 a drainage trench was dug to take rainwater from the church – and many skeletons were found. It was clear that the

The stone at Happisburgh Church, commemorating the men of the *Invincible*. The inscription reads: 'On 16 March 1801, HMS Invincible was wrecked off Happisburgh when on her way to join a fleet with Admiral Nelson at Copenhagen. The day following, the ship sank with the loss of some four hundred lives. One hundred and nineteen members of the Ship's Company lie buried here. "And the sea gave up the dead that were in it..." Revelations 20:13. This memorial stone was given jointly by the Parochial Church Council and the officers and Ship's Company of the HMS Invincible, 1998.' (Photograph by author)

old legend was true: the men of the *Invincible* were buried there and Mary Cator had been right. On 24 July 1998 a stone – given jointly by the present-day *Invincible* and the Parochial Church Council – was placed in the churchyard, dedicated to the memory of those who died on the *Invincible*.

1915 saw a major storm which flooded the marsh at Southery to a depth of 5ft. There were also two shipwrecks at Sheringham. The first was the steamer *Penarth* from Cardiff; the ship struck Sheringham Shoals and the crew took to the lifeboat, but it capsized and threw them all into the water. The ship broke in two and was sunk within an hour and a half of striking the shoals; although the 27 crew struggled to cling to their upturned lifeboat, they lost hold one by one. The trawler *Glen Proseen* of Aberdeen saw the boat and came to their rescue, and skipper Stephen Nicoll said that they picked up the seven survivors one by one. Three were 'very far gone', and although his crew gave artificial respiration one died from exhaustion. The Sunderland steamer *George Royle* was also wrecked, and all the 20 crew were lost. The Cromer lifeboat was out at 1.30am but it was too late to save the ship. They did, however, manage to save a ketch carrying coal on their way back to the lifeboat station.

1975 saw a blaze cause £150,000 worth of damage at the Bure Court free house in Wroxham; it started at noon, just before opening time, and spread through the roof – within five minutes the whole place was ablaze.

17 March

Norwich was hit by fire in 1811 when R. & S. Culley's warehouse in St Peter's Street burned down. The fire started at 1am; luckily, Benjamin Culley had stayed in town that night, in a room that would otherwise have been empty, and was woken by smoke. He roused the family, and the bell at St Peter Mancroft was tolled to warn neighbours of the fire. The *Norfolk Chronicle* reported that a large quantity of sugar and over 60 chests of tea burned, and 'the column of flame which rose from them was truly awful' – in fact, they said it was the worst fire in the city since Mr Ward's house caught fire on Ber Street nearly 45 years before.

By 2 o'clock in the morning, the city engines were there along with crowds of willing helpers – but, as the newspaper pointed out, water was scarce 'and we regret to say lost through the pipes'. The engines were as hopeless as the pipes, 'out of repair and inefficient'. The crowd helped to haul cheese from the shop and furniture from the house into the street. The doors of the Guildhall were opened to receive the goods, but then a rumour spread that there was gunpowder in the cellars. It wasn't true, but nobody was prepared to risk it and the goods stayed in the street.

Within the hour, the soldiers from the Horse Barracks arrived with their fire engine. By this point, the warehouse had been burnt to the ground and the shop and house were both on fire. Alderman Cole got the engine into the garden of Miss Weston's house next door, with the help of others, and the firemen managed to save her house and Mr Priest's laboratory. But when the fire threatened to spread, the people in the houses on the corner of St Giles Street started emptying out their belongings, and then John Freeman's house caught fire. The upper storey contained 'unwrought stuff for cabinet-making' and the top two storeys were lost.

The fire raged until 5 o'clock in the morning, and the ruins were still red-hot two hours later. Culley's losses were reported at £3,600 and Freeman's at £600 – between them, the equivalent of nearly a quarter of a million pounds in today's money. Luckily, no lives were lost, though two workmen were injured in the fire-fighting. The *Norfolk Chronicle* noted that the Pope's Head Inn 'had had a wonderful escape, almost surrounded as it was by fire'. Though it also said that there had to be a guard for the next day and night by the Norwich Battalion of Volunteers and the Rifle Corps, 'many depredations having been committed during the conflagration'.

Both Freeman and Culley put notices in the paper thanking people for their help – and letting their customers know that they were still very much in business!

18 March

1943 saw the worst air raid of the year in Norwich. F.W. Harmer's clothing factory on St Andrew's Street was burned to the ground, and two people there were seriously hurt.

20 March

1897 saw a major fire at Thetford at the Pulp Manufacturing Co., which started in the old papermaking works. The alarm was raised at 7pm and the fire brigade got there fast, but hundreds of tons of rags, paper and wood pulp were already in what the *Norfolk Chronicle* described as 'a mass of flames'. Hundreds of helpers managed to confine the fire to the block and saved the drying shed and the manager's house, but several thousands of pounds' worth of damage was caused. Between 60 and 70 people were thrown out of work, mainly women and girls.

1939 saw a serious explosion at Great Yarmouth electricity power station when a transformer blew. A second explosion occurred as four police officers arrived, and one came out of the building with his clothes on fire. Great Yarmouth and Lowestoft had no power for an hour, and candles were used to light the hospital until the power came on again. Onlookers said they saw a blue-green flame go through the windows on one side of the building at the time of the second explosion. Five men were taken to hospital, one badly injured; sadly, John Smith, the turbine driver, died two days later. An inquest held in May found that the explosion was caused by a rat, which had its paws on one terminal and its tail on another.

1961 saw the worst floods across the county since 1953. At Great Yarmouth the pleasure steamer *Resolute* was swept from its moorings (but later recovered). St Margaret's Church in King's Lynn was flooded to a depth of 15in when the Great Ouse poured over the quays. (See 11 March for photograph.)

21 March

1962 saw a three-hour blaze at Leziate, when fire broke out in the early hours at the main electrical workshop at the British Industrial Sand Works. The fire brigade managed to confine the blaze to one section of the shed and stopped the flames spreading to 20 diesel locomotives.

22 March

1873 saw James Darken's music warehouse at London Street, Norwich, go up in flames. The shop sold harmoniums and pianos, and also had a circulating music library; around £1,500 of damage (equivalent to over £91,000 in today's money) was caused.

1965 saw a huge fire in the dispatch and finished products departments at the Hartmann Fibre Factory in Great Yarmouth. The alarm was given at 3am after egg trays, flowerpots and food containers went up in flames. Despite the 25mph wind, the seven fire brigades with 10 fire engines managed to save the building. Two firemen were taken to hospital with eye trouble from smoke after the fire was extinguished.

23 March

In 1614, according to the 19th-century historian William Richards, much snow melted suddenly, and most of Marshland was flooded.

1898 saw a major fire in Dove Street, Norwich. Artist Mr E. Pocock rented the upper room in the building housing Sutherland's draper's shop and lived there with his parents. That evening he noticed the smell of smoke and went to investigate; he found the front room full of it and realised that there was a fire in the shop below. He sent his father to fetch the fire brigade, and carried his mother – who had fainted – outside to safety. The fire spread so rapidly that he didn't even have time to put his boots on, let alone rescue any of his paintings or property, and he lost everything – and it was uninsured. The fire spread from the draper's shop to the roofs of the neighbouring shops, Mr French's fish restaurant and Mr Jillings's hairdresser and tobacconist. Because the road was narrow, it was hard for the fire brigade to reach the flames, and it took them two hours to get it under control. Mr French had just moved, so he wasn't insured; his roof, the top room and the property in it were lost.

1915 saw another wreck on Sheringham Shoal, when the *Empress* of Sutherland struck the shoals during a gale. The crew fired distress flares, which were seen at 6pm, and the Sheringham lifeboat crew went out; the ship by then had broken its back and the crew of 21 had taken to the ship's boats. They were rescued by the lifeboat crew and taken to safety.

In 1933 Sprowston postmill caught fire when someone lit a bonfire on the edge of Mousehold Heath and the flames spread to the gorse. It was a windy day and the debris blew on to the canvas sails and set the mill on fire. The mill was also known as Old Crome's Mill, as it was the subject of Crome's painting *A Mill on the Heath*.

24 March

1895 saw what the *Norfolk Chronicle* described as a hurricane 'such as never been known in living memory'. The storm, with gusts of up to 60mph, started at three and lasted for an hour and a half, and did tremendous damage. In Norwich, whole rows of houses had tiles stripped from their roofs; roofs were blown in, garden walls came down, trees fell, and chimneys came down across the city. Pottergate was impassable due to the number of tiles and slates that had crashed on to the ground. Chamberlin's sign in the Market Place was wrecked; the railway roof was damaged and the *Norfolk Chronicle* reported that the zinc ridging was 'blown off like paper'. The worst damage was at Norwich Workhouse, where £2,000 worth of damage was caused (equivalent to nearly £165,000 in today's money). The roof of the chapel was blown into the air, and part of it fell on store rooms and sleeping quarters – luckily, they weren't occupied at the time. Half the roof fell inside the chapel and went into the dining room below; again, it was fortunate that it was empty at the time. A hundred and twenty children were terrified when a chimney fell through the roof of the Mission Rooms at St Martin at Oak during Sunday school; nobody was hurt, but they were all very scared. Surprisingly, only one person needed to be taken to the Norfolk and Norwich hospital: 15-year-old Charles Robertson, who sustained a fractured skull in Ber Street. Seven trees were blown down in Chapelfield Gardens, including a black poplar whose roots stretched for yards under the lawn, which were torn up when the tree toppled. A hundred trees were blown down in Tuck's Wood at Lakenham, and 200 in Catton Park.

Over the county, things were also grim. Over 2,500 trees were uprooted at Marsham, a barn was blown down at Buxton, people were lifted off their feet, and the mill at Acle was damaged and the wreckage strewn for 40 yards. Great Yarmouth saw gale force 10 winds; tiles were off everywhere, and the flagstaff at the signalling station in front of the Sailors' Home had to be held down by eight men when one of its stays snapped. There was enormous damage in the Rows; two roofs were blown in at Row 109 (the Lion and Lamb Row). Plate glass in the market place shattered; the *Norfolk Chronicle* referred to 'a tornado' along the Southtown Road. Chimneys came down – including the huge chimney at Southtown Steam Laundry, which crashed through the roof. At the beachfront, sand was 'whirled in dense clouds all along the coast and obscured the view'.

The newspaper devoted a page and a half just to listing the damage. Village by village and town by town, it was the same: roofs denuded of tiles and slates, chimneys blown down, glass shattered, trees crashing everywhere. At Old Buckenham, the water in the river was 'blown like clouds of smoke'. At Coltishall, Bullard's maltings was blown down, with the loss of 2,000 coombs of barley (a coomb is a measure equivalent to four bushels or a little under 8,900cu in); water was taken out of the river and carried for 100 yards, where it seemed like heavy rain. A hundred trees came down at Coltishall Hall, and 200 trees came down at Felbrigg, including a cedar tree thought to be 200 years old. At Cromer, people were blown over, and at Ludham the mill was blown down. At King's Lynn, the storm was the worst for over 30 years, and several thousands of pounds' worth of damage was caused, including the Corn Exchange roof being blown off. The roof of Oxnead Hall – 46 yards long – came off in one piece and demolished a conservatory. Two thousand trees came down on a plantation at Sandringham, and hundreds came down at Sproule. At Wymondham, the Alma plantation at Kimberley – which had been planted to celebrate the Crimea – was swept away, and 73 trees were blown down on the road between Wymondham and Dereham. At Swanton Morley between 300 and 400 specimen trees at Bylaugh Park were blown down. At St Faith's workhouse, the roof was badly damaged. At Swaffham, the Morse and Woods brewery was wrecked when a chimney smashed down into the boiler, broke the steam traps, and the ruins landed in 50 gallons of beer that was brewing; there was £1,000 damage to the malthouse and the kiln roof was blown off.

25 March

1975 saw staff at the Maid's Head Hotel in Norwich re-adopting 19th-century methods and taking hot water to guests in pitchers, after a fire in the boiler room involving a tank with 1,800 gallons of fuel. Sixty staff and guests were evacuated and three fire engines had the blaze under control with foam within five minutes; because the door to the boiler room was closed, the fire was starved of oxygen and firemen managed to contain the blaze to the boiler room. Two boilers were put out of action, and the standby boiler was only able to supply half the hotel, so hot water was rationed. Repairs were expected to take around six weeks at a cost of £8,000.

26 March

1968 saw a £40,000 blaze at a potato store in Costessey. The flames were less than 6ft away from fuel tanks; luckily the wind changed direction and blew away from the tanks, saving hundreds of gallons of petrol and diesel. Four engines fought the blaze, which broke out just before 6pm; the fire was under control in three hours, but the buildings, three vans, hundreds of tons of seed potatoes, lots of straw and a potato grinding machine were lost.

27 March

In 1908 there was a major fire in Attleborough, which gutted the steam mill and granaries in Hargham Road. Although the fire brigade were quickly on the spot, they couldn't save the mill. A nearby windmill was scorched, but the wind was blowing in the opposite direction so it was saved. The damage was estimated at £1,000 (the equivalent of nearly £72,000 in today's money).

1916 saw what the *Eastern Daily Press* headlined as 'a March blizzard', and *The Times* described as a terrible snowstorm 'accompanied by a wind of great violence'. By 7pm Norwich was cut off by the snow, but the next day saw the real tragedy, when the Jersey ketch *Dart* ran aground. The crew couldn't see through the blinding snow. Captain James Kent and the mate lashed themselves to the main rigging, and his 81-year-old uncle, Charles, and 17-year-old William Meers lashed themselves to the fore rigging. They spent the night exposed to the elements, until the lifeboat reached them at 7am. William died in the lifeboat. At the inquest, the lifeboat crew said they didn't see the ship sooner because of the snow and only one flare had been sent up. Although they were probably near enough to send rockets with lifelines from the shore, it wouldn't have worked because the crew were too exhausted to tie the ropes to themselves. Lifeboat crewman Edward Bensley got into the rigging to rescue the men and put a line round them so they could be taken to safety; he said before he cut them free, the captain was so exhausted that he simply swung from side to side. The octogenarian Charles Kent simply commented that he didn't think he'd go to sea again.

1938 saw a major fire causing thousands of pounds of damage at Savage's saw mill in King's Lynn; the glare was seen for miles around, and the whole mill was ablaze within minutes. Firemen were called out of cinemas when a special 's' was shown in the corner of the film to warn them that there was a blaze and they were needed. The roof collapsed within five minutes, though the fire crews had it under control within half an hour and confined it to one building. It was thought that a fuse shorted and the spark set light to sawdust, which smouldered for a while before the fire broke out.

1987 saw a storm with high winds (including gusts of 100mph) and rain. Several lorries were turned over by the winds, a bus shelter was blown over, and 5,000 homes were left without electricity.

29 March

Good Friday 1929 saw a major fire at Roudham Heath, following a week of outbreaks in the area. Five miles of heath stretching as far as Brettenham were ablaze, and the fire was visible in the evening over a 10-mile radius. Workers from Lord Fisher of Kilverstone's estate spent seven hours beating out the fire until it was under control; they saved several plantations but 300 acres of heath were destroyed and many pheasants were suffocated by smoke. The *Eastern Daily Press* said that the fire was unprecedented in local history 'for its fierceness and the area involved', and people in the area said it was worse than driving in dense fog.

1952 saw the worst blizzard in East Anglia since 1916. Four inches of snow fell on the Saturday night and caused traffic chaos; 30 passengers spent the night on a bus in Beetley. In the afternoon, there was a 50mph gale at Great Yarmouth, which brought sand 2ft deep on to the Marine Parade.

30 March

In 1273 Norwich saw its worst floods since 1258. The damage was said to be worse than that done by the Disinherited Barons when they sacked the city in 1266.

31 March

1862 saw an accident at Mace & King's circus at St Stephen's Gates, Norwich. Spectators had come to see a boxing match, but it was so popular that the weight of the supporters in the elevated seats broke the supports. The centre of the pit fell; many were bruised and shaken, and one man broke his leg.

In 1908 a huge fire started in Lakenham mill; both it and the Cock Inn next door were destroyed.

1969 saw a huge fire at the Albany Hotel (formerly the Grand Hotel) in Cromer. Martin Lax, the 60-year-old caretaker who was partially deaf, was trapped inside, but neighbours and firefighters worked together to find him and lead him to safety at 1am. Seventy-five firemen and 11 engines fought the blaze; many doors were closed, which helped the fire not to spread, although the heat along corridors blistered walls and doors and made fittings crumble. The gas feeder pipe was damaged, but fireman John Folds from Cromer got into the basement through thick smoke and managed to turn the gas off before the roof fell in.

1971 saw 85 firemen and 11 appliances fighting a huge blaze at a depot belonging to Pointer Group Transport Ltd in King's Lynn. Most of the cold store was destroyed, and a 10,000sq ft building containing 500 tons of canned food was also destroyed. Asbestos sheets in the walls and roof exploded, but the fire crews managed to save the 10,000sq ft transport section, and a dozen road tankers were moved to safety. Half a million pounds' worth of frozen fruit and vegetables were lost.

1976 saw four firemen blown out of a smouldering turkey shed at Weston Longville. They were trying to locate the source of the smoke when there was a blast at roof level and flames rushed from one end of the shed to the other. Luckily, the building was empty as it was being prepared for 17,000 day-old chicks the following week. The building was destroyed 'in a ball of fire'.

April

'April showers' definitely rings true in Norfolk, with major floods around the county. It was a very wet month in 1446; there was a storm in the North Sea and a significant tidal surge, which caused thousands of deaths in coastal areas. Records also refer to an earthquake in Norwich in April 1446. It was wet in 1607, too, and there were major floods at King's Lynn.

It has also been a disastrous month for fires – particularly for the Britannia Pier in Yarmouth, which burned down twice in April in the space of 40 years. (And also in between in August!) April also saw huge wartime damage in Norwich, in the first of the 'Baedeker' raids.

1 April

In 1607, according to the 19th-century historian William Richards, there was a high tide which broke Catt's bank and drowned Clenchwarton; in King's Lynn the water flowed up to the Tuesday Market Place cross.

1754 saw Baconsthorpe parsonage, its stables and barn destroyed by fire. The parsonage had previously been destroyed by lightning in 1692 and rebuilt.

In 1775 there was another large fire, this time in Norwich. It started in the chimney of Mr Fielding's house in St Giles and spread to the house of glover Benjamin Hugman, opposite the Curriers Arms. The *Norwich Mercury* noted in disgust that during the fire someone stole a box from him containing 'plate, rings and cash' worth £30 (around £2,500 of today's money).

2 April

1973 saw a hurricane sweeping East Anglia; the wind was recorded at 85mph at Gorleston and 75 knots at Great Yarmouth. Two men were killed when a 30-tonne pine tree collapsed on their car at Scoulton. Four helicopters battled through the gale to rescue 16 men from the coaster *Amberley* 23 miles off Cromer; the ship was carrying coal when it began to list to starboard. The nearest ship was three hours away, and they radioed for assistance, saying that the ship was not steering properly. The waves were 10ft high and the ship's decks were awash when the helicopters winched the crew from the ship in hail and more than 60 knots of wind and took them safely to Wells. Hundreds of trees were blown down in Norfolk, including 300-year-old pollarded beeches at Fellbrigg. Caravans were smashed to pieces; Cromer was littered with tiles blown from roofs and New Street was closed because of the danger of falling tiles – traffic found it difficult, too, as a furniture van was blown over on its side. A 300ft cedar tree at Swardeston Vicarage associated with Edith Cavell (it was said that she was sitting under it when she got the telegram calling her back to Belgium) was blown down.

3 April

1938 saw poor Horsey battered by floods yet again; the high tide was the worst since 12 February 1938 and the wind was 50–70mph; much of the material in the new defences was moved, the railway was wrecked, and 7,000 acres were under water.

In 1912 the windmill at Hargham Road in Attleborough, which had survived the 1908 fire (see 27 March), was gutted by fire. The fire started near the cap of the mill and burned downwards.

4 April

In 1817 there was a tragic incident on the river at Norwich when Wright's Norwich and Yarmouth steam packet blew up just as it was pushing from its moorings near Foundry Bridge, with 18 adults and two children on board. *The Times* said that 'the vessel was rent to atoms, so that little remains entire'. Mr Agg, opposite whose premises it happened, rushed to help. Three women, three men and a child were killed instantly; six women with fractured arms and legs were taken to the Norfolk and Norwich hospital, and one of them died later. Of the six people who remained unscathed, the *Norfolk Chronicle* reported that incredibly one of them was actually standing over the boiler when the explosion happened. And the remaining child – a two-month-old baby – slept through the whole thing, though sadly his mother died. According to 19th-century historian A.D. Bayne, a £350 subscription (the equivalent of nearly £19,000 in today's money) was raised to help the families of those caught up in the explosion.

In 1925 there was a fire in the long narrow range of wooden buildings of J. Youngs & Co's woodworking business in Chapelfield Road, Norwich, which the *Norfolk Chronicle* described as the 'most spectacular fire in Norwich for 10 years'. The buildings were gutted, but the paper noted a real act of heroism by unemployed carter Samuel Beck, who saw the fire engine going up St Stephen's near midnight, followed it and discovered a policeman trying to get a horse out of the stable. Beck broke a window in the back and climbed into the building; he found the horse, whose coat was alight, put a sack over its head and a rope round its neck, and led it out to safety. He suffered burns to his hands but was more concerned about the horse's welfare.

1939 saw a major storm in Norwich, when 0.57in of rain fell in just 45 minutes and there was flooding throughout the city. Lightning struck the tower of St Edmund's Church in Fishergate and brought stonework crashing through the roof of the factory next door; luckily it occurred at lunchtime so nobody was hurt.

5 April

1978 saw the Royal Links Pavilion at Cromer in flames. The Cromer ambulance gave the alarm at 5.30pm when they were on their way back to hospital from an emergency and saw flames going through the roof and thick smoke. One young girl watching the blaze said that the flames looked like a big genie. Luckily the building was empty; the police closed the road, and 30 firefighters from three fire brigades fought the flames. The roof fell in, and the blaze was out within an hour; the building was gutted, and there was a pall of smoke for an hour afterwards.

7 April

1941 saw the worst air raid of World War Two in Great Yarmouth; an estimated 4,000 incendiary bombs fells that night. However, due to news restrictions during the war, the incident was only mentioned in the *Eastern Daily Press* as occurring to an 'East Anglian town'.

8 April

1963 saw the Caister lifeboat rescuing eight crew from the Lowestoft trawler *Kirkley* when they had to abandon their ship on the Scroby sands. The crew tried to launch their lifeboat, but the trawler keeled over and put a hole in it. Water was up to the top bunks in their cabin when they managed to launch the rubber dinghy; the lifeboat rescued them from the dinghy.

1971 saw a £10,000 blaze at a London Street jeweller's in Norwich; jewellery, silver and glassware were damaged, and the building itself would cost several thousands of pounds to repair. The fire smouldered for two hours in a window, and then a passer-by noticed smoke at 2.30am and raised the alarm. Four engines had the blaze under control in half an hour.

9 April

1976 saw a fire at Norwich publishers Hughes & Coleman. The blaze started in a first-floor store room in the afternoon, but it took some time for firemen to get the blaze under control, as their job was made more difficult by exploding gas cylinders. One fireman injured his hand when he slipped on the asbestos roof, and books, cards and stationery worth several thousands of pounds were damaged by fire and water.

10 April

In 1810 there was a fire in Dereham – serious enough to destroy four houses and a barn.

12 April

In 1902 Winterton post mill was demolished in a hurricane. The *Eastern Daily Press* said that 'an eerie and all pervasive noise was heard far out to sea', but nobody realised it was the wind – and within seconds there was torrential rain and a gale force wind. The mill owner, realising that the mill was in danger, ran outside, intending to stop the fan wheel operating. But he was too late – the mill crashed to the ground. Luckily, unable to see in the dark, he ran into a tree and was delayed in reaching the mill; this saved his life.

In 1924 the mills and box-making department of Jewson's on the corner of Colegate and Calvert Street, Norwich, were gutted by fire. The only thing left of the 100ft by 30ft mill was a pile of beams. According to the *Eastern Daily Press*, the fire was 'so bright that the cathedral spire stood out sharply'; Porter's steam bending shop next door didn't suffer much damage because it had a sprinkler system, and the timber sheds and their contents were also saved. There was one casualty during the fire; fireman Mr Hardiment fell from the roof and hurt his back.

1995 saw a serious fire at the Assembly House in Norwich. The roof had only been refurbished five months previously in a £250,000 programme – but that day an electrical fault in heating and ventilation equipment caused a fire in a store room. The alarm was raised, but the fire spread quickly and wrecked the roof – historic buildings consultant Dr Bill Watson said that the roof was 'probably irreplaceable', and Timothy Colman, the Lord Lieutenant of Norfolk, added, 'We have lost a priceless and much loved piece of our heritage.' The fire also destroyed much of the interior, including the music room where the composer Liszt had played in 1840. More than 100 firemen fought the flames, and many of the paintings and furniture were saved from the house. Large areas of wood panelling and Georgian plasterwork also survived, and the roof was rebuilt. The Assembly House was reopened on 13 February 1997.

13 April
1856 saw a huge gas explosion in Bank Plain, which ended up with the roof of Gurney's Bank House being lifted and the windows blown out. Mr Utting, the clerk, smelled gas. He entered Mr Mottram's office with a lighted candle – and there was an immediate explosion. The *Norfolk Chronicle* reported that 'the ceiling was raised so that the gas escaped to the rooms above' – luckily, nobody was hurt.

14 April
1991 saw a fire at Horning Pleasure Craft, which caused £150,000 worth of damage. The general manager, Charles Brown, was on his way to bed when he noticed that the security light was on in the boatyard. He saw an orange glow that meant fire, so he raised the alarm. Forty firemen fought the blaze in strong winds; meanwhile, Charles brown and his chief engineer, Arnold Gowing, went to the other side of the dock through thick smoke to start up as many boats as they could and lead them out. Five cruisers sank and seven were damaged; it's thought that the fire spread so rapidly due to the inflammable polyester resin used in the construction of the boats, but it was not known how the fire started.

15 April
In 1845 the brig *Nautilus* of Aberdeen was wrecked between Sheringham and Wells. The lifeboat at Sheringham rescued the crew of eight and took them to the landlady of the Crown at Sheringham, who kept spare clothes there for shipwrecked sailors. The ship itself broke up on 21 April.

16 April
In 1795 Pockthorpe windmill, near the barracks on Mousehold, Norwich, caught fire around midnight; the flames took hold rapidly and the mill was gutted before firefighters could get there. The *Norfolk Chronicle* reported that 'the effect of the light upon the surrounding objects, and the stillness of the night, rendered the scene awfully grand'.

In 1925 there were gale force winds which ripped the R33 airship at Pulham off its mooring mast. The airship drifted with its crew of 20 and was blown across the North Sea to the Dutch coast. They finally managed to get the damaged ship under control and were all safely back in England eight hours later. George V presented the crew with watches after the event.

17 April
In 1914 there was a huge fire in Great Yarmouth, when the Britannia pier caught light – less than four years after the pavilion reopened after being burned down. The new pavilion was a huge building – 140ft long and 60ft wide, with a domed roof 60ft from the deck of the pier and

an 80ft tower either side. The watchman on the pier heard a loud explosion just before 4am; he thought it was a warning from the lightship to vessels at sea, but then he saw flames coming from the building. The strong wind from the east meant that the fire was raging within a few minutes, and by 5am the pavilion was what *The Times* described as a 'shapeless mass of twisted girders and charred woodwork'. The only things that escaped were a cash register and a limelight box; the London entertainment troupe the Mountebanks lost all their things. The damage was estimated at £15,000 (the equivalent of nearly £1 million in today's money), and the fire was blamed on the Suffragettes, who'd recently made 'inflammatory speeches' (a perhaps not unintentional pun from *The Times*!) and whose handbills were found littering the gardens near the pier the following morning.

In 1965 a three-minute whirlwind hit Hunstanton. The flagpole of the Golden Lion hotel snapped, postcards were swept up and scattered like confetti, and rubber balls bounced all the way down the street.

18 April

1973 saw an emergency in the Cathedral Close in Norwich, after a nine-inch main in the Lower Close exploded at 8.20am while workers were laying replacement piping. Police cordoned off the area for two hours and offices were evacuated. Nobody was hurt, but the gas burned violently and three fire engines had to use foam to subdue the surges of flames while the gas board sealed the mains.

19 April

In 1960 a carelessly thrown cigarette set light to Pretty Corner, near Sheringham. Fifteen acres of young pine trees and 15 acres of heath were burned. It was difficult to get water to the area, and a fire brigade spokesman said they were lucky that the fire was going downhill so they could beat it out – had it gone uphill they wouldn't have been able to stop it.

20 April

In 1954 the Britannia Pier at Great Yarmouth burned down for the fourth time. The night watchman saw smoke in the building at 12.35am, just five minutes after making his hourly 'all's well' report, and within 10 minutes the fire had taken hold in the Long Bar, which ran 84ft across the pier between the theatre, the ballroom and the restaurant. The fire destroyed the 1,300-seat theatre, the ballroom, the restaurant, amusement booths, children's rides, the merry-go-round and the Peter Pan railway that had only been installed the week before.

22 April

1928 saw a major fire in the south of the county, when the Elizabethan mansion Lynford Hall, near Thetford, burnt down. It had recently become the Australian Farms Training College; the fire started in the east wing and spread quickly to the main buildings. Molten lead from cupolas and turrets streamed down and hampered the work of the Brandon and Thetford fire brigades. One fireman was injured, and the house was gutted.

The dry weather in the spring of 1929 led to a major heath fire on 22 April in the west of the county which lit the countryside for miles. The fire spread from Grimston and Roydon through to Gayton and Gaywood; at midnight men were still trying to beat it out.

There was a fierce storm in Norwich in 1931; lightning struck the chimney in a house in West End Street, but luckily nobody was hurt. Landlord Mr Richardson said that a ball of fire the size of a cricket ball hit the window at the Rainbow Tavern in Old Palace Road, bounced across to a mirror 30ft away, then disappeared. At Potter Heigham, residents heard a huge explosion and saw a blue light; luckily, the only damage was some broken windows and a severed phone line to the railway.

23 April

The 'Great Blowe' took place in Norwich in 1648, after the citizens thought that their Royalist mayor John Utting was going to be taken to London. A crowd gathered in the market place and turned on the Puritan aldermen; they broke into the houses of several Puritan leaders, including Thomas Ashwell and Adrian Parmenter. They marched on Committee House in Bethel Street, where the county arms and armour were stored together with 98 barrels of gunpowder. When a shot from inside the building killed a boy in the crowd, the crowd stormed the building. Gunpowder had been spilled through Committee House – and when it caught light all the barrels of gunpowder went up. The explosion destroyed Committee House and blew out the windows of St Peter Mancroft Church, St Stephen's Church and many neighbouring houses. Forty people were killed (three of whom were buried at St Peter Mancroft, whose parish register notes that they were 'slain by gunpowder') and 120 were injured. Special parish rates were levied to meet the cost of repairing the churches.

Following extensive investigations, on Christmas Day 1648 108 rioters were tried in the Guildhall. Twenty-six of them were fined £30 (the equivalent of nearly £3,000 in today's money), seven were imprisoned, two were whipped and eight were hanged in the castle ditches on 2 January. Mayor Utting rode to London himself the day after the Great Blowe, to avoid further trouble. He was sentenced to six months in the Fleet prison and the town clerk John Tooley was sentenced to three months, and they were fined £1,500 (the equivalent of nearly £138,000 in today's money) between them. The ruins of the Committee House were pulled down, and in 1713 the Bethel Street hospital was built on the site by Mary Ann Chapman.

25 April

In 1507 the first of two enormous fires hit Norwich. It started in the Popinjay Inn at Tombland and spread all the way to St Andrew's; it lasted for four days and burned over 700 houses. (See also 4 June.)

The great fire of Watton broke out in 1674 and destroyed much of the town, including 60 houses, barns and stables. The damage caused was around £7,450 in buildings (the equivalent of nearly £781,000 in today's money) and £2,660 in goods (the equivalent of nearly £279,000 in today's money). The King's Brief meant that people who'd been involved in a disaster of fire or flood could seek recompense by having a Royal Proclamation read out in churches in the surrounding parishes; the money collected was meant to be used for rebuilding the destroyed property. The fire was so bad that the King's Brief for Watton was allowed to be read until 20 September 1675. (According to parish records, the congregation of Wirksworth raised 16 shillings, 11 pence and a farthing.) The clock tower in the middle of Watton was built five years later and contained a bell, supposedly to warn the inhabitants in case a serious fire ever happened again.

1916 saw a severe naval attack on Great Yarmouth and Lowestoft in World War One; the bombardment started at 4.15am and lasted for about 50 minutes. At the end of it, 19 people had been wounded and four had been killed. Several fishing premises were on fire or had been partially destroyed; some roofs had collapsed, and windows were blown out.

1981 saw 90mph winds across the county. The Waveney valley was flooded, and the River Bure flooded between Buxton and Aylsham; the water was 2ft deep at Millgate.

26 April

1941 saw one of the worst raids in World War Two; 23 people were killed and eight were injured when the Ferry pub at Horning was bombed that evening.

The Briton's Arms at Elm Hill, Norwich, the only building in the street to survive the fire of 1507. (Photograph by author)

The clock tower at Watton, built in 1679, though the clock itself dates from 1825 and the cupola comes from the town's market cross which was demolished in 1920. There is a hare-and-barrel design in the spandrels which is a rebus for Watton, i.e. 'Wat' (hare) and 'tun'. (Photograph by author)

1964 saw the worst fire at Thetford Chase for eight years. The alarm was given at 8am and the fire was under control in 40 minutes, but even so 40,000 pines were destroyed and the smoke could be seen 10 miles away at Thetford and 6 miles away at Watton. There were two other forest fires that afternoon: 100 acres at Horsford and 25 acres at Salhouse, badly burning several thousand young trees.

27 April

In 1931 a storm stopped the trams on three routes in Norwich; the cars were stranded at around 9.30 in the evening, and it was over four hours until the current was restored to get them back to the depot.

In 1942 the first of the 'Baedeker' raids flattened Norwich – the Luftwaffe High Command decided to hit the places in Britain that were marked in Baedeker's guide as having great historical significance, in reprisal for the assassination of Heydrich, Himmler's deputy, in Czechoslovakia, and Norwich was one of its main targets. Between 25 and 30 planes dropped 185 high-explosive bombs weighing a total of more than 50 tons over the course of two hours from 11.40pm, and the fire was visible for miles as Norwich burned. Six hundred people were injured and 162 were killed; many were buried under debris. Streets were flattened, particularly in the Heigham area (the City Station, Oak Street and Dereham Road); the city station was burned to a shell and the water mains were smashed, hindering attempts to put out the flames. An estimated 7,000 homes were damaged in the raid; St Augustine's School was hit by a 500kg bomb and was gutted. But there were also stories of heroism that night; 15-year-old John Grix lied about his age so he could ride his bike in the Messenger Service and lead firemen to the reported incidents. On one occasion that night, as he rode past a broken window, his hands were sprayed with acid, but he didn't tell anyone he needed first aid until he'd finished his work.

1976 saw a blaze at Great Walsingham which gutted four homes. The fire started in the roof of a pair of houses, then strong winds helped it leap across the gap to the next pair of houses and set light to them, too. A builder working nearby saw what he thought was a chimney fire and phoned the fire brigade; meanwhile, the occupants of the houses saved as many of their belongings as they could. Five brigades fought the fire and got it under control, but the ceilings fell in and the top floors of both houses were gutted; the ground floors were also badly damaged. Luckily, nobody was hurt, and the families were able to stay temporarily with family and friends locally.

1981 saw the 170ft-long coaster *Wegro* forced on to the beach at Great Yarmouth, when she tried to ride out a storm with 50mph winds and her anchor didn't hold. The crew were uninjured and the two young passengers were rescued, but the problem was refloating the ship – it meant digging out the sand and a groyne, checking the boat for damage and then a bulldozer digging a trench so the ship could refloat at high tide. The crew allowed tours of the ship in return for a donation to the lifeboats; and the ship was finally refloated on 2 May.

28 April

In 1805 fire broke out at Hellesdon mill. Within an hour and a half of its discovery around 1 o'clock, the mill was destroyed except for a part of the west end. The part that was saved had been undergoing repairs and a quantity of oil was stored there – if the flames had reached it, the fire would have spread rapidly, so a firebreak was made by cutting the timbers away. The damage was estimated at £3–4,000 (the equivalent of between £173,000 and £231,000 in today's money), but only a small part of that was insured. The mill was rebuilt, but was eventually pulled down in 1920.

29 April

According to the 19th-century historian Browne, the spire of Norwich Cathedral was struck by lightning in 1601 and the top 20ft fell down. The 18th-century historian Francis Blomefield is slightly more expansive; hail started at 5pm and 'caused a great darkness' (which fits the profile for a tornado). After the thunder there was 'a noisome stink of brimstone' in the cathedral; John Colne was walking in the cathedral with William de Borne at the time and was struck to the ground by lightning. The top of the spire fell down, and the damage was estimated at £500 (the equivalent of nearly £70,000 in today's money).

1773 saw a fire at Thompson, which gutted the houses of James Perfit and cordwainer William Bokenham; two other cottages also caught fire but were saved. The same day, there was violent hail in Horstead; from 3–4pm there was thunder, hail and snow in Norwich, and the *Norwich Mercury* said that the hail was 'remarkably large'.

In 1941 Norwich saw heavy bombing over the King Street and Carrow Hill areas. There was much damage at Colman's (where it took five hours to get the fire under control, and the oat and flour mills were gutted), Boulton & Paul, and Laurence, Scott and Electromotors, but incredibly only one person was killed.

In 1942, during the second 'Baedeker' raid on Norwich, around 40 aircraft flew over the city, concentrating on the commercial area and dropping 112 high explosive bombs and incendiaries. It was a windy night, which fanned the flames, and the city burned for hours. Another 69 people were killed and nearly 90 were badly injured – the casualties were lower than expected because many people had already left the city for the night. Some reports say that a third of the population left to spend the night in fields or shelters outside the city.

St Stephen's Street was flattened, and Curls (now Debenhams) and Bunting's (now Marks & Spencer) were demolished. St Benedict's Church was blown up – only the Norman round tower was left, and most of the remains of the gate were blown up. Westwick Street was also badly hit. Nelson Street School went up in flames, as did Bishop Hall's palace (the Dolphin Inn) on Heigham Street, Barker's Engineering Works, the Clarks shoe factory, St Mary's Silk Mills, the printing works on Chapelfield and Caley's chocolate factory – the fire ripped through 1,000 tons of chocolates and the packaging, and the two six-storeyed buildings were gutted. In Earlham, St Thomas's Church was gutted; in Wensum Park, a 1,000kg bomb landed in a fishpond and exploded a couple of hours later.

Norwich, war damage at Caley's chocolate factory, 1942. (Picture courtesy of Norfolk County Council Library and Information Service)

The Hippodrome was also bombed, killing the stage manager, his wife and the trainer of a troupe of performing sea lions. Buddy, known as 'the world's greatest comedy seal', died soon after – probably from a broken heart, because photographer George Swain in his studio next door heard the seal flapping through the theatre crying for his master.

John Grix was out again on his bike – even being blown off it five times didn't stop him doing his job. He was awarded the British Empire Medal for his work that night.

30 April

1777 saw a house gutted at Billingford; it burned down in an hour, and the damage was estimated at £120 (the equivalent of over £11,000 in today's money).

May

The old nursery rhyme says that April showers bring forth May flowers – well, in Norfolk, those flowers appear to be flames. Most days in May have seen huge fires, some of them equivalent to million-pound blazes in modern times.

1 May

1708 saw Holt devastated by fire. Apparently it burned with such fury, the butchers couldn't save the meat from their stalls – and much of the town was destroyed within three hours. The church was badly damaged; its thatched chancel was burned, lead melted from the windows and the flames spread up the steeple. Overall, there was around £11,000 of damage (the equivalent of nearly one and a quarter million pounds in today's money).

1779 saw a huge fire at Sea Palling, which started when hot ashes were thrown out; a high wind spread the flames rapidly, and nine houses, three barns and a granary were lost.

1942 saw an air raid over Norwich; 700 incendiary bombs landed over Heigham Street, Oak Street, Duke Street, St Andrew's Street and London Street, causing fires in many factories and businesses, including Harmer's clothing factory, the Free Library, and the Norwich Corporation Electricity Works.

The town centre at Holt. (Photograph by author)

2 May

One of the most shocking tragedies happened in Great Yarmouth in 1845, when the suspension bridge collapsed. Nelson the clown from Mr Cook's circus had been advertised as travelling from a drawbridge on the Quay to the suspension bridge in a bath drawn by four geese. Even though it was raining, thousands of people stood on the sides of the banks to watch. People thronged the bridges, too – and when Nelson was sighted, people rushed to the side of the bridge to see him. One or two rods were seen to give way and people shouted a warning, telling everyone to get off the bridge, but it was too late. The chains snapped and the bridge went down. *The Times* reported that between 300 and 600 people went into the water – many of them children. Carpenter's wife Mrs Gillings caught her child's clothes in her teeth and paddled them both to safety. Twenty-seven little girls were rescued on the west bank and put straight to bed at Vauxhall Gardens; as soon as they revived, more took their places. But others were not so lucky; in one house on the east bank, only three out of 68 people revived. Rescuers searched for bodies until 9.30pm, then put tide nets each side of the bridge to stop any bodies being carried out to sea. In the end, 79 people drowned, and the suspension bridge is carved at the top of nine-year-old George Beloe's grave in St Nicholas' Churchyard, Great Yarmouth.

1888 saw a fire destroying nine cottages at Hockering. The fire spread rapidly through the first block of three houses; a few minutes after the discovery was made, the roof came down. High winds drove the flames over to a block of three houses 60 yards away; by the time East Dereham fire brigade arrived, they were in ruins. Between the two blocks of houses, there was another on the opposite side of the road; that, too, went up in flames, and because the buildings were 300 years old they contained a lot of dry timber and burned rapidly.

3 May

1890 saw a fire at the West End Furnishing Store in St Giles, Norwich. At 10.30pm a shopboy was extinguishing an albo-carbon gaslight when the flame caught the lace curtains and set them alight. He pulled the curtains down, but it was too late – the fire spread to the contents of the shop. According to the *Norfolk Chronicle*, the alarm bombs exploded; they said that some reports claimed it took the fire brigade 10 to 20 minutes to get there (and at walking speed it would take three minutes, at most). A crowd had gathered and hooted and jeered at the firefighters. The flames reached the first floor, and the fire crews were worried that the coach-building factory of Mr Thorn would go up next. Assistants removed vehicles from the coachbuilders, and soldiers and civilians helped take hoses up the ladder because the water pressure was too low to get the water jets high enough. The fire was contained to Mr Cole's furnishing store and Mr Thorn's roofs; the chief constable's official report was scathing about the soldiers and their 'improper interference', saying that the fire brigade had to struggle for control of hoses. (However, he changed his mind a week later – see 10 May.)

1964 saw a fire in a Great Yarmouth house, just after the family had finished redecorating. Mrs Anchor, rescued six of her eight children from the fire by carrying them down a smoke-filled staircase, while another child jumped out of his bedroom window on to an outbuilding, and her 11-year-old son fought the blaze with buckets of water until the fire brigade arrived.

Engraving of the collapse of the suspension bridge, 1845. (Picture courtesy of Norfolk County Council Library and Information Service)

The gravestone of George Beloe who was killed in the suspension bridge disaster. Although the stone is much weathered, you can still see the picture of the suspension bridge carved at the top of the it. (Photograph by author)

1965 saw a freak storm in King's Lynn. Lightning hit a tree and left a 4ft hole in the ground beside it; windows were blown out of neighbouring houses and the water main was fractured. One elderly neighbour was flung into the air by the explosion and bruised his back, but recovered. The lightning strike damaged the roots of the 60ft tree, which was deemed dangerous and had to be cut down.

1976 saw a storm which heralded a temporary end to the dry spell (though it soon started up again and there was a heatwave and dry spell until September). Lightning struck the spire of Croxton Church, and firemen faced a difficult climb up the 55ft spire. They went up a ladder, then clambered along rafters. The fire was between the boarding and the slates, so they had to strip part of the roof to fight the blaze. A tarpaulin was used afterwards to protect the spire from further damage until the slates could be replaced.

4 May
Norwich was badly hit by fire in 1413; the blaze destroyed St Andrew's Hall, Norwich (which at the time was the Dominican friary, and two of the friars there were killed), then spread throughout the city.

1970 saw an 80-acre blaze at the heath at Dersingham. Seventy firemen from eight brigades fought the blaze with 11 engines, despite the fact that the flames were leaping 20ft above them and there were clouds of dense smoke. The fire came within 10 yards of nearby cottages, and the flames were higher than the house; the fire crews had the blaze under control within 90 minutes, but needed to damp down the area for hours afterwards. There were also two other major heath fires that afternoon: five acres at Blackborough End and three acres at Kelling Heath.

5 May
The Battle of Ringmere took place just south of Thetford in 1010. Ulfcytel fought against the Danes, who were led by Sweyn's ally, Thorkell the Tall; he lost, and the Danes spent the next three months burning East Anglia. The *Anglo-Saxon Chronicles* mentions that the Danes burned Thetford and Cambridge and 'even the Fens'.

1991 saw 150 villagers evacuated from Kelling on the north Norfolk coast after chemical tanks containing 24,000 litres of toxic material were washed ashore.

6 May
In 1928 Great Yarmouth saw a huge blaze at the maltings of R. Watling & Son, which took firefighters seven hours to subdue. The exact cause was not known but was believed to be overheating in the maltings.

1978 saw a disaster when the 12-tonne Greek tanker *Eleni V*, carrying 16,000 tons of oil, collided with the French merchant ship *Roseline* off Winterton. The 39 crew were all saved, unhurt, but an oil slick of 15,000 square metres (containing 1,000 tons of oil) developed. The oil started to come ashore, and crews worked 16-hour days to clean it up. Eight spraying vessels were used to disperse the oil; pups and seals were huddled in the middle of Scroby

Sands trying to avoid it. Beaches on a 20-mile stretch between Winterton and Lowestoft were affected, and the worst area was at Corton in Suffolk, where the oil was ankle-deep in pools 10ft wide.

James Prior, the Conservative MP for Lowestoft, told Parliament how angry local people were that the hulk was left to go 'careering up and down the coast for the past three weeks giving out oil at odd intervals and that the powers that be have been unable to make up their minds'. There were plans to sink the hulk in deep water on 29 May, but they were scuppered by fog. The ship was finally blown up by divers from the Royal Navy on 30 May, using 2½ tons of explosives 26 miles off Lowestoft. The blast was heard 44 miles away. However, a week later *The Times* reported that oil was still a threat to the East Coast beaches, and the spraying vessels had no effect on oil slicks six miles off shore.

Overall, Norfolk had to remove 20,000 tons of oil-drenched sand and shingle and transport the mess to refuse dumps inland.

8 May

1956 saw a huge heath fire at Bawsey. Seventy acres caught light, and it took six brigades three hours to subdue the blaze.

9 May

There was a huge storm at Great Yarmouth in 1925, with hail and lightning. At 3.30pm there was a sharp flash and flames were seen coming from the Isolation Hospital at Gorleston; it hadn't been unoccupied since 1912 and was kept in case of emergency outbreak. There was no water supply except butts and an old-fashioned pump with a long iron handle, so the fire engine couldn't be used. Within an hour, only the chimney (which was first struck) was left; the fire was fortunately out by 5.30pm.

10 May

1890 saw a huge fire at Boulton & Paul in Norwich which caused around £4–5,000 of damage. The fire was discovered just before 11pm, and an alarm bomb was exploded. Behind the Hop Pole pub there were tongues of fire, and it was obvious they were coming from the wood yard. King Street to Mountergate was blocked by spectators, and the glow was seen nearly 20 miles away at Attleborough and Diss. Many onlookers got into other wood yards and sat on the roofs of outhouses to see the fire; although the general confusion made it hard for the police to get through to fight the fire, they managed to drive the flames back and saved the factory and house next door belonging to John Hotblack. Colman's floating fire engine also steamed up the river to help. This time, the chief constable's official report praised the soldiers. The fire was under control by 1am and was then damped down.

2005 saw Hunstanton Pier completely destroyed by fire when a blaze swept through CHS Amusements. The fire destroyed a three-storey building at the entrance to the pier; the café, amusement arcade and play area were gutted and all their contents lost. The fire started some time before 5am, but because the structure was so badly damaged – the steel was left twisted and cracked, and it was unsafe for investigators to go in – the cause remained unknown. Sixty firefighters were called to the blaze, and the cost of the damage was estimated at £1.5 million.

11 May

1815 saw drama in Great Yarmouth when a press gang from the *Cadmus* landed. The crew was attacked by a mob, who stoned the press gang and destroyed their gig. At the assizes on 14 August 1816, seven people were indicted for riotously assembling and rescuing from the press gang a person who had been impressed. Six of them were found guilty and sentenced to nine months' imprisonment in the following December.

1927 saw a disastrous fire at Wroxham, when Wroxham Cottage, the home of Major D.G. Astley, was gutted. At 5.30pm the gardener saw smoke on the roof and raised the alarm, but the fire took hold and it was clear that the house was doomed. A hundred people helped to rescue the contents of the house, but, although the fire brigade arrived quickly with 1,200ft of hose, the building was gutted before they got there.

1943 saw the last air raid in Great Yarmouth where there were fatalities; 49 people died that night. Over the course of the air raids in Great Yarmouth, 2,639 houses were destroyed or needed to be demolished, and 1,500 were damaged badly enough for the people who lived in them to be evacuated while the houses were repaired.

1973 saw an 81-year-old man in Mundford rescued from a burning house by diggers. Mr Hawkins only had one lung and was resting in bed when the fire started at around midday; he was alone in the house as his wife had taken their granddaughter shopping. Neighbours tried to rescue him with a ladder, but he refused to go; eventually he was lifted to safety in the bucket of a digger by workmen on a nearby building site.

14 May

1924 saw a storm after a heatwave, with much lightning over Norwich. Cromer was flooded and three houses were struck by lightning in Mundesley, but luckily nobody was hurt. Wymondham saw a major tragedy; hail began at 8am and houses were flooded. At 12.30pm, five-year-old Herbert Bennington came home from school and was playing with a friend near the bridge when he fell into the swollen river. A schoolfriend raised the alarm, but Herbert's body was found 100 yards from where he fell in.

1934 saw a tornado at Cromer. At 7 o'clock in the evening the wind, which had reached speeds of 80mph, whipped the sea into the air 'like a cloud of smoke'. One observer said it was like a small waterspout, around 15ft high. At Sheringham, tents were blown out to sea, houses were stripped of tiles, and the roof of a shed was blown 50 yards and knocked a cyclist unconscious; he was carried to safety.

15 May

1973 saw a huge fire at a potato warehouse in St George's Street. The building had a 100ft frontage and it took 30 firemen and seven engines to subdue the blaze, but the potatoes were mainly intact, apart from a bit of smoke damage.

16 May

1934 saw a major fire at Colegate, Norwich, at Mr Gazey's cycle shop on the corner of Coslany Street, thought to be caused by an explosion in carbides in the shop. A neighbour heard an explosion and saw flames shooting out of the house; Mr Gazey jumped out of a ground floor window and his hands and face were burnt, but luckily his wife and child were away for the weekend so were uninjured. The fire spread across the street and scorched the top of the trees in St Michael's Churchyard; the fire brigade managed to contain the blaze, and Mr Gazey was treated at hospital.

17 May

1974 saw a blaze at Felthorpe woods which started behind the sawmill; a strong wind drove the fire in a 100-yard swathe which affected six acres of young pines. It took four fire engines three hours to put it out and damp down.

18 May

1895 saw a major gale, and the Short Blue fishing fleet at Great Yarmouth was badly hit. The Yarmouth smack *Royal Standard* was lost, and one of the crew was killed. At Sheringham, many fishermen lost crab pots – their livelihood. At Hunstanton, the brig *Amelie*, laden with pit props, capsized when its mast crashed down; the nine crew clung to the side and were rescued by the Hunstanton lifeboat crew. However, the sea was so rough that the crew couldn't land at Hunstanton; they had to take the stranded sailors to Heacham instead. The brig became a total wreck.

1964 saw a 3ft flood in Norwich after an 18-inch water main burst at the junction of Mousehold Lane and Plaford Road. The *Eastern Daily Press* described a 'tidal wave' going down the street, which flooded gardens and left sandy mud behind. The water settled at the bottom of Plaford Road; it was 3ft deep, but luckily stopped within inches of going into the house. The flood actually happened at 4am but was not discovered until 6am, when Mr Clarke got up and saw the state of his garden.

20 May

In 1847 there was a second fire that year at Mr Kitton's warehouse in Rose Lane. It started in the distillery connected with the manufacturing of anti-friction grease. The alarm was raised at 1 o'clock in the morning and two engines came, but the fire had already taken such a hold they could do nothing – the buildings were gutted. The neighbour's property was threatened, and because there was a delay before the engine could work, 50 policeman and watchmen set to work with buckets. The *Norfolk Chronicle* commented that very few of the people watching the blaze would help – and that the fire was thought to be started by 'an incendiary'.

1971 saw a huge fire at the factory of chipboard makers Airscrew Weyroc Ltd in Thetford. At 4am the fire was seen near the base of the fuel tanks, which contained 1,000 gallons of petrol and diesel; then the flames leapt 20ft to the top of the tanks. Workmen used extinguishers and the blaze was out by the time the fire brigade arrived; however, the fire brigade spent a while damping down afterwards.

21 May

In 1382 there was a violent earthquake at Yarmouth, according to Holinshead (other chroniclers place it a month later). Much damage was caused; Holinshed adds that a 'watershake' followed three days later.

1879 saw a fire at shoe manufacturer's Willis & Southall in Norwich which caused £1,000 of damage. It broke out in the rivetting room at around 8pm and the blaze was visible above the roof; however, it was subdued in 20 minutes and confined to area. The Norfolk Chronicle said this was due to the small portable fire engine. The losses were insured – but the tools belonging to carpenter John Rice from Wounded Hart Yard, which were also lost, sadly were uninsured.

23 May

There was a major fire at Cawston in 1783, when a fire broke out in a wood store belonging to the baker. Luckily his house and bakery were saved, although the flames apparently blew over to four houses next to the churchyard and burned them down, as well as damaging the chancel of the church. The Norfolk Chronicle reported that 'by the exertions of the people little damage was done to it, and the town, after being given over for lost, preserved without further damage by their activity'.

In 1854 there was a major storm over Norwich between 3 and 4 o'clock in the afternoon, with much thunder and lightning. Bixley mill was struck by lightning and damaged, and a man near Trowse was knocked unconscious.

In 1852 there was a serious fire in Norfolk Hotel, St Giles' Street, Norwich. The Watch Committee held an inquiry into allegations about the water supply not being sufficient and the fire engines being inefficient; the Norfolk Chronicle felt that the water company did their best, but the problem lay with Superintendent Mr Dunne, who simply didn't direct the 58 policemen present to fight the fire properly.

1865 saw an earthquake which was felt across the coast from Scratby to Lowestoft. The Norfolk Chronicle was sceptical about it, saying that the rumour couldn't be traced back to a reliable source, but added that 'in absence of other news this has been the "sensation" topic of the week'. Apparently church bells rang on their own, glasses jingled, and people were woken from their sleep.

1946 saw a huge forest fire, which started at Ling heath near Brandon; 14 different fire brigades joined together to tackle the fire, which affected 400–600 acres of trees mainly 10–15 years old. They managed to stop it reaching the bomb dump at Elveden, and the fire was out by 6pm.

1964 saw a fire that smashed hundreds of clock faces at clock makers Metamec Ltd in Dereham. Fire broke out in the wood yard, and although the fire brigade stopped it spreading to piles of timber in the yard the heat of the blaze damaged the clock faces.

24 May

In 1744 the Norwich Mercury reported there was a fire at Stoke Paper Mill House; the house and part of the mill were burned to the ground, along with an engine worth £100 (the equivalent of nearly £150,000 in today's money). The editors were shocked that much of the property that had been rescued from the fire and carried into the neighbouring meadow for safety was stolen by passers-by.

1970 saw Norfolk in the middle of a heatwave – and a 100-acre blaze damaging grass and woodland in the middle of Holkham Nature Reserve. Five fire brigades fought the blaze, which started on Burnham Overy sand dunes.

27 May

In 1832 there was a fire at the factory of Grout Baylis & Co in Barrack Yard, in the Denes, Great Yarmouth; the five-storey factory was enormous, 105ft long, 55ft wide and 50ft high, and cost £7,000 to build in 1818. When the fire was discovered in the fourth storey of the building – which was used for silk throwing and weaving – the alarm was raised by ringing the hospital bell, the church bell and sounding the Great Eastern bugle. Many people came to help, and the firemen got there fast – but the fire spread rapidly. The firefighters managed to save the building next to it, but at 2 o'clock in the afternoon the factory's roof fell in. The roof of the steam engine building was destroyed, but the engine itself was unharmed. However, the losses – estimated at £12–15,000 (the equivalent of between £860,000 and £1.1 million in today's money) were uninsured, and nearly 500 factory girls were out of work.

28 May

In 1931 there was a major storm at Dereham, starting at noon and lasting for two hours. Lightning struck Quebec Hall; the building had a lucky escape, because although the bolt smashed a window, destroyed a radio set and tore up flagstones near the radio's earth, then set fire to a curtain, the fire was quickly extinguished.

1947 saw a series of forest fires at the Sandringham estate. The first outbreak started on 28 May and covered 300 acres; there was another outbreak the following day. Fourteen brigades banded together to fight the fire, aided by German prisoners of war, and although it was out by dusk on 29 May there was another outbreak on the following day.

2006 saw a fire at Caister when a teenager left a basket of washing on top of the cooker and accidentally knocked the switch turning a ring on before he went out. The clothes caught fire and spread to a basket of shopping on the kitchen worktop, and the deodorant exploded. It caused £35,000 of damage, including a cracked wall; the blast lifted the roof off the building and blew the windows out. Three crews fought the blaze; happily, one of the family's pet dogs was rescued and the other one had already escaped.

31 May

The weather was rough in 1646 – there were tornadoes at Thetford and Brandon Parva, following an extremely hot day and a violent hailstorm. According to the *Norwich Remembrancer*, it was even worse in 1767, with 'the most tremendous storm ever remembered' – many people were hurt and the bridge at Harford outside Norwich was swept away.

In 1802 Swanton Morley paper mill suffered serious damage in a blaze, and all the paper was lost. The damage was estimated at £4,000 (the equivalent of nearly £275,000 in today's money).

In 1856 there was a bad fire in Sadd's Yard off Coslany Street in Norwich; Ineson's rag and bone merchants was destroyed, along with Fisher's building workshop and Turner's paint shop.

Wells-next-the-Sea narrowly escaped disaster in 1927 when workmen were preparing to tar the road and the tar boiler tilted; tar overflowed into the fire box and the machine was quickly on fire. The horse was released so it didn't get hurt, but the heat was so great that the workmen couldn't smother the flames with sand. The fire brigade managed to put it out with four fire extinguishers; the *Eastern Daily Press* soberly related that if it had happened in a narrow street instead of the wide part of Freeman Street, 'much damage must have resulted'.

1931 saw a cloudburst early in the morning which centred on the Waveney valley. Roads were flooded up to a foot deep in water, and mangolds were washed out of fields.

1978 saw three fire engines and firemen working for three hours to subdue a blaze at East Winch common. Hundreds of nests and rare plants were destroyed, as well as snakes, lizards, and toads, and three hectares of the 80-hectare reserve were ruined. The wind kept changing direction, hampering the fire crew's efforts, and the soil was peat, which meant that the fire could suddenly break out just when everyone thought it had been extinguished. The cause of the blaze was unclear, but conservationists – who had cleared four tons of rubbish from the area on the previous weekend – thought that maybe it had started with the sun shining through broken glass.

June

June has been the season for riots in Norfolk; the events that sparked the big riot of 1272, which saw the city of Norwich excommunicated by the Pope, took place in June, as did the Peasants' Revolt of 1381 and Kett's Rebellion of 1549 (see 27 August for details). June also saw the second wave of the Baedeker raids in Norwich in World War Two.

June has also been a month of fires. Many villages and towns in Norfolk have had a 'great fire' in their history; in June, fire ravaged Attleborough, Foulsham, North Walsham, Thetford and Wymondham.

In 1559 there was a major fire at Market Street in Attleborough which basically wiped out half the village. Although I have been unable to pin the fire down to the exact day, the rector wrote in the parish marriage register between the entries for 13 June and 10 August 1559: 'This yeare was the Towne of Atleburgh in the streete there of the markett street then burnt.'

1 June

There was a major fire at Thetford in 1697; a collection to relieve the suffering was made at St Stephen's Church in Norwich, two months later, when the King's Brief was read.

1797 saw a mutiny on board the North Sea Fleet at Yarmouth, and the *Norfolk Chronicle* reported that several sail of the line hoisted the red flag of defiance.

The Griffin at Attleborough, next to the church: the first building erected after the great fire. (Photograph by author)

1889 saw a major storm across the county. A cottage was destroyed by lightning at Hickling, and there was damage to fruit trees around Gorleston. Hail weighing 3–4oz, and measuring 4in in circumference, fell in an area which stretched between Swaffham, Docking, Harpley and Thornham. There was much damage to glass houses, and livestock were cut and bruised. Over £1,000 of damage was done to grain crops lost at Docking. At Swaffham Mr Lindsey at the corner of Lynn Street lost 90 panes of glass in his house due to hail the size of hens' eggs; the *Norfolk Chronicle* listed many other people who'd lost well over 20 panes of glass.

2 June

There was a huge tempest in Norwich in 1772, according to the *Norwich Remembrancer*; the brass works of a clock were melted by lightning, which also hit the White Horse in Bethel Street and the chimney at Mrs Wright's house at St Lawrence. The *Norwich Mercury* added that glass in a dressing room at the Mayor's house was silver side up when the storm struck and it was cut in half by the lightning; in one Norwich pub a dog standing between a person and the fireplace was struck by lightning and killed.

1799 saw a tragic accident when a pleasure boat sailing from Heacham to King's Lynn overturned; 12 out of the 24 men, women and children aboard drowned.

1886 saw a whirlwind at Sparham. Farmer Thomas G. Nelson gave an eyewitness account in a letter to the *Eastern Daily Press* saying that he saw 'a very black cloud rising in the south west, with a light cloud almost like steam underneath, which came up very quickly with a peculiar roaring, whistling sound'. What he described next was a classic tornado: instead of rain, the wind brought hail. It then blew all the tiles off the house, mowed five trees down, blew eight chicken coops over a high fence – they landed 50 yards away – and snapped off the top of an oak tree, blowing it 60 yards. It was all over in two minutes and Mr Nelson said that none of his neighbours noticed anything – the wind moved in a swathe and left a zigzag pattern across a field of wheat.

1928 saw an enormous fire at Yarmouth, when Jewson's timber mill caught light just before 6pm; the *Eastern Daily Press* reported that the fire 'seemed to develop in an instant', and because the buildings were wooden the fire quickly became an inferno and spread to the five-storey building of Clark's flour mill. Spectators on the other side of the river, 150ft away, could feel the heat of the fire on their faces. By 7pm the flour mill was 'in a lake of fire', and 40 minutes later the roof burned away, leaving a crater of fire with flames 12ft high. Even at 10pm it was reportedly as light as day – and it was not until seven the next morning that the firefighters could relax.

In 1964 £25,000 worth of sweets and rock were damaged at the Great Yarmouth factory of H.M. Docwra Ltd. The fire was discovered at 7.30am by workers arriving early, but the fire brigade couldn't stop the blaze wrecking the stock.

3 June

1780 saw a major storm at Norwich; according to the *Norfolk Chronicle*, the thunder shook all the houses to their foundations.

1973 saw a huge blaze at a disused maltings in Thetford. The blaze lit the sky over the centre of town and destroyed much of the roof, but the four crews managed to confine the blaze to the 100ft range of buildings.

4 June

In 1507 the second of two serious fires that year hit Norwich (see also 25 March).

It started on Colegate, in the house of a French surgeon called Peter Johnson, and burned for two days in the area from Colegate to Coslany. It destroyed 360 houses in Norwich as well as St Michael's Church. In May 1509 the city's rulers ordered that all new buildings had to be roofed with 'thaktyle' and not thatch, with a fine of 20 shillings (the equivalent of nearly £500 in today's money) for not complying. The rules became more detailed still in 1570, when it was decreed that roofs had to be made of tile, slate or lead, and every church had to have buckets and a ladder. The poet John Skelton wrote of the fire, 'All life is brief, and frail all man's estate. City, farewell: I mourn thy cruel fate.'

1922 saw a major fire at the International Stores in Attleborough, opposite the church. At 5am Mr Daines was woken by smoke; he managed to get his wife and child out safely, but the fire spread so rapidly that he had no time to get anything else out of his home. The heat was intense, and the fire brigade worried that neighbouring buildings would go up – particularly as they had problems getting water. Eventually they pumped water from the pond at Attleborough Hall; by this time it was obvious that it was too late for the shop, but they fought the blaze for five hours and managed to contain it while townspeople helped to rescue the neighbours' property from inside their houses.

1958 saw freak storms causing fires and floods across the county. Gorleston had 1.3in of rain in four hours and water was knee-deep in the streets. The ground floor of Blickling Hall was flooded to a depth of 3½ft, and Aylsham fire brigade spent a long while pumping it out – even though they were pumping out at the rate of 1,000 gallons a minute! They had to open the lock from the lake to let water into the River Bure. Cars on the main road were stranded with water up to the door handles. Pupils at Bradwell School were stranded, and two thatched cottages at Hoveton were damaged by fire – firemen couldn't reach them as the road in Horning had flooded to 18in.

5 June

There was a huge fire in 1846 at St James' Factory in Norwich, which started when the boiler overheated. Although the walls were fireproofed, the roof wasn't, and the fire went through the roof and spread to the drying and preparing rooms. The blaze broke out just after 4am and the watchman discovered it and raised the alarm half an hour later. Although the engines came immediately, it took half an hour before they could get to work. Soldiers and workmen set up a human chain with buckets, but even so by 6am the *Norfolk Chronicle* reports that the flames had a 'terrific appearance'. The firefighters worked without regard for their own safety – one workman got on to the roof, took it off and broke down some of the walls, so the fire wouldn't spread to the longer rooms. Sailor Mr Allen carried a pipe on to the roof next door, so water could be directed on to the flames. However, despite their hard work and bravery, the roof of the engine house fell in and much of the stock was burnt. Sadly, a thousand people were put out of work because of the fire damage.

1867 saw the outhouse belonging to confectioner Mr Ives in Howard Street, Great Yarmouth, on fire. At 2 o'clock in the morning the alarm was raised when flames were spotted in the loft used as a carpenter's workshop by Mr Crome and Mr Ives jnr. The fire brigade arrived to face an enormous blaze – luckily there was no wind as there would have been much more damage. The fire engine belonging to Grout's silk mills came to help and the fire was contained, but the loft and the warehouse were destroyed. The damage was estimated at £800 (equivalent to nearly £48,000 in today's money) – and the *Norwich Mercury* commented that it broke out the day before they were planning to start negotiations to sell the business.

1962 saw a major fire in a garage store in Watton. A thousand gallons of oil and 200 gallons of paraffin went up; each drum 'went up like a bomb', according to eyewitnesses. It took three hours to get the blaze under control; luckily the fire brigade managed to contain the fire and it didn't affect the main garage, cars or the tyre store.

7 June

In 1931 the largest earthquake recorded in the UK hit the region. The epicentre was at Dogger Bank (approximately 120km north east of Great Yarmouth), and the earthquake measured 5.5 on the Richter scale. *The Times* reported that 'an earth tremor of greater severity since any experienced in this country since the East Anglian shock in 1884 [the Colchester earthquake on 2 April 1884] was felt… shortly before half-past one yesterday morning'. The tremor lasted for half an hour; there were cliff falls at Mundesley and chimneys down in Cromer, but according to the *Eastern Daily Press* the only casualty was in Northampton where a canary broke its wing.

1964 saw a major storm across the county. At Blofield one of the four pinnacles on the church tower crashed to the ground when it was hit by lightning and just missed the war memorial. In King Street, Norwich, lightning hit the chimney of the Kingsway pub, demolishing it and twisting part of the kitchen sink; landlord Mr Cubitt was having his lunch when the storm hit, and the next thing he knew he was on the floor. At Crostwight, lightning sheared off a chimney and cracked the gable end of a house; its owner was standing 4ft away, holding a garden fork, and was thrown to the ground. He was shaken but unhurt; he remembered seeing a reddish flash and hearing a huge crash, while his wife saw a blue flash go through the house. The storm also caused floods; the Norwich to Beccles road was 6in deep in water.

1978 saw 30 firemen fighting a blaze at the stable block of Scottow Hall near Coltishall; the stables were gutted and tack was destroyed. Miss Wynn Wilson woke to find the stables on fire; luckily no horses were there, but she had to rescue seven dogs. The fire lit up the sky for miles around, but was out by 1am. The same night, Coltishall Cricket and Bowls Social Club burned down; the fire spread so quickly that by the time the fire brigade got there, the building was gutted. Further south, in Norwich, the roof of the Salvation Army Citadel in Magdalen Street was ablaze. Because the lining of the roof was timber, the fire flared in the gap between, so the fire crew had to cut the lining of the roof ahead of the flames and pour water into it. They managed to contain the blaze, but the damage was estimated at thousands of pounds.

8 June
In 1811 there was a severe storm in Norwich.

9 June
1867 saw a large fire at Mr Barnes's engineering shop in Southtown near the bridge at Great Yarmouth. The previous day, smoke had been seen coming from his loft, but the fire turned out to be very small and was quickly extinguished. Mr Goode, the blacksmith who owned the property next door, visited 20 times that day (rather obsessive – but, as the *Norfolk Chronicle* pointed out, he had an interest as his buildings could be threatened by any fire) but couldn't smell any burning. However, as soon as the church services had finished that evening, much smoke could be seen from the loft and there were large flames. The whole building went up, and although the fire brigade were there quickly, the paper notes that their engines were 'poor quality instruments'. Grout's silk factory sent their engine over and the fire was contained to Mr Barnes's property. It was under control by 9pm, but the insurance didn't cover all the patterns, moulds, engines and machinery.

10 June
In 1667 there was a major fire at Thetford.

1964 saw a huge storm at Reedham; it lasted for half an hour, and the 'penny-sized hailstones' (old money) broke windows and glasshouses and damaged crops. The head of the village primary school collected some of the hailstones and said they were over an inch in diameter – some were over 1.5in.

1978 saw a major fire in Tombland, Norwich, when Ethelbert House (Boswell's) caught light. It took nearly 60 firemen to subdue the blaze and the damage ran into tens of thousands of pounds. The buildings on either side were at risk, so the fire crews had to cut through the roof to save them; owner Hy Kurzner was in tears when he was called to the scene at 3am.

11 June
The great fire of Wymondham occurred in 1615. It was believed to be started by three gypsies – William Flodder, John Flodder, and Ellen Pendleton (who pretended to be John's wife) – and Margaret Bix. They originally intended to set a fire in Norwich, but the keeper of their lodgings thought they were unruly and locked them in. They moved to Wymondham instead and started the fire. Pendleton claimed that Lord Stanley employed 'wandering companies' to burn down Puritan towns; however, it's very likely that they started the fire for revenge because they didn't get enough when they begged in the town. A contemporary broadsheet, *The Araignement of John Flodder and his wife*, said it caused £40,000 of damage, but the true cost was more like £15,000 (the equivalent of nearly £1.9 million in today's money). The fire was thought to be started in two places: one around the Market Place and one in Vicar Street. It destroyed the market cross,

the schoolhouse, the vicarage and the guildhouse; the worst affected areas were Vicar Street, Middleton Street, the Market Place and Bridewell Street. The following December, John Flodder was executed at Norwich for arson.

1939 saw a major fire at Hunstanton pier. Miss Doris Bassford of Leicester and Miss Winifred Taylor of Wembley were sitting at the end of the pier when they saw smoke. People waded out into the sea and told them to jump because they were trapped – although the sea was only 4ft deep and the drop was 30ft, they threw their handbags into the sea and jumped to safety. They were shocked but luckily unhurt; the concert hall, cafés and waiting rooms were burned out and fell into the sea. Hunstanton fire brigade and the ARP auxiliaries tried out their new equipment for the first time; it poured 500 gallons of sea water per minute at a pressure of 150lbs on to the flames. The fire was thought to be caused by a smouldering cigarette end.

The market cross at Wymondham, built in 1617. The crossed spoons and spigot carved into the timbers are the town's arms, adopted from the major industries in mediaeval times: spinning and making wooden domestic equipment such as spoons. (Photograph by author)

1973 saw a fire in the basement of Jarrold's office equipment department. It took 35 firemen four hours to control the blaze, but the 30 employees were safe. Staff had tried to extinguish it, but the heat and flames were too much. The fire crews used special foam for the first time during their four-hour fight to subdue the blaze.

12 June

In 1925 there was a strange coincidence in a tragic accident at Great Yarmouth, when the Newcastle steamer *Norsman* collided with the Glasgow steamer *Burnside* in dense fog. There was no time to launch a lifeboat because the *Norsman* sank in three minutes; the crew of nine were dragged down with the ship. Two of them drowned, but the *Burnside* rescued the remaining seven. By an odd coincidence, the captains of the ships discovered that they were old shipmates who hadn't seen each other for 13 years.

1941 saw bad air raids over King's Lynn. Exactly a year later, King's Lynn was hit by another bad air raid. Four bombs fell, hospitalising 17 and killing 43; among these were 18 civilians and 24 servicemen who were killed by a single bomb which destroyed the Eagle Hotel.

13 June

Hackford Church burned down in the great fire of Reepham in 1543, along with most of the high street, because the river was almost dry so there was no water to put the fire out. It was never replaced, and when the tower became dangerous in 1790 it had to be pulled down. A note in the parish register says that on this day in 1790 Mr Samuel Sewell (a roofer who'd replaced the leads on St Mary's Church in Reepham with slate) fell off the top 'and had like to have been killed'.

In 1964 there was a huge storm across the county. Houses at Wells were struck by lightning, a chimneystack collapsed at Dereham and there were floods at King's Lynn. There were also power failures across the county.

14 June

1890 saw a suspected case of rabies at New Buckenham. A liver and white spaniel had bitten over 10 adults and several children; Edward Cunningham of Buckenham shot it, and when the vet from Harleston did a post mortem he said that the dog had rabies. The *Norfolk Chronicle* commented that the dog 'probably came out of Suffolk'! Mr Miles sent his son, one of the children who'd been bitten, to Paris to be treated by Louis Pasteur.

1968 saw oil spreading across seven miles of beaches in east Norfolk. The oil appeared in an 18-inch wide strip from Caister to Winterton; at Scratby, patches of the oil spread to 20ft. Scrapers worked to clear it off the sand.

15 June

In 1770 there was a major fire in Foulsham which destroyed 14 buildings and damaged many more. The fire started on one side of the market place in a barn at 1pm; unfortunately, the General Stores contained gunpowder and there was a huge explosion. The parsonage and the 14th-century church were badly damaged, and three of the five bells were melted. A collection was made at Norwich for the relief of sufferers and to help rebuild the church.

17 June

There was a huge thunderstorm across part of the county in 1774 at 4pm. Lightning damaged the Church of St Peter's, Southgate, in Norwich, as well as firing a house and barn near Loddon. There was also much storm damage at Acle.

A violent thunderstorm in 1926 saw Norwich flooded again; half an inch of rain fell in five minutes, followed by a hailstorm where the hail was between a quarter and half an inch in diameter. The *Eastern Daily Press* described Guildhall Hill as a 'millrace', and because the wooden paving blocks in the streets around the market place rose up it looked as if the middle of the market itself was rising up. The department store of Curl Bros in Orford Place (now Debenhams) was flooded to a depth of 3ft; staff made a human chain of buckets up the stairs so the water could be thrown into the gutters. The scalding yard of Young's brewery on King Street was 3ft deep in water, and it was ankle deep at Heigham Street; houses were flooded at Heigham and St Martin's, but fortunately nobody was hurt. Sadly, at Ditchingham, George Hambling was not so lucky; he was hoeing in a field when he was fatally struck by lightning.

Two years later, there was a huge fire in St George's Street, Norwich, when the paint and oil store of Gunton Sons & Dyball, opposite the Technical Institute, caught fire. Although it wasn't a windy day, the way the building was constructed (to allow fumes to escape) meant that draughts fanned the fire; the *Eastern Daily Press* described the building as full of 'blood-red flames and belching masses of choking smoke'. Nobody was hurt, but several thousand pounds' worth of damage was caused.

1935 saw a severe fire at the new dye works of Fras. Hinde & Hardy in Oak Street, Norwich. Mrs Pughe, the manageress of the Empire Cinema next door, told the audience to go home, and 81-year-old Mrs Jex was taken from her home in Howman's Yard to a safe place. The factory covered a large area of Oak Street; the *Eastern Daily Press* reported that the flames at their worst were as high as the chimneystack.

1965 saw a blaze at the warehouse of Henry Sutton, fish exporters in Great Yarmouth. The warehouse contained tons of shruff (a mixture of shavings and sawdust, used in the process of curing herrings) and bystanders said that the smoke really hurt their eyes. Six fire engines fought the flames and had the fire under control within an hour.

18 June

1611 saw a tragic accident at the Gild Day pageant in Tombland, Norwich, when Thomas Anguish was about to become mayor. Fireworks were set off but some misfired and the crowds rushed away, fearing that they'd be hurt. Around 33 people fell and were crushed to death by the weight of people rushing over them; they were buried in St Simon and Jude's Churchyard, the next day, and fireworks were banned from the mayor's day celebrations in future.

19 June

Trinity Sunday in 1272 led to a three-day riot between the citizens and the monks in Norwich over tithing rights and the rights to the Trinity fair in Tombland. The cathedral prior brought in some armed men from Yarmouth (Norwich's traditional rival at the time) and they killed and wounded several people and looted property, as well as allegedly burning down some houses. The citizens complained to the king – but they also took matters into their own hands, and on 8 or 9 August they burned down the Ethelbert Gate. In the fracas that followed, some of the wooden buildings in the close also burned down. Henry III came to sort it out; he clearly saw blame on both sides as he put both the city and the priory under separate wardens. Thirty citizens were hanged, and their bodies either drawn and quartered or burned. However, after his death the new king, Edward I, ordered an investigation. The jury decided that the prior was guilty of murder and robbery and the fires by the citizens were mainly accidents. This sparked a diplomatic incident because then the whole town was excommunicated by the pope! It was finally settled in late 1275, when the citizens had to pay the prior 500 marks for six years (a mark was ⅔ of a pound – so this was a total of 3,000 marks, or today's equivalent of over a million pounds), give the priory a gold pyx weighing 10lb, and make new gates for the priory. In return, the pope gave the city a General Absolution in 1276.

In 1842 there was a severe gale and thunderstorm near Norwich. The vanes of the sails of Catton mill were ripped apart and scattered across neighbouring houses.

1922 saw the workhouse at St Faith's partly destroyed by fire. Mrs Florence Savage came on duty at 9.30 that night; all was well until 4.40am, when she smelled burning. She saw smoke coming out of the workhouse master's sitting room and discovered that the room was alight; quickly, she closed the door to stop the fire spreading, woke Mr and Mrs Bowman (the workhouse master and matron) and started rescuing the bedridden elderly in the workhouse. Mr Bowman grabbed an extinguisher but the flames were too much. He didn't stop to dress properly or even put his shoes on – he rode a bicycle to the post office, wearing only his trousers, and asked them to phone the fire brigade. Then he assembled the villagers (despite the fact that his bare feet were badly cut with glass and stones) and got them to help evacuate the elderly residents. Eight men, nine women and three babies were brought down from their first-floor bedroom windows in slings made of blankets, via ladders, and amazingly nobody was hurt. The fire brigade used 3,300ft of hose to reach the river; they had the fire under control in an hour and confined it to the main block, then spent the next five hours damping down. Forty inmates were taken to Aylsham workhouse; the board decided to close the St Faith's workhouse as it was 'a death trap', but they praised Mr Bowman as 'a hero' for his work in the rescue.

1964 saw a fire in the newly enlarged drapery shop of Rust's in Cromer. Employees were having lunch in the canteen above and the storeroom and heard cracking; then one of them realised the floor was red hot and there was a fire. Some of the assistants tried fighting the blaze with extinguishers, while others tried to salvage stock; Miss Pearman was overcome by the smoke while rescuing the stock but recovered outside the shop.

20 June

There was a tragic accident in Great Yarmouth in 1781; the *Norfolk Chronicle* reported that some gunpowder had been drying in the yard of Mr Riddlesdell the gunsmith in Howard Street when it caught fire and blew up. Mr Riddlesdell and his assistant were both badly hurt, the windows and part of the shop were destroyed, and several houses in the neighbourhood were damaged.

21 June

According to the 18th-century historian Francis Blomefield, in 1592 it rained from 21 June until the end of July, causing much damage to the hay and corn.

There was violent hail at Norwich in 1759; the *Norwich Remembrancer* reported that some stones were 2in long and weighed ¾oz.

A further storm hit in 1772; lightning hit a church at King's Lynn, and some roads were under 12in of water.

In 1834 there was a severe storm in the county and many cattle were killed by lightning.

1967 saw a £250,000 blaze at Hopton Constitutional Holiday Camp, when the dance room, beach club, bars and billiard rooms caught fire. It started at around 1pm and smoke was seen by a workman laying felt strips on the roof. He gave the alarm, but the blaze was so fierce that a fire engine was scorched by the heat, and holidaymakers later said they could feel the heat from 200 yards away. The fireman drained the pond at the camp dry, then had to fetch water from the village pond, a quarter of a mile away. However, the blaze was under control two hours later, and holidaymakers were able to go into the damaged dining hall for a late lunch. It was the second large fire at the camp; the previous one in March 1963 had seen the place rebuilt.

1989 saw the electricity in the Thetford area cut off after a 10-acre fire destroyed wooden pylons. Forty firemen fought the blaze at Barnham Cross Common, which was fanned by strong winds; they had to use sprays as there was a risk of electrocution if they used jets – the power might pass through the stream of water.

22 June

There was a bad fire in Norwich in 1776, starting at the premises of cabinet maker Samuel Cooper in Whitefriars; it burned down his house and that of William Woods in less than an hour. The houses of George Gibbs and Cave Burridge were also destroyed.

1933 saw a whirlwind in the Hingham area. Farmer Mr Burt heard a sound like a plane flying very low and saw a black cloud approaching. The whirlwind threw water from the pond into nearby trees, ripped a thousand tiles from cowsheds, threw chicken houses into the air and then crossed the road and snapped the top off a tree before blowing itself out.

1934 saw a massive fire at the Theatre Royal, Norwich, described as 'one of the fiercest fires ever seen in the city'. The fire was spotted by assistant cashier Miss Bardwell, who heard a 'clanging sound' just before 2 o'clock. She saw flames licking at the bottom of the safety curtain and called for help. However, the theatre acted as a kind of wind tunnel and the building was gutted within a couple of hours. Alfredo and his Gipsy Orchestra, who were playing at the theatre, lost much of their property, though Alfredo's favourite violin was saved. Acrobatic dancer Miss Valmar said that her father climbed into the dressing room and saved her dresses and shoes; he pushed them out of the window and she caught them.

1940 saw the first death in Norfolk caused by an air raid in World War Two, at Diss.

23 June

There was a flood in Norwich in 1703; the Wensum overflowed after heavy rain.

24 June

Feltwell saw a major fire in 1782, when a pea-stack belonging to Mr Grimwood caught fire. The flames spread rapidly, wiping out two large barns, 20 loads of hay and a dove-house; the wind carried it 30 yards away to the parsonage house, which was lost together with its barn, stables and other buildings, along with most of the furniture 'and two fat hogs', according to the *Norfolk Chronicle*. A fortnight later, the paper reported that the fire had been started by Mr Grimwood's maidservant – and the damage was thought to be around £2,000 (the equivalent of £178,000 in today's money).

In 1946 Wroxham was hit by a 'whirling cyclone'. Large trees were uprooted, roofs lost tiles, and fields of corn, sugar beet and cabbages were flattened – as was the glass roof of the pig pens at Wroxham Sale Ground. Over 100 homes were flooded and more were damaged by the loss of chimneys, tiles and windows. Three 180ft by 30ft glasshouses were smashed, and three hours after the storm people were still picking up lumps of hail as big as a fist. At Dereham the downpour was so fierce that people couldn't see the buildings on the other side of the street. In Norwich the rain was so forceful that it blew manhole covers 2ft into the air on Earlham Road.

25 June

The great fire of North Walsham occurred in 1600. Over 118 houses, 70 shops, barns stables and outhouses and the market were destroyed. It's thought that the fire started at about 6am in the house of a 'poor and lewd person' called Dowle; he fled, was apprehended and put in jail. The damage was thought to be around £20,000 (the equivalent of over £2.7 million in today's money).

The market cross at North Walsham, replacing the one lost in the fire of 1600. (Photograph by author)

In 1801 there was almost a disaster at Norwich Cathedral, when plumbers who were repairing holes in the lead went to lunch without securing their fire properly first. The fire took hold and over the next two hours, until the blaze was extinguished, nearly 45 yards of the roof and lead were destroyed, with an estimated damage of £500 (the equivalent of over £26,000 in today's money).

In 1817 the *Norfolk Chronicle* reported there was a severe hailstorm in Stoke Ferry and Wereham; some of the hailstones were 6in in circumference! Unsurprisingly, many windows were broken and sadly many rooks were found dead afterwards.

26 June

26 June 1381 saw the end of the Peasants' Revolt in Norfolk. It began when, in 1377, a poll tax was levied at 4d a head, regardless of income (this was equivalent to two days' wages for a peasant), to help pay for the cost of the war against France. There were three poll taxes in four years – and when Richard II raised the tax to a shilling per head, the equivalent of nearly a

week's wages, the peasants had had enough. They started to rebel; led by Wat Tyler, they burned tax records and marched to London to demand fair treatment from the king – in particular, fair wages and an end to the feudal system.

Geoffrey Litester (or Lister), a dyer from Felmingham, helped to gather dissidents at Mousehold – but the unrest in the county was not just about getting fair treatment for the peasants. The rebels invited Sir Robert Salle to join them – they hoped that because he was not born a noble, he might sympathise with their cause. When he refused, the crowd turned on him and killed him. Litester invaded the city, beheaded a JP, established himself at Norwich Castle (as 'King of the Commons') and then seized and publicly burned the deeds and court rolls of Carrow priory.

Litester's men then turned on Yarmouth; they plundered the town, burned the town charters, and broke into the jail – where they killed three of the four inmates just because they were Flemings.

When Wat Tyler was killed during a summit with Richard II at Smithfield on 15 June, Litester decided to try and negotiate a settlement. He sent some of his men to London with the money he'd taken from Norwich and two hostage knights – but they met Henry Despenser, the soldier Bishop of Norwich, just outside Newmarket. Despenser had heard the news of the rebellion and marched from his manor in Burleigh to deal with it. He cut off the heads of Litester's three men and displayed them on a pillory, then gathered his forces to fight Litester. Litester retreated to North Walsham, where he was defeated by Depenser. He was tried, then hung, drawn and quartered on 26 June; the quarters were displayed at Norwich, Great Yarmouth, King's Lynn and North Walsham to dissuade other potential rebels. The battle site was marked by three stone crosses, of which two remain on the Norwich Road at Walsham.

There was a disastrous fire in Norwich in 1839 at the cabinet maker Mr Bush's workshop in Roache's Court, off Fisher's Lane. The *Norfolk Chronicle* described it as 'one of most destructive seen in the city for years'. The fire broke out at 4 o'clock in the morning then spread to the shavings; a small boy saw the flames and raised the alarm. Four engines came to put out the blaze, but there was no waterman and no water supply for 20 minutes and the factory was destroyed, as well as the tools and furniture.

Carving of Bishop Despenser from a misericord in St Margaret's Church, King's Lynn. (Photograph by author)

The fire also spread to the silk weaver's next door. Fireman Mr Levy went on to the roof to pull up the lead and direct the water pipe on to the flames, but the roof fell in. He was buried in the ruins, but he escaped unhurt apart from having a scorched face.

The fire also spread to another neighbour, tailor John Galey. Although the fire was put out by 9 o'clock, much had been lost in the fire, including the roofs of the houses and their furniture. One mean-spirited thief even stole the material meant for clothes for the silk weaver's 10 children; nobody stopped him because they thought he was moving the material safely out of the fire's reach. The *Norfolk Chronicle* urged the public to start a subscription to help the three families.

JUNE

27 June

Following the April raids, the Baedeker raids on Norwich began again in 1942. Bombers dropped around 22 high explosive bombs and 20,000 incendiaries, which gutted 117 houses; 30 shops and offices and 29 factories were destroyed. Over 650 fires were reported. A thousand incendiaries fell on the cathedral, but Reginald Pallent and his team of firefighters tackled the fire on the roof and managed to stop the cathedral burning down. Two houses in the close were destroyed. The Norfolk and Norwich hospital was hit – including the nurses' home, the main operating theatre and four wards. Ber Street was badly hit, with both Bonds department store and the Church of St Michael at Thorn being flattened – it took 10 days before Bonds was cool enough for staff to get into the strong room. St Julian's Church in King Street was blown up. St Paul's Church in St Paul's Square was gutted by fire, as was the Jewish synagogue in Mountergate. Amazingly, only 16 people were killed and 15 seriously injured. According to the city engineers, the cost of repairs for air raid damage during the war was £1,060,000 – and over a quarter of this was for materials and haulage. 23,450 ceilings were repaired, 2,300 chimney stacks, and 19,850 doors and window frames – and an incredible 610,000ft of glass was used to repair shattered windows.

1970 saw a freak storm over west Norfolk. There was a two-hour cloudburst, with 3.07in of rain falling at West Winch and 2.64in at West Runton. The drains at King's Lynn and surrounding villages couldn't cope with the deluge; the floods were up to 2ft deep. At South Lynn an 85-year-old was flooded out for the 31st time. The King's Lynn fire services had to pump out 150 homes.

28 June

In 1912 Foulsham mill burned down. The fire was discovered at 1am and the alarm was raised by ringing the church bells, but although the fire brigade was there quickly the mill was gutted within an hour. The sails crashed down but luckily didn't hit the engine house next to the mill. The fire brigade managed to confine the fire to the mill, so the engine and flour grinding plant were saved; two hours later they were still damping down, and large beams that were still smouldering were removed from the mill. The damage was estimated at £1,000 (the equivalent of over £68,000 in today's money).

1976 saw a huge fire at the stores department of contractors May Gurney at Trowse bridge. The storemen tried to use extinguishers but the flames were too much, and in the end nine fire engines were needed to fight the blaze. Gas cylinders were dragged clear, but one fireman was hurt when an explosion blew him backwards.

29 June

In 1271, according to the 18th-century historian Blomefield, 'on St Peter and St Paul's day' lighting struck Norwich Cathedral while the monks were at prayer and two pillars were thrown down; luckily, the monks escaped unhurt.

1933 saw a major fire at fish curer Henry Sutton's premises in Great Yarmouth, just off Battery Road. The alarm was raised at 7.45pm; onlookers saw flames on the roof of the four-

93

storey building and slates fell. Sailors from HMS *Warspite* came to help and kept the crowds out of the firemen's way, but at 10pm the fire gained new vigour and was still burning fiercely at midnight, although the fire brigade managed to confine the blaze to the building.

30 June

1881 saw a huge fire in Colman's mustard packing department at Carrow Works in King Street Norwich; the glare was reportedly seen as far away as Ely, as a light in the sky. The fire was spotted just after 11pm by a watchman, who raised the alarm. Employees came to help with the firm's own fire engines, and the city fire brigade was also asked to help. The building was enormous – 120ft by 40ft, seven-storeys high, with 200 windows. There was no wind that night, but the building burned rapidly – as the *Norfolk Chronicle* said, the floors were 'more or less saturated with mustard oil'. Chimneys fell and the building was gutted; however, the fire crews managed to stop it spreading to the warehouse or paper mill.

Norwich, mustard packing section at Colman's destroyed by fire.
(Picture courtesy of Norfolk County Council Library and Information Service)

31 June

1883 saw violent storms across the county. The *Norfolk Chronicle* described the thunder over Norwich as 'remarkable', and unlike the usual sound because it was 'first a sharp, crackling crash and then a kind of prolonged fusillade'. Heavy rain was blown by the gale so the water looked like steam vapour. Heigham was flooded, and the Old Palace Road in Norwich looked like a canal. Three people were killed by lightning in the storm. Twenty-five-year-old team-man William Gould took shelter in a barn with two of his colleagues at Mr Keable's farm in Earlham; the barn had a metal weather vane on the top shaped 'like a running fox', and when the lightning struck it, the current went down into the barn and hit him on the right temple, killing him outright. The roof of the barn caught light; the fire brigade managed to put the fire out within two hours and saved the other farm buildings, but the barn and the granary were destroyed. Also in Norwich, Benjamin Deacon, a pedlar who lived at Fishgate Street, sheltered under an elm in Grove Road with his wife; lightning hit the tree, stripping the bark from it. Mrs Deacon was stunned, but Benjamin was killed. And finally, at Broom Green, Mr Grove was covering a haystack when lightning struck him, killing him instantly.

July

July is one of the hottest months of the year, and many heath fires have taken place during the month. 1990 in particular was very dry – the fire service answered 860 calls that month regarding grass, heath and crop fires due to the dry conditions.

But July has also been a stormy month – in July 1730, according to the 19th-century historian Charles Palmer, there was a remarkable storm and tempest, and hailstones of 'prodigious magnitude' fell over Great Yarmouth. July has also seen thunderstorms lasting for three days and floods caused by the storms.

2 July

In 1910 a waterspout was seen at Hunstanton at 10am. The *Eastern Daily Press* reported that it was a beautiful sight, and the base of the spout was seen at Heacham. When it reached the shore, it turned into a whirlwind and went over the green, but clearly the wind had lifted above the ground because the only damage reported was 'whisking over a large seat' and sand spread from the beach on to the green.

In 1946 it was the warmest day of the year, at 87°F – and ended in a huge storm, the second in just over a week. Two farm workers were killed at Horning when they sheltered under a haystack and were hit by lightning; at Fersfield Aerodrome a 1,000-gallon petrol tank exploded when it was hit by lightning, but luckily nobody was hurt. The *Eastern Daily Press* reported that west Norfolk was hit by hail 'as big as plums and bantam eggs'. One farmer at East Winch lost 260 panes in a greenhouse, and another at Tottenhill lost half his crop. Reepham church tower was also hit by lightning.

3 July

There was a major fire in Dereham in 1670. 170 houses burned, £19,500 of property was destroyed (the equivalent of nearly £2.4 million in today's money), five people were killed and many horses and cattle were lost. The 19th-century historian William Richards notes that the citizens of King's Lynn collected £110 in a subscription for them (equivalent to over £13,000 in today's money).

Fire hit Norwich in 1804 – on the Tuesday, malt in a kiln belonging to the brewery of Prentice & Co. in King Street overheated and set fire to the malting office. The fire was discovered between midday and 1 o'clock and the alarm was raised. According to the report in the *Norfolk Chronicle,* 'the engines immediately hastened to the spot, where the inhabitants, with the most commendable zeal and alacrity, soon assembled in great numbers, and, by their indefatigable exertions, added to the well regulated assistance of the military and the garrison'. The fire was out by 4 o'clock – but despite the best efforts of the firefighters, the malt kiln, granary and a dwelling house were destroyed, and a couple of neighbouring properties were damaged. The damage was believed to be around £1,000 – the equivalent of nearly £65,000 in today's money.

JULY

4 July

There was a huge storm in 1819. The hail caused £600 worth of damage (the equivalent of nearly £35,000 in today's money) to the wheat and barley crops of just one farmer, William Ungless of Whitwell, near Reepham.

5 July

1888 saw a severe thunderstorm across the county. A thatched barn at Caston was hit by lightning and the roof caught light. Villagers tried to clear the house's contents so the fire wouldn't spread, but a gable wall fell down on an elderly man, Robert Perry. Rescuers pulled him out, but he died from his injuries. In Norwich there were no human losses, although there were floods after a torrential downpour at midday: the basement at Curls was flooded to a depth of 3ft.

In 1932 there was a major fire at the Saturn Shoe Works in Fishergate, Norwich. Most of the workers left at 6pm, and all was well when the caretaker did his inspection round half an hour later. However, 10 minutes after that, smoke was spotted coming from the top of the three-storey building. A clerk who was working late in the office tried to investigate but was forced back by the smoke; the fire brigade was there quickly, but by then the top storey was already in flames and the roof fell in. By 9pm most of the fire was out, but the premises were gutted.

1946 saw another huge storm, only three days after the last, which caused landslides and flooding. Norwich had almost 2in of rain. At Cromer the fire brigade had to pump out 20,000 gallons of water from the furnace retorts of the gas company; for the second time in four days the basement of the Melbourne Hotel was flooded to a depth of 9in. There was extensive damage to crops; hundreds of acres were wiped out at a cost of tens of thousands of pounds.

1976 saw the RSPCA making daily boat patrols on the Broads to save birds after an outbreak of botulism wiped out scores of swans, ducks and geese.

1985 saw a severe hailstorm which stretched from Norwich to the coast, involving golf-ball sized hail. Norwich had an inch of rain in 15 minutes, and the flood damage to the Theatre Royal was estimated at £20,000.

6 July

1784 saw the footpath over the New Mills at Norwich give way; luckily, nobody was hurt.

1863 saw a tragic accident at the Burgh Water Frolic which had terrible echoes of the suspension bridge disaster in May 1845. The wherry *Ruby* had been chartered by Mr Longhurst of the Foundry Arms in Great Yarmouth; at the inquest, Daniel Hogg the nut seller said around 100 passengers were on board. They all rushed to the starboard side to see the famous yacht, the *Red Rover*; the stanchions couldn't cope with the sudden pressure and gave way, so the hatches fell down on the heads of people on the lower deck. Nine people fell overboard but were rescued; sadly, Charles Rushmer and James Tripp weren't so lucky, because they were killed when the falling hatches dislocated their necks and fractured their skulls.

In 1932 there was another Norwich shoe factory fire, this time at Sexton's in Coslany Street. The roof and the offices on the top floor were alight, but the workers in the factory beneath were unaware of it! It took two hours to subdue the flames; the top floors sustained a lot of damage, but the lower storey was relatively unscathed.

1957 saw storms across the county in which three people died. Lightning struck a tent at Mundesley, killing a schoolboy and knocking two others semi-conscious. Lightning also blinded a man driving a van in Outwell; he drove into a creek, and both he and his wife died.

7 July

1784 saw flooding at Norwich when a 'severe tempest' started at 5.30am. A chimney was knocked down by lightning at Bramerton; it went through the bedroom shared by three children and two servants, shattered the window, the went down the bell wire and dissolved a lead bell in the parlour. Luckily, nobody was hurt. The farm belonging to Mr Skinner outside Burlingham was burnt down by lightning; again, luckily, nobody was hurt.

There was a severe thunderstorm in Norwich in 1833. The day had been sultry; at 10.30 in the evening the tempest started. At midnight, there were two crashes, and the *Norfolk Chronicle* reported that a ball of fire 'the size of a man's hat' fell on the thatched roof of the Black Tower. The fireball set light to the interior of the tower; the top floor was filled with astronomical equipment, which the inhabitants threw out of the window to save it – though sadly it smashed. In the middle storey, two women were asleep and were unharmed; on the ground floor, two young boys were shocked insensible. Water – 'except for the torrent that rolled down the hill' – couldn't be got to the tower to put out the flames, so everything but the furniture (which was taken outside) was lost. The *Norfolk Chronicle* said that 'the appearance of the blazing tower on the old city wall… formed a scene of awful grandeur' and many people gathered to watch it.

The lightning also hit a cottage at the end of a row on Bracondale Place. Weaver John Dye, his wife and five children and his loom were all safe, but the lightning actually came into the house, broke the windows, damaged a clock, pulled the nails out of the back of the sofa and cut it in half so the room was strewn with feathers. John's brother Samuel was by the door and the lightning severely scorched his right arm, thigh and lower body; the paper reported that although he was presently unable to leave his room, he was safe.

In 1924 fire broke out at Costessey Mills at 9am. The fire brigade arrived quickly but the fire spread rapidly, and the five-storey building was reduced to ruins with all the floors collapsing within an hour. It was windy so the fire brigade couldn't cross the bridge over the stream by the mills and had to fight the fire from 120 yards away. Police Constable Porter heard a cat crying, so, regardless of the risk to himself, he entered the building, crawled through the smoke and rescued the cat. The damage was estimated at £10–15,000 (the equivalent of between £392,000 and £588,000 in today's money).

1976 saw a huge grass fire in South Wootton which severely threatened homes. Nine fire crews fought the blaze and finally managed to stop it when it was only 6ft away from houses. The fire started on the side of the bypass; fanned by a strong breeze, in less than 30 minutes the flames had covered an area half a mile long and 100 yards wide. People used buckets to try and stem the flames, but the water supply dried up. Volunteers joined police and firemen using beaters to try and stop the fire; many families had oil-fired central heating and were worried that the oil tanks at the bottom of their gardens would blow up. In the end, the gardens of six houses were in ruins, and the fences, garages and sheds in the area were also affected.

That day there were 80 calls to the county fire service about grass fires. Four fire engines attended a huge blaze at Bowthorpe which involved 200 acres of grass and 70 acres of barley; houses were also threatened at Brandon where the fire went straight across a firebreak dug by mechanical diggers, but the fire crews just managed to stop it before it reached houses.

1978 saw a fire at sea, when the engine room of a dredger 14 miles off Great Yarmouth caught light. Two lifeboats were launched and a helicopter winched down firefighting gear. The blaze was extinguished but one of the 11 crew was injured.

8 July

Freak weather hit Blakeney in 1843 when a whirlwind appeared out of nowhere and lasted for a quarter of an hour. In that short time, it managed to carry away several yards of a 2ft-thick wall, blow a man off a threshing machine, take the roof off the White Horse and rip hatchings from fishing smacks.

1893 saw thunderstorms which lasted for three days. In Norwich a house in Edinburgh Road was hit by lightning, and a terrace in St Paul's was flooded. At Fakenham, the thunder was so bad that, according to the *Norfolk Chronicle*, 'several persons suffered severely from fright'; there was also widespread flooding. At Walsingham corn was damaged by hail. At Great Massingham, lightning struck the heath and burned gorse; five men hoeing turnips in a nearby field had a narrow escape when the lightning struck, and two of them were confined to bed the next day. The rain was torrential; Cromer had 4.48in of rain in 24hr, and just over half of that fell over the course of just one hour. At Long Stratton, Thomas Francis and William Nodd took shelter under a tree; when the lightning hit, Nodd was killed and Francis was injured.

1948 saw gale force winds across the county and the Cromer lifeboat went to the rescue when the 650-tonne French collier *Francois Tixier* sprung a leak five miles off Sheringham; the crew couldn't pump out the water in the terrible weather conditions and the ship was sinking. The Sheringham lifeboat was already out, so the Cromer lifeboat went to the rescue. When they reached the ship, it was listing to port and the lifeboat couldn't get close, so they used the breeches buoy to save 11 of the crew. Another was being dragged to safety when the collier capsized, throwing the captain and remaining three crew members into the sea. The lifeboat crew plucked them from the waves, but the sea was so bad that the lifeboat ended up landing at Great Yarmouth. It was Henry 'Shrimp' Davies's first rescue as a coxswain, and he was awarded the French maritime medal for his bravery.

9 July

There was a huge storm in 1853, when rain fell for three hours. The *Norfolk Chronicle* reported that it 'hadn't rained so fast in Norwich for 10 years'; there was vivid lightning, the sewers burst in London Street, and houses had to be pumped out in Exchange Street. At Bracon Ash, lightning set fire to a barn and severed the shafts of the threshing machine from its body. The streets in North Walsham were flooded to a depth of several feet, and, around the county, bridges were forced up and crops damaged.

1940 saw the first of 46 air raids on Norwich during World War Two. Incendiary bombs hit Barnard's factory at Mousehold, leaving two dead and five wounded; four high explosive bombs fell on the Boulton & Paul riverside factory, leaving 10 dead and 70 injured. More bombs fell on Carrow Hill; no air raid warning was given and the attack came just as the Colman's factory workers were leaving for the day, killing 26 women. Four more fell on Thorpe Station, causing serious injuries and fatalities.

1976 saw the county's chief fire officer Frederick Western warning the county that the fire risk in Norfolk was 'at crisis point'. He appealed to farmers not to burn stubble and to picnickers not to discard bottles, tins or cigarettes which could start a blaze; that day alone the fire service had had 70 calls about heath and grass fires. By the middle of the next month, the *Eastern Daily Press* reported that firemen were working 18-hour stretches to keep up with the blazes in the driest summer in memory.

10 July

1972 saw a blaze gut a Norwich store, and demolition crews had to spend the night working on the dangerous building. The owner of C&G Stores in Magdalen Street lit a Tilley lamp and it blew up in his face; 15 tons of candles caught light and the flames spread quickly, wrecking £13,000 of clothing and general goods. The fire started at 3.30pm, and 35 firemen managed to confine it to the shop and extinguish it within two hours.

1974 saw a £50,000 grass feed blaze on a farm at Wormegay, which started in the grinding area of a grass drying firm. Nine hundred tons of grass and grass meal caught light and the fire spread quickly. Nine fire engines from seven fire brigades fought the blaze; they used the farm pond and a swimming pool, then set up a relay system to bring water from an open source a mile away. The fire crews were still fighting the blaze a day later, using earth-moving machines to shift the burning feed.

11 July

1968 saw what the *Eastern Daily Press* called an 'incredible' storm. Hundreds of trees were blown down and it was estimated that 1,100 phones were out; power lines were also blown down. Cars at Cromer were having trouble staying on the road, and one woman was actually pushed into the path of a car by the wind – luckily, she was unhurt. There was much damage in the harbours at Overy Staithe, Brancaster and Wells – at the latter, the sea came up to the boundary wall on the road.

1995 saw a storm after the end of a heatwave, caused by a combination of high temperatures and high moisture in the air. The storm started a little south of the county in Lowestoft at 5am and had moved in a swathe across the county to King's Lynn by 10am. At least eight houses were struck by lightning; a home in Whissonsett was gutted, with the loft and first floor lost in minutes when it was hit by lightning. The phone lines came down and there were power cuts; the heavy rain (29 mm in Norwich) made drains overflow, causing floods.

12 July

In 1946 a sawmill burned down in North Walsham. The outbreak was discovered at 3am; it's thought that it started in an underground furnace used to drive the steam engine. Firemen stopped the blaze spreading from the sawmill to the timber yard, and it was under control two hours later.

1965 saw the biggest fire ever seen at Thetford, when the new factory at Thermos Ltd caught fire. The fire broke out at three and the fire brigade arrived within 10 minutes but realised they needed more help. By 3.30am there were nine fire engines and 75 firemen fighting the blaze. It was under control in one and a half hours, but even so the factory was gutted and 750,000 glass flasks exploded with sounds like gunshots that could be heard all over Thetford. The glow from the flames could be seen for miles. Half the roof fell in, but the firefighters were about to contain the blaze so it didn't reach the acetylene cylinders at one end of the store and propane gas tanks outside.

1971 saw 2,000 fish dying in the River Wensum after a rain storm that evening. A sudden surge of rain water swept waste material (which had been stored in the storm sewers during the dry spell) into the river. The waste material absorbed all the oxygen in the water and the fish were killed; they were seen lying under Bishop's Bridge in Norwich.

2002 saw a serious fire in Sculthorpe Watermill. It was restored at a cost of £400,000 and reopened in January 2003 by the fire crews from Fakenham and Great Massingham, who had saved the building from being completely destroyed.

14 July

1859 saw a fire at Noble's the organ builder in Pottergate, Norwich; the entire stock was destroyed. Next door was the hospital for the West Norfolk Militia invalids; according to the *Norfolk Chronicle,* 10 invalids escaped 'in great alarm, and only partially dressed'.

1932 saw major storms in the south of the county. Four cottages near Diss were struck by lightning; Mr Brown, in one of the cottages, had a very lucky escape. He was standing near the kitchen door, rocking the baby in its pram, when lightning struck his foot, took a chunk of leather out of his shoe near his big toe, then went past the pram into the wall.

1968 saw major floods hitting the county – for King's Lynn, it was the second time in four days, because householders had just finished clearing up when the sewers burst again. East Runton suffered the worst floods for 50 years after half an hour of torrential rain; one yard, opposite a blocked drain, was flooded to a depth of 2ft. Sheringham had floods up to 5in deep, and Cromer was flooded in Church Street.

1977 saw a £50,000 blaze at Ayton Asphalt in Wymondham. Bitumen burst into flames when it was being transferred from a storage tanker to a road tanker, and four storage tanks and three sheds were destroyed. Workers heard an explosion and rushed out to see the tanker ablaze. Fifty firemen and 10 engines fought for two hours to stop the blaze reaching nearby diesel and a 2,000-gallon tank of white spirit. The black smoke was visible for miles around – and police had to seal off roads and halt the trains until the blaze was under control.

15 July

1817 saw a huge northerly gale, and the salt marshes near Wells were inundated by a high tide. At Warham, the villagers tried to rescue the sheep on the marshes by taking the boats out, but the sheep had been shorn the previous week and the *Norfolk Chronicle* reported that the cold sea numbed their joints and they couldn't move. The shepherd, clearly devastated at the idea of losing his flock, tried so hard to move them that he ignored how tired he was and almost drowned. Sadly, 300 sheep were lost, including '11 score stock ewes' belonging to Mr Moore and 60 or 70 belonging to Mr Bloomfield.

16 July

There was a major storm in the county in 1769; hail destroyed 60 acres of wheat at Welney, belonging to Mr Emblin, and destroyed the crops of neighbouring farmers.

1863 saw a serious fire in Dereham which started in the hayloft of builder William Hubbard at about 9pm. The fire brigade were there within an hour and the fire – which could be seen from several miles away – was out by 3am. The fire destroyed the workshops, costing £2,000, and did £400 of damage to the warehouse next door (between them, equivalent to over £160,000 in today's money). Goods and furniture from nearby houses was put in the Corn Hall to keep them safe from the fire, but the *Norfolk Chronicle* reported that much was broken or stolen.

1973 saw an hour of storms over the Norwich area during the evening rush hour; a restaurant in Coltishall was flooded to a depth of 14in.

17 July

In 1901 there was a major fire at Snelling's candle factory in Rampant Horse Street, Norwich. The fire started in the lard room, and everyone thought it would destroy the neighbours (Goose, the printer and stationer, and Thompson the tinsmith). Rescue workers got barrels of tallow out of the factory, but the heat caused the wood to swell; the barrels burst and liquid tallow ran all over the road. And the firemen had a narrow escape when the roof fell in – one was stunned when the roof fell on to him but clearly wasn't badly hurt as the newspaper reported that he soon got back to work.

1971 saw a massive heath fire in Holt. Forty firemen fought the blaze with seven engines; the water had to be ferried from the hydrant half a mile away. The smoke could be seen for miles, and 80 acres were burnt; at one point, the fire almost encircled the firemen, but they managed to walk to safety.

1975 saw torrential rain which caused utter chaos in Dersingham. The rain washed tons of silt into the village from the surrounding hills, and the post office was flooded to a depth of 12in.

18 July

The great fire of Dereham took place in 1581; it destroyed most of the town, recorded as '52 tenements and 350 houses of office,' and caused £14,000 of damage (the equivalent of nearly £588,000 in today's money). A poem by local man Arthur Gurney called *A Doleful Discourse and*

Ruthfull Report of the great Spoyle and loss by Fire in the Towne of East Dereham explained that there had been a drought for the previous month; the fire started in Church Street, then spread to the market place and westwards. The church and Bishop Bonner's cottage survived, and the town was rebuilt by 1597. The poem gives a dramatic flavour of the day:

'For after it had once begonne to fume,

Against the winde, and with the winde it went,

It leaft no side, but eftsoones did assume,

All that it toucht, and no way would be pent,

Till my long streetes, on both sides it had brent,

And made them lowe and leauell with the grownde,

And of my coyne, had molten many a pownde.

…the brandes, they whirld so fast aboute,

They burnt my Pumps, I wor my welles right out.'

There was a severe thunderstorm over the county in 1816, and Norwich was particularly badly hit by lightning in the afternoon. The storm exploded over a house in St Giles' Gate, where two people were sheltering in a doorway. Lightning went through the roof of a house and literally shocked the inhabitants – a man was knocked down and had numb legs, while his son's side and shoulders were seriously burnt (to the point where the medical attendants were surprised it was not fatal) as well as being blinded and his hair being singed. Two women and a child were lucky to escape with one of them having only a slight burn to the cheek. The lightning also damaged the house, but ripping the window off the bedroom and chucking it down the stairs.

1971 saw Sporle School badly damaged by fire, three days before the end of term. Books, equipment and furniture were lost. Three brigades arrived to tackle the fire, but the roof collapsed just as they got there. It took three-quarters of an hour to get the blaze under control. The children were given the Monday off, then it was planned to give lessons in the school field on the Tuesday and a school trip on the Wednesday.

19 July

Great Yarmouth was flooded in 1931; the *Eastern Daily Press* reported that a thunderstorm started at 1am and rain fell in torrents for an hour. Several roads were well under water, despite new pumps at Northgate Road; one new motor car drove on the pavement past the Apollo Tavern and its wheels sank into a flowerbed!

19 July 1940 saw an air raid over Norwich over the Bull Close and Botolph Street areas; fortunately, people sustained only minor injuries.

1977 saw a dramatic nine-and-a-half-hour rescue by the lifeboat at Caister, when a catamaran broke down in Hewett gas field; the boat had been hit by squalls and run out of fuel. A North Sea gas platform saw the boat in trouble and reported it to the coastguard; the supply boat *Boston Hornet* towed them out to meet the Caister lifeboat, who then towed them to safety at Happisburgh.

20 July

In 1656 there was a major storm in Norfolk. A pamphlet dating from 1656 in the Colman Collection in the Norfolk Heritage Centre refers to a whirlwind and thick darkness, with 5in hailstones. In Norwich, 'the loud claps from the clouds so amazed the people that they thought the spheres came thundering down in flames about their ears', and because the hailstones were bigger than oranges, all windows facing south and south east were shattered. It caused around £3,000 of damage; another storm caused damage across 30 miles of the county, and the lightning set crops on fire.

1900 saw a storm across the county at midnight. Cattle were killed by lightning at Foulsham; bullocks were killed and crops were damaged at Little Cressingham. At Elmham, a haystack caught fire when it was struck by lightning, and Wymondham suffered hail as big as bantam's eggs which smashed all the glasshouses in the area.

1903 saw major rain across the county, with 2in falling within 24 hours. The *Eastern Daily Press* remarked that 'unusually there was no thunder'. There had been an inch of rain the previous day, too, and the paper said that it was the worst rainfall since August 1879.

There was a major thunderstorm in the county on the evening of 20 July 1929, followed by a tidal wave early the following morning. Two thatched cottages at Happisburgh were hit by lightning and caught fire; villagers couldn't save the cottages but managed to save their contents and stopped the fire spreading next door to the oil store and cycle shop belonging to Robert Hemp. The newspaper gave a 'special mention' to Miss Gertie Hemp and the officers of the local Girl Guides and Brownies who helped. At Cromer, it was the worst storm in several years; onlookers described the sky at 2am as 'like a rainbow'. Lightning was going off at 70 flashes a minute and thunder was 'like the sound of big guns'. At Brisley Manor, lightning struck a chimney, smashed stone and glass and travelled to the floor below; Mr and Mrs Brody and their two sons had a lucky escape, as they were thrown from their beds but were not hurt. Later in the morning, the *Eastern Daily Press* reported that there was a tidal wave from Yarmouth right the way down the coast to Hastings – luckily there were no fatalities in Norfolk.

1932 saw a major storm across the county. In Norwich, the force of the water pushed up manholes at Unthank Road and the junction of Mile Cross and Drayton Road. Cromer saw its worst storm for 20 years, with ¾in of rain recorded during the storm; cellars were flooded to a depth of 18in and at the East Coast Garage firemen worked for an hour to pump out 20,000 gallons of water.

21 July

Norwich was hit by fire six times in two days in 1928 – starting with a fire that threatened the War Memorial cottages on Mousehold Heath. The following day, the fire broke out there again and also at the nearby pavilion; around an acre and a half of heathland was destroyed near the cottages.

1965 saw two heavy thunderstorms – one in the afternoon and one in the evening – which caused severe flooding in Norwich. The Salhouse Road was closed to traffic due to a flood 3ft deep under the bridge.

1973 saw a two-hour cloudburst in the afternoon over north Norfolk. Floods were severe at West Runton, where water was knee-deep outside the Village Inn and 6in inside. The North Walsham road to Norwich was impassable.

22 July

The next four Norwich fires over that weekend in 1928 were in different parts of the city; first of all, a fire at Eaton in a field by Bluebell Road, then a disused brickyard on City Road, and then Dereham Road allotments; finally, farmer Mr Gowing at Lower Helleson lost 50 yards of fence – but he was very lucky that it didn't spread to the field, which contained 23 acres of barley.

1942 saw air raids over Sheringham, killing nine people, and Cromer, killing 11.

23 July

In 1717 there was an odd incidence of subsidence at Mannington; according to the *Norwich Remembrancer*, three oaks, together with their roots and the ground around them 'sank in front of astonished beholders'. It seemed the soil was a layer of gravel, over the top of quicksand, which in turn was over subsidence-friendly clay.

1774 saw a major fire in Heigham, which started at 2pm and 'raged with great violence', according to the *Norfolk Chronicle*, in the tanning yard of John Tinkler in Heigham. It also spread to Mr Smith's tanning yard next door, but the fire crew prevented it spreading further. Three men climbed on to the roof of an outhouse to damp down the flames, but the roof fell in and one of the men was badly bruised.

In 1968 61-year-old Billy Rudrum fought a blaze single-handedly at a Great Yarmouth fish and chip shop in St Peter's Road. Two fryers and six customers were taken to hospital with burns. Billy saw the flames as he walked past, went to the shop opposite and got an extinguisher, then stopped the draught fanning the flames in the fryer by closing the doors. He'd managed to put out the blaze by the time the fire brigade arrived. Afterwards, he simply told the local paper that 'anyone would have done the same thing in the circumstances' and added that he was not scared as 'I never am nervous'.

1971 saw a huge fire at A. King and Sons, metal dealers, on Hall Road in Norwich, causing £15,000 of damage. The fire broke out among railway sleepers that had been impregnated with creosote, and spread to a diesel locomotive containing £7,000 worth of scrap metal; the blaze was thought to have been started by oxy-acetylene and propane cutting. When the flames got very close to a high voltage transformer, the fire brigade cut off the power supply to safeguard against further damage. Five engines were needed to fight the blaze, and there was a dense pall of smoke over Lakenham.

24 July

1972 saw 0.64in of heavy rain, causing floods in Great Yarmouth and Gorleston – but that was just a warm-up for the storm that happened a week later. (See 1 August.)

26 July

1772 saw a storm across Norwich, and lightning caused damage at St Andrew's and St George's Colegate. Peter Nevil of St Martin's was hit by lightning, which rendered him temporarily speechless and broke his arm; a dog belonging to Mr Mann of St George's Colegate was killed when it was struck by lightning.

In 1946 storms hit Norwich; gusts of winds were measured at 40mph and nearly an inch of rain fell in 15 minutes. The metalled surface of the road at Unthank Road and Earlham Road was forced up by torrential rain, and there was subsidence at the corner of Rupert Street and Essex Street. That evening, it was so dark at 7pm that cars actually had to use their headlights.

1974 saw a sawmill and timber worth £8,000 burned at Letheringsett. Three brigades took an hour to bring the fire under control. The smoke could be seen five miles away, and police had to stop traffic on the A148 Cromer–Lynn road because the smoke was so dangerous. When the fire brigade arrived, the sawmill had already collapsed, and 25 tons of timber were lost. The fire crew's efforts were hampered by the fact that there was no water on the site and the nearest hydrant was a quarter of a mile away in the village. The cause of the fire was unknown.

27 July

1879 saw a landslip at Attleborough. Mr Gathergood, a farmer from Rockland, was crossing his field of turnips in Attleborough when he heard a noise like the roar of a cannon. Suddenly a piece of earth 24 yards in circumference sank out of sight, replaced by a pool of water. The water subsided the next day to 12ft below the surface, and eventually the chasm was measured at 35ft deep, with 'perfectly perpendicular' sides. The cause of the subsidence was thought to be heavy rainfall, but locals had a saying that putting anything in that field was like throwing it away, so clearly some kind of subsidence had occurred before – and the previous year, a horse ploughing the field sank into the earth up to its neck.

1900 saw a huge fire in Fishergate in Norwich; at around 9pm Porter's Sawmills and timber yard 'became suddenly one mass of flame'. The blaze could be seen for miles, and Soman's Shoe factory also caught light; the two premises were gutted, but ABC wharf and Mr Skipper's box shop were saved. Five fire brigades had the flames in hand by midnight; at 3am the fire was still going but it was under control. The firemen had to cover their face with wet cloths to stop being scorched by the intense heat. The fire caused several thousand pounds' worth of damage; luckily it was all insured.

28 July

In 1753 most of the flax room at the city bridewell in Norwich was destroyed by fire.

29 July

1932 saw a huge fire in Allen's Lane, just off Newmarket Road in Norwich. At 1 o'clock in the morning, Albert Bilham was woken by his dog barking; when he looked out of the window, he saw flames in his wood and paint store. He called the fire brigade and, together with neighbours, managed to move most of the vehicles from six lock-up garages; however, the petrol tanks of a baker's van and a private saloon car exploded. The wood and paint store was also gutted.

1971 saw a huge amount of rain – Gorleston had 3½in of rain in less than 24 hours, flooding several cottages. Norwich had 2in and Loddon had 2.56in. At Yarmouth, the flooded roads brought traffic to a standstill, and at North Walsham the Norwich road was flooded to a depth of between 2–3ft.

2000 saw two major fires in the county. At 9.30am 50 firemen were sent to Hepworth Minerals and Chemicals in Leziate (a firm producing silica sand for industrial purposes – and incidentally the quarry where some episodes of *Dad's Army* were filmed). An asbestos-clad building 80 metres square, containing propane and gas cylinders, had caught light and toxic chemicals were stored nearby. The seven crews got the cylinders out and managed to contain the fire within an hour, although they needed to spend another three hours damping down. At Cromer, even more firemen were needed – 11 fire engines and 90 firemen spent two and a half hours fighting a blaze at the Edinburgh House flats, which spread from the kitchen to the whole building; the blaze was thought to have been caused by a candle. Two teenagers helped to save their family; 13-year-old Adam Dobson woke his family and threw his mattress out on to the rear balcony to give everyone an escape route, and his 15-year-old brother Arran-James held their young sister below the smoke level to avoid the fumes.

30 July

In 1625 the plague hit Norwich. According to the 18th-century historian Francis Blomefield, the previous week people had been told to keep their dogs and pigs indoors or they would be killed. But on 20 July the authorities stopped watching the city gates because the city had been infected by the plague. On 19 September the Black Tower on the Butter Hills was used as a reception for the infected poor; on average, more than 40 people died in a week, though in the worst week of the plague it was almost double that. The plague finally ceased in December 1626, and during that period 1,431 people died from it.

1940 saw an air raid over Norwich. Bombs fell on Surrey Street, wrecking two buses, and also the Ber Street area, leaving one person dead and several injured.

In 1965 there was a dramatic rescue off Scroby Sands when 35-year-old engineer Harry Dickie was rescued by the Gorleston lifeboat. The water pump of his 2.5ton sloop packed up and the engine failed, so he sent up distress flares at midnight. The lifeboat went out, but when they threw a rope to him he went overboard. The crew pulled him to safety and towed him in; coxswain George Mobbs said that another hour and Mr Dickie would have been where the trawler *Yarmouth* was wrecked, and he wouldn't have had a chance.

1976 saw firemen using an unusual method to put out the flames, when fire broke out in a 120ft straw store on a farm at Hainford. The water was running low, so the seven fire engines had to put their hoses into the dyke and spray liquid pig effluent on to the flames. The straw had been stacked in the building because of fears of rain; the blaze destroyed 40 tons of pig bedding and machinery. However, the 800 pigs were saved and nobody was hurt.

2002 saw flash flooding in the county due to torrential rain. Marham had nearly 2in of rain, and Thetford, King's Lynn and Downham Market were flooded.

31 July

In 1834 there was a major storm around Diss. Lightning hit a windmill on Stuston Road; the sails were ripped off and Mr Leathers, working inside it, was knocked to the ground by the lightning, and his hair was singed and his face was scorched. He did, however, make a full recovery.

1946 saw a big fire at Thetford when R.J. Goddard's carpentry shop caught light. The fire broke out just after 1pm, when most of the staff had gone for lunch; apprentice Alan Frost saw smoke from the shop and raised the alarm. By mistake his call was put through to Bury rather than Thetford, so by the time the fire brigade arrived the flames were rising 80–100ft into the air. It spread to the timber stores, paint and oil stores, shop and office; although the fire was under control by 3pm, the wooden buildings were gutted and Goddard's lost all their stock-taking records and tool kits.

1951 saw a huge storm across the county. Worsted parish church was hit by lightning and a pinnacle crashed through the roof, causing much damage. Three houses at Wymondham were also hit; the Meale family had a lucky escape, because lightning hit the chimney at 5am and ripped a hole in the wall between the bedrooms of the parents and their daughters. The children's beds were covered in rubble but nobody was hurt. The lightning also ripped a hole in the gas main, but the fire brigade managed to turn off the gas before it caught light.

2006 saw a huge crop fire at Pulham St Mary, needing 100 firefighters to tackle the blaze. A hundred tonnes of baled straw was destroyed and 300 acres of land were damaged.

August

Harvest time is usually associated with sunshine and plenty – but it has not always been the case. In 1252, according to the chronicler Holinshed, there was 'great death and murrain amongst cattle, and specially in Norfolk'. Apparently dogs and carrion feeding on the bodies of the cattle died immediately, so people didn't dare eat beef.

August was also a bad month for Norwich when it came to the plague. In August 1578 the plague hit the city badly for the fourth time since its first visit in 1349 and wiped out nearly a third of the population. According to the 18th-century historian Francis Blomefield, 2,335 English and 2,482 'alyan strangers' (i.e. Flemish weavers) died. The mayor issued proclamations that anyone who had a plague sore was not allowed into the city until they'd been clear of them for 20 days. If you lived in an infected house but didn't have the plague, you had to carry a 2ft-long white wand and you were banned from public places. The parish clerk or sexton had to pin a paper on the door of every infected house, with the words 'Lord have mercy upon us' written on it, and the paper had to stay on the door until the house had been free from the plague for a whole month. In August 1603 plague hit Norwich yet again and remained for almost a year; nearly 3,000 people died from it during that period.

And one of the worst floods ever occurred at the end of August in 1912.

1 August

In 1842 there was a terrible accident in Ber Street at the Greyhound Gardens, when acrobat and tightrope-walker Alleni 'descended in a chariot of fire' – the rope broke, and he fell 30ft.

1898 saw what the *Eastern Evening News* called 'an irreparable loss' when the subscription library was burned down in a fire that caused an estimated £100,000 of damage (most of it insured just a couple of streets away, at Norwich Union) and saw the largest number of firemen working together in the city on a blaze that took six hours to subdue. Outside Cambridge, the subscription library was the biggest of its time in East Anglia. The library began in the porch of St Andrew's Hall, grew to take over the Chapel of the Duke of Norfolk in St Andrew's Street, and then in 1784 a new building was opened on Guildhall Hill. But it was gutted completely on 1 August 1898, when fire broke out at the ropemaker Daniel Hurn's. Mr and Mrs Booth, who lived around the corner in London Street, were walking through the area at 4am when they smelled burning and saw tar running down the gutters. Realising that something was wrong, they raised the alarm. The city fire brigade were there on the spot within minutes, but by 4.30am the fire had spread to Self the gas-fitter's shop, and to the cloth department at Chamberlin's. Mr Hurn and his assistants were helped from the house – Daniel Hurn was so shocked that he had to be carried from the house.

The servants and assistants sleeping at Chamberlin's took their personal belongings to the Guildhall for safety. The Carrow and Anchor Brewery fire brigades were in place by 6.30am, but half an hour later the library caught fire. Mr Quinton, the secretary of the library, asked the firemen to put ladders up to the roof – but they didn't have any long enough, and the library ladders were too short. The flames took hold and in three-quarters of an hour the entire 60,000 volumes burned, including the irreplaceable Norton collection of foreign dictionaries, natural history books and scientific books. The roof caved in and the galleries collapsed. The ropemaker's shop collapsed wall by wall, and if the wind had been blowing in the opposite direction the whole of Dove Street and Lower Goat Lane would have burned down! Luckily the fire didn't quite reach Mr Bagley's furniture workshop in Pottergate, which was well-stocked with seasoned timber and would have gone up in seconds.

The cost of the damage at Chamberlin's alone was estimated at £80,000. And the secretary of the library, Mr Quinton, said that if ladders had been available the library could have been saved. Ironically, just before the fire broke out, the library catalogue had been finished and was about to go to the printer's. The library reopened on 2 August 1899, at a cost of £1,719. But thousands of rare books were reduced to ashes – and it was to happen again, less than a century later.

1940 saw an air raid over the city. The paint shop in Boulton & Paul's at Riverside was hit, killing nine; then the airmen sent machine gun fire towards Thorpe Station and Prince of Wales Road, killing more.

1970 saw a disastrous fire at Garland's department store (now the site of Habitat). It started with a chip pan fire in the restaurant and turned into a million-pound blaze; it took nearly 70 firemen three hours to stop the whole of London Street being gutted, and the thick black smoke was visible from five miles away. A human chain rescued 7–8,000 pairs of shoes from J. Buckingham & Sons (Norwich) Ltd on the corner of Swan Lane, and at one point Bedford Street seemed in danger.

1972 saw sunshine at Great Yarmouth but an incredible 5in of rain in just two hours in Norwich. Floods were up to 4ft deep. A footpath in Hughenden Road collapsed on to the railway line, sending tons of earth cascading down. The casualty department in the Norfolk and Norwich hospital flooded; the lifts were out of action, with 18in of water in the lift shaft, and £3,000 of medical supplies in a store room were ruined. The rain was heaviest at Costessey, which had 5.46in of rain. Bertram Books on Guardian Road suffered a six-inch flood, ruining thousands of books at an estimated damage of £1,000. There were 18in-deep floods on a 200 yard stretch of the main road at Toftwood, Dereham, when culverts failed, but it drained away by the afternoon.

1994 saw yet another bad fire in Norwich, when the central library caught fire at 7.30am – this was the worst library fire in Britain since World War Two, and it spread rapidly through the open-plan building. The thousand-degree heat wiped out two-thirds of the Colman collection and countless rare archive material; the entire lending library (125,000 lending and reference books) were lost, along with 25,000 local history books and 75 years of newspaper cuttings, and the smoke could be seen from six miles away. Fifteen fire engines and 150 firefighters were in attendance, and Anglian Water was asked to increase the pressure on the mains to give the firefighters more water. Salvage started at 10am, and most of the flames were out by noon. Malcolm Bradbury commented that he was sick to his stomach and 'cannot think of any other building... that I would feel more terrible about its burning down'. The books which were damaged by fire or water were frozen to stop more damage occurring. Local bookbinders worked on some of the volumes, including the 16 volumes remaining from the hundreds in the St Peter Mancroft Parish Church library. A temporary library was set up in Ber Street on 14 February 1995, and the replacement library was opened in the Forum in November 2001. The first of the 120,000 books back on the seven miles of shelving – as voted for by readers of the *Eastern Daily Press* – was Thomas Paine's *Rights of Man*.

2 August

In 1280 Norwich Cathedral records note that there were storms and floods for two days, which caused considerable damage across East Anglia.

There was a severe storm in Norwich in 1643, according to 18th-century historian Francis Blomefield, which killed more than '40 combs of fish in the city river'.

1873 saw the worst thunderstorm in Norfolk since 9 August 1843. There were a few drops of rain, but then at 11pm the storm hit. The wind was at hurricane force and the rain was torrential from midnight to 3am. The show in the sky was spectacular – the *Norfolk Chronicle* described 'fine blue sheet lightning and bright pink globular interspersed with forked lightning' – but, together with a hurricane-force wind, it left a trail of damage which wrecked crops and ripening fruit and left trees down across the county. In Norwich, roads were flooded – particularly in the areas of Heigham, King Street and Clarence Harbour Road. There were floods in city cellars; grocer Edward Wild lost £200–300 worth of sugar, candles, soap and cheese.

Wymondham had hailstones that were half an inch in circumference, and there was 3ft of water in some streets. Two mills were wrecked at Wreningham and Wymondham; at Garboldisham, two sails were torn off a windmill and hurled 200 yards away. Thetford flooded; Bridge Street was under 15in of water. In Diss, many houses had broken windows, thanks to hail the size of walnuts. At Great Yarmouth, homes were flooded to a depth of up to 3ft. Cromer lost part of the cliff. At Tivetshall, 22-year-old George Winterton was killed by lightning as he walked out of his bedroom.

At Wells, the church tower was hit by lightning. Flints flew hundreds of feet away as the tower burst into flames. The *Norfolk Chronicle* said that the parish fire engine was old and 'useless'; the fire brigade was fetched from Holkham but it was too late for the church. At 7.10am, the clock stopped and the bells (which were mostly molten from the intense heat) fell. Two hours later, the church was a ruin.

In 1942 another Baedeker raid on Norwich destroyed Hurrell's shoe factory in Magdalen Street, Page the house furnishers in St John Maddermarket and the Sexton shoe factory in St Mary's Plain.

1972 saw subsidence in Norwich as a direct result of the floods the previous day. A 6ft hole opened on Earlham Road, which spread across an area of 20 yards; the hole was 10ft deep.

3 August

In 1761 a fire at Fincham destroyed several houses.

In 1804 there was a major thunderstorm in the county.

There was also a major storm in 1879; at Garboldisham, two sails were torn from the windmill and the wind blew them 200 yards away.

1900 saw a severe gale across the county which did much damage to orchards and stripped tiles from roofs everywhere. There were severe dust storms on the north Norfolk coast early, but luckily it was a neap tide so there was not major flooding. The lamps at Cromer were 'twisted like wirework', according to the *Eastern Daily Press*, and boats were smashed at Hunstanton. The ketch *Hopewell* was grounded at Wells and filled with water, and the seas were too heavy for distress flares to be sent up; because of the rain and mist, the ketch wasn't found for another four and a half hours. The Wells lifeboat was launched at 8.30am, even though the wind was against her and the seas were tumultuous, and rescued the crew – just in time, because by 1pm the ketch was wrecked.

4 August

In 1738 there was a major fire at Fakenham which destroyed 26 houses.

In 1932 there was a major fire in Great Yarmouth, when the £10,000 Floral Hall on Britannia Pier was burnt out. The fire was discovered just after 4am, but had already taken such a hold that the pier employees couldn't put it out. They called the police, who brought three fire engines to the pier, and four lines of hose were fed from tanks down the pier to the hall. The firemen quickly realised that the hall couldn't be saved, so they contained the damage by putting a screen of water between the hall and the concert pavilion. The windows of the building next to the hall were cracked by the heat, and according to *The Times* the paint on the walls 'hung in festoons' – but at least the rest of the pier was saved. There was a trail of debris stretching half a mile into the sea, and the fire consumed two grand pianos, a complete set of band instruments and over 1,000 chairs; the mini golf course on the pier was also burned in places. The fire was out soon after 6am, but the cause remains a mystery.

5 August

In 1931 there was a major thunderstorm across the county, causing flooding. The *Eastern Daily Press* reported that rain was torrential over Thetford; Bridge Street 'became a stream' and was 18in deep in water at one point! Residents tried to sweep water out of their houses, and those without flood boards spent an hour mopping up. The paper notes that 'inconsiderate drivers of motor vehicles' rushed through at 'a smart pace' and swept yet more water into the houses. It was described as the worst flood since August 1879.

6 August

1897 saw a fire at Cullingford's paper mills in St Martin's Plain, Norwich. The mills had burned down the previous year, and the replacement two-storey building had a corrugated iron roof; 30 tons of waste paper was kept on the top floor, and the ground floor housed machinery and the boiler. When workers left at 6pm, all was well – but half an hour later the fire was spotted and the alarm was raised. Three fire engines were there within 10 minutes and an invalid was evacuated from a nearby house; although the roof fell in, the fire was out within an hour, and the crews spent two hours damping down.

In 1932 there was a blaze in St Peter's Street, Norwich, which started in the confectioner's store at the end of Wounded Hart Lane. The alarm was raised at 7pm, and the fire was under control in half an hour. On the same evening, in Aylsham, Mr Betts was not so lucky – a blaze in his shop caused £600 damage to books, magazines and sweets. His mother smelled smoke, and when Mr Betts went to investigate he saw the fire. He raised the alarm, and neighbours formed a human chain of buckets; the fire brigade were soon there and put the fire out, but the front of the shop was ruined. The cause of the fire turned out to be a melted gas pipe.

In 1941 the Cromer lifeboat crew rescued 88 people from a convoy of six steamers which were stranded on Haisboro sands. In September, Henry Blogg was awarded the RNLI gold medal for the third time for his bravery and was also awarded the British Empire Medal and the George Cross. The first steamer was almost submerged when Blogg drove his lifeboat again and again over the deck, until he'd rescued the 16 crew. He rescued 31 men from the second steamer, then drove over the submerged deck of the third and held the lifeboat against the bridge, while 19 crew jumped aboard. The fourth steamer was in more shallow waters; Blogg kept the lifeboat alongside until the crew jumped in. Despite the fact that the lifeboat had three holes in its side and most of its stern and 15ft of its fender was torn away, he kept going until he'd rescued all 88 people.

In 1947 there was a huge fire in Queen's Road, Norwich, at the animal feed manufacturers Steward & Case. The fire started between midnight and 1am; one neighbour said that flames 20ft high were coming from the roof, and the glow was seen all over the city. Tons of molasses were ablaze in the mill; however, the fire brigade managed to save the petrol store and fertiliser store, and the blaze was under control within an hour.

1956 saw subsidence in St Stephen's Road, Norwich. A passer-by noticed the road sinking slightly outside a tobacconist's shop; when he came out a minute or so later, the hole was 6ft wide! No traffic was allowed on the road unless they were going to the hospital. Later in the month the city engineers excavated the hole to a depth of 45ft and discovered that there was a major collapse in the main sewer after heavy rain.

1973 saw a blaze at the Red Lion hotel in Cromer. The fire in the downstairs bar was thought to have started in an electrical beer cooler. Staff led the 70 guests to safety and two fire engines had the blaze under control in 20 minutes.

1987 saw a fire at Church Street flats in Cromer; the fire brigade rescued 13 people and were awarded a Certificate of Commendation for their work.

7 August

1872 saw major floods at Walsingham, when heavy rain made the stream overflow its banks. By 6pm the water was across the meadows, and by 7pm the flood were 3ft deep in 22 houses. Forty women and children were rescued from their upper windows; they were brought down by ladders or carried out in the arms of rescuers, and all stayed the night with neighbours who hadn't been flooded. An hour later, the water was 5ft above its normal level, and the villagers got permission to knock holes in the abbey walls to drain off some of the water. By 9 August they were able to put a temporary dam across the street and the clean-up began. The *Norfolk Chronicle* reported that 'sturdy housewives' had to deal with 'a dark muddy deposit' on the walls and floors which had 'a fragrance by no means healthy or agreeable'.

1899 saw a fire at Leake & Sons' oil mill at King's Lynn, which contained 100 tons of linseed, 12 tons of oil and a quantity of oilcake; the damage was estimated at £10–12,000. The four-storey building, dating from 1888, was next to Purfleet (a tidal tributary). The 80 employees had left on 5 August, ready for the bank holiday weekend, intending to be back on Tuesday. No artificial light had been left on and the boiler furnaces had been raked out. On the evening of 7 August, people could smell something burning; just before midnight flames were spotted in the centre of the upper building – and the fire was spreading. The fire brigade came out, but the engine wouldn't work as the water gauge had burst; there were no gauges in stock so they had to find one in town before they could fix it. In the meantime, the new steamer engine was sent into action; however, it pumped 400 gallons per minute and the water supply was not strong enough to cope, so the crews had to keep stopping and filling the engine. The mill was in flames, the roofs and floors fell, and oil tanks burst. Sparks and burning linseeds went on to roofs and shipping; lit debris fell on the deck of Leake's lighter ship, destroying it. Two hours later, the fire was under control, but the fire crews had to deal with the huge heap of burning material in the middle of the ruins for the rest of the day. The local paper noted that Mr Marriott's mill, which had been on the site previously, had burned down in August 1860.

1937 saw a major fire in Hunstanton, when the 600-seater St Edmund's café burned down. It was thought that the fire started in the kitchen. A concert was about to start in the Lounge Concert Hall next door when the alarm was given. The fire crews worried that a 4in gas main in the middle of the building might explode, but they couldn't turn the gas off. They used sea water and hydrants and managed to save the concert hall, but the café, together with its furniture, the day's takings and staff belongings, burned down. The heat was intense, and one fireman was injured by scorching to his head.

1951 saw a huge storm in the night; nearly 2in of rain fell, and Cromer was particularly badly hit by floods. The fire brigade spent almost 12 hours from 10.45pm pumping out water.

1971 saw a deluge over the weekend. The roads were flooded again at Yarmouth – just a week after the last flood. Cromer streets were flooded to a depth of several inches, and a shop in Mundesley had a 4ft flood. Swannington had an inch of rain in an hour; Bergh Apton had the same amount of rain in the same time, but with the addition of 2in of hail.

1973 saw yet more subsidence in Earlham Road, Norwich, when a water main burst in the centre of a roundabout at the junction with the ring road at 7am. The water spouted 6ft in the air from the 24in main near a defective sewer. Although the damage was repaired quickly, it caused the road to sink; a hole 25ft deep appeared just two hours later. It was filled in, and police kept an eye on the area overnight in case more subsidence occurred.

The disused Briggate Mill, near North Walsham, caught fire in 1975; firemen managed to contain the blaze, but the three-storey building was badly damaged.

8 August

In 1808 there was a major storm over Norwich. The *Norfolk Chronicle* of 13 August described it rather laconically as a 'slight thunderstorm Monday last' – then added that it was a cloudburst which inundated the streets. Clearly the rain was heavy and fast, because the noise of the water falling on the leads of the cathedral actually drowned out the noise of the thunder! The cellars and kitchens in St Stephen's Street, London Street and White Lion Lane were deluged, and reportedly over 150 pails of water were taken from Dr Beckwith's house in Dean's Square. As a result, a Special Committee was set up to investigate the sewers and stop it happening again.

1935 saw the worst thunderstorm in living memory and the worst downpour since 1912 in Cromer. One and a half inches of rain fell in 40 minutes; the main streets resembled rivers and held up traffic. The flood waters met on the corner of two streets on the west cliff; water poured over the edge and tore a hole in the slope 30ft in diameter and 12ft deep, sending 50 tons of cliff crashing to the promenade below. Firemen pumped 40,000 gallons of water from the basement of Stead & Simpson in an hour and a half, and staff in Woolworth's gave customers boxes to stand on because the shop floor was 4in deep in water.

1959 saw a fire at the church in Morley St Botolph, which gutted the nave and bell tower. Flames rose 30ft in the air and firemen at Hingham, four miles away, could see them. The fire was first seen at 9pm and was out by 3.30am, but the bells were still shedding red-hot sparks.

1965 saw a fire at the store where all the gifts and prizes were held at Great Yarmouth Pleasure Beach; although workers formed a human chain to rescue the prizes, thousands of pounds' worth of prizes and gifts were burned. Smoke was first seen at the greyhound racing stall, but the flames were too much for the extinguishers. Holidaymakers were asked to leave for safety's sake, and the fire brigade put out the blaze.

9 August

1787 saw a severe storm in Norwich. Lightning blazed across the city from 9–11.30pm and two women were struck by thunderbolts but recovered; thunder shook the whole city at 1am, and citizens were relieved when the storm finally abated four hours later.

In 1843 there was a major storm – *The Times* reported that it affected the whole country. The day had been a sultry one, and then at 7.30 in the evening the storm burst over Norwich. There was a tremendous hailstorm, with the hailstones reportedly 1¼in in diameter – as a result, ice lay four to five inches deep across the city. The first floors and cellars of houses in Surrey Street, St Stephen's Street, Rampant Horse Street, the Market Place and London Street were flooded and the audience in the Theatre Royal couldn't get out because of the water. In Red Lion Street, the flood caused an abyss to open up in the cellar of the Coach and Horses pub – beer barrels disappeared into it, and the crack was large enough to endanger the neighbouring properties. When the Lamb Inn flooded, there was no loss of human life, but the landlord's little dog drowned; the Market Place turned into a lake and the hampers belonging to the traders just floated on it; and four cartloads of ice were taken from Messrs Barber's grocer's shop in Old Haymarket. Most of the windows on Ber Street and King Street as far as Foundry Bridge were smashed. The windows in the workhouse were broken, and the

3ft flood in the yard surged into the house. The Corn Exchange lost around 700 panes of glass; the cathedral was flooded and men spent the whole of Thursday baling it out. On Bracondale, Mr Bell's horticultural establishment was wrecked – 20–30,000ft of glass was smashed and all the plants ruined, at an estimated cost of £3,000. Mr Gurney lost several thousand panes of glass in his conservatory at Keswick and many valuable plants were damaged there, too.

The storm didn't let up – at 2 o'clock in the morning the *Norfolk Chronicle* reported that 'a surface of flame spread across the heavens, followed by a clap of thunder which seemed to rend the welkin'.

The county was just as badly affected; most windows facing the storm in Thetford were broken, cellars were filled with water, and warehouses and shops were flooded to a depth of 2ft – and it took nine men three hours to get the water out of the Bell Inn. Horses on the coach from Lynn were up to their chests in water in Thetford. At Yarmouth, there was lightning from 7.30pm on the Wednesday until 3am on the Thursday, with hail at midnight. Crops were destroyed at Bunwell, Wreningham, Carleton Rode, Fundenhall and Hethel. Little Cressingham was so badly flooded that cattle were forced to swim in the fields, and villagers had to be rescued from their bedroom windows. And even the birds didn't escape: after the storm, the *Norfolk Chronicle* reported that one man picked up the bodies of 100 sparrows in his garden.

There was another bad storm the following day and a further storm five days later. The newspapers reported that total losses from the storms came to £30,770 (the equivalent of nearly £2.4 million in today's money).

1931 saw similar bad weather; there was a major thunderstorm at Great Yarmouth at 5pm which lasted for 20 minutes and flooded roads, shops and houses. On Northgate Street, according to the *Eastern Daily Press*, the water was over the top of knee boots. King's Lynn was also flooded, and residents had to bale water out of their houses; the pinnacle on the south tower of St Margaret's Church was struck by lightning, but luckily there was no serious damage. At around 2.15am there was a whirlwind at Mattishall, which broke telephone posts, blew a stack across the road, and wrecked poultry houses – one poor man saw three or four henhouses coming straight towards him! Houses also lost lots of tiles. A similar whirlwind hit Cromer half an hour later, and a ridge of tiles from the West Cliff Hotel was blown 100 yards up the street.

1965 saw holidaymakers helping to save Ranworth's thatched church. The alarm was raised at 11.30am when one man saw a small circle of fire on the roof while cine-filming from the church tower. Another climbed up a drainpipe with a fire extinguisher strapped to his belt, in an attempt to limit the damage. The fire destroyed a large part of the chancel roof, but there was little other damage; the firemen managed to save the church's treasures, including the Sarum Antiphoner (a psalter dating back to 1400), the 15th-century painted screen between the chancel and the nave, a 16th-century chalice and a 13th-century paten.

1972 saw a huge heath fire at Salhouse, when 11 acres burned; five brigades fought the flames for half an hour before getting it under control.

10 August

1125 saw a major flood along the east coast; the *Anglo-Saxon Chronicles* refer to the floods occurring on the feast of St Lawrence, and many people drowned.

The weather in 1935 was the complete opposite – tinder-dry – and 10 August saw a major plantation fire at Weybourne. It started on Saturday morning, and the blaze stretched for a mile and a half; firemen had to fight the flames for 16 hours, but by the time the blaze was subdued 150 acres of gorse and bracken were destroyed. Due to the dry weather, fields also caught light at Wymondham, Thetford, Reepham and Great Witchingham, and stacks caught light at Dereham and Bressingham.

1967 saw storms across the county which lasted for three hours. A malting flooded at Beccles; and lightning struck the 200-year-old Dial House at Thetford, damaging the roof and part of the house next door. Firemen had to pull slates off the roof so they could dampen the reeds underneath them.

11 August

There was a major storm in Norwich in 1768, resulting in a boy being killed by lightning near the Brazen Doors.

1873 saw a huge fire at Boulton & Paul's in Rose Lane, Norwich, which spread to Turner's Yard, causing damage of £10,000 (the equivalent of nearly £650,000 in today's money). The horticultural department covered half an acre and included a lot of inflammable material. A woman in a nearby cottage saw the flames between 5 and 6am and raised the alarm; by the time the fire brigade got there, the blaze had already taken hold. Men from Boulton & Paul's helped the fire brigade train nine jets on the flames, but even so the roof fell in somewhere between 6 and 7am and a body of flames shot up into the sky. Charred embers were found as far away as Chapelfield. The fire was under control within two hours, and the fire crews contained the blaze – but the windows in nearby cottages had burned and the horticultural buildings were destroyed along with their contents, including 300 lawnmowers. Between 70 and 100 workmen lost their tools, which were uninsured, and were temporarily laid off. It was thought that the fire was caused by the stick of a rocket from the fireworks at the Hop Pole gardens going through glass in the roof of the horticultural buildings.

12 August

In 1582 there were major thunderstorms and hail in Norfolk – and what may well have been a tornado. The chronicler Holinshed talks of 'rain with hailstones like to the rowels of spurs, two to three inches about'. Between North Walsham and Worsted, corn was beaten flat to the ground and trees were torn up. At 'Hening' (presumably Horning), the door of the church weighing over 300lb was lifted up and thrown over the font, and the top of the church was 'riven up'. At 'East Russen' (Ruston), barns were blown down.

1884 saw a storm which was described as 'tropical in violence' at Great Yarmouth. The rain came down so hard that it looked like a thick mist, and hail was as large as marbles. There were floods in the streets and the water seeped into houses, too. At Ludham, lightning set fire to two cottages – they were lost, along with their entire contents. Luckily, nobody was hurt.

1897 saw a fire at Denmark Street in Diss, which caused £6,000 of damage – not all of which was insured. The rear of Mr Dykes's furniture shop had a three-storey store; part of the buildings were used by Mr Bartrum as a carpenter's shop. Flames of 'a considerable height' suddenly appeared, and the fire spread to the roof of Mr Gaze's pig saleyard next door and the roof of Mr Pearse's cottage. Two elderly and infirm people were evacuated to the hospital. The Eye fire brigade arrived but the flames were in hand – though the store had been gutted, as had Mr Pearse's cottage and the pig pens, and there was some damage to cottages in the Beehive. Mr Pearse also lost all his tools. The fire was out by midnight, but the cause remained unknown.

14 August

1873 saw a major fire at the engineering works of Holmes & Sons in Cattle Market Street, Norwich, which started at 11pm in the smithies and spread rapidly. Three troops of the Dragoon Guards and Norwich Rifle Volunteers were needed to help the fire brigade control the blaze, and the damage ran to £10,000 (equivalent to over £600,000 in today's money). People who were just coming out of the pubs helped to take machines out of the showrooms. The fire was out two hours later.

1928 saw an alarming fire at Norwich when the top floor of Hovell's basketmakers caught light, threatening the Bridewell, the Wild Man pub and neighbouring shops. The alarm was raised at 10pm and the fire brigade were soon there and managed to contain it.

1960 saw the worst storm at 'dry' Docking in living memory. Homes were evacuated when flood water reached a foot deep in houses.

1984 saw a huge fire at Norfolk Textured Yarns in Cromer, where the asbestos roof exploded in the heat; over 20 firemen fought the blaze, which partly destroyed the factory.

15 August

In 1832 cholera hit the county. In August a cholera epidemic started at King's Lynn; at least 120 people were infected and 35 died over the course of 17 weeks. The epidemic also started in Norwich on this date in 1832; the official return on 18 October said that the total number of cases in Norwich was 320, with 128 deaths.

The disease had spread outside the city earlier in the summer – and it also exposed the extreme poverty in which people lived. In June the *Norfolk Chronicle* reported that cholera had been at Cawston since Friday 25 May, starting with Mr Kemp who had to be carried home from work. The paper reported that his house 'presented a scene of wretchedness and filth as has seldom been witnessed'; there were no beds or furniture 'nor every necessity to make use of'. He died 20 hours later; then his small son became sick and died. A total of seven deaths were reported in Cawston, and 10 more were expected during the next few days.

1843 saw an enormous fire raging in Norwich at the Cavalry Barracks. It started in the forage barn around 7pm and spread to the left wing; when the wind rose, it was thought that the whole barracks might be lost. The fire engine at the Barracks was out of order, so the men worked with buckets to try to douse the fire. The soldiers got out as much as they could – bravely trying to rescue things even when the roof threatened to fall in. Crowds watched from St James' Hill and reported that the heat was unbearable as far as 60 yards away from the Barracks. Norwich Union sent their fire engines to help, but, due to lack of water, it was a while before they could get to work – so the human chain with buckets continued to work as hard as they could. Even so, the *Norfolk Chronicle* reported that the area 'resembled a vast furnace covered with brilliant flame', because the rafters were burning on the ground after the roof fell in.

Finally the fire was put out – and the newspaper thought it was caused by children playing with matches.

1978 saw two fire crews fighting a blaze for 12 hours at a Dutch barn in Forncett St Peter. The fire started in the early afternoon when workers were unloading straw; the barn, which contained 160 tons of hay and 120 tons of straw, was gutted. The fire crews were able to contain the fire so it didn't spread to a silage heap or cattle sheds, but there was £25,000 of damage.

16 August

1971 saw two whirlwinds at South Lopham which just missed a house. The first one went through the garden at 1.40pm, then swept up straw in the field next door. The second one, half an hour later, also squeezed past the side of the house and did no damage.

1975 saw a huge fire at Syderstone which flared up over a half-mile front and destroyed 500 acres. It spread quickly through shoulder-high bracken and gorse, and the fire could be seen 10 miles away. Eleven fire engines, with help from three more from the US base at Sculthorpe, managed to subdue the blaze.

17 August

1776 saw a fire at Hethersett when bricklayers put slaked lime into a hole then put straw on top; it caught fire and burned a barn down. There was also a bad storm reported at Thetford.

1878 saw a four-acre fire at Bagshaw's paper mills in Coslany Street, Norwich; it was seen between 1 and 2am and the alarm was raised. The fire was under control within two hours but took a lot longer to put out and caused several thousand pounds' worth of damage to the engine room and paper loft; the heat was so intense that part of the zinc roof of the engine house melted. Mr Bagshaw went into the stables and turned off the gas mains, even though the building was in flames; the four horses were rescued. Cottages nearby had melted glass and blistered doors, and many properties in the densely populated area were damaged by water. Thirty men and between 40 and 50 women were temporarily laid off. And the cause of the blaze? The *Norfolk Chronicle* said that 'the origin of the fire is involved in mystery'.

There was a huge storm in 1924 which involved a cyclone, near Aylsham. The *Eastern Daily Press* reported that a 'wind of great velocity' came from Haveringland, Mr Howes of Silvergate, Blickling, had a narrow escape – he was milking cows in his barn when the cyclone hit and stripped the tiles from the roof. Luckily he was unhurt, but apple trees were uprooted, branches severed from oaks, sheds carried away and tiles stripped from neighbouring houses.

18 August

There was a massive storm on the evening of 18 August 1858, with torrential rain and hail and much lightning. A bolt of lightning hit the barn belonging to Mr Drane at Newfoundland Farm in Cringleford; he managed to save most of his pigs and carthorses, but he lost the barn and 340 coombs of wheat (a coomb is a measure equivalent to four bushels or a little under 8,900cu in). He sent his farm lad over to his son's in Little Melton in a pony and trap to tell him about the disaster – but they'd travelled less than a mile when lightning hit the pony and killed him. The poor lad was terrified but managed to get back to the farm and tell his master what had happened. Meanwhile, the fire engines had been called; they managed to save the farmhouse and the neighbours' property, and the *Norfolk Chronicle* reported that 'Mr Drane was very obliged to Mr English and the fire brigade'. The storm was county-wide; lightning also destroyed a house and cottage at Kenninghall and killed a horse at Thornage.

Following the cyclone of the previous day in 1924, there was a cyclone at Swaffham, which threw a tree across the road at Tank Lane, damaged houses in London Street and stripped the vicarage roof. The storm also raged at Calthorpe, where the Dunning family had a very narrow escape. At around 1.25pm, Mrs Dunning had gone into the scullery to return a washtub, Mr Dunning was about to go back to work as a farm labourer after his dinner, and five of their nine children were in the living room near the dining table. 17-year-old Wilfred was by the window and saw a great flash of light in the room, like a ball of fire – the noise made him temporarily deaf. Mr Dunning was thrown to the floor by the door with two-year-old Jack. Lightning smashed the chair from under the eldest son, Charles, and the brick paving under his chair was smashed to 1½in in depth before the lightning burst through the front wall of the cottage, leaving a hole 2ft square. The four-year-old girl, who was playing with a doll in a pram, was incredibly lucky – when the Dunnings surveyed the ruins of their cottage, they discovered that the pram had a bent wheel and a crack in one side of its wooden body, but their daughter was unhurt. The four-room cottage was completely wrecked.

In 1933 Norwich fire brigade was kept incredibly busy. It started when the biggest fire for years broke out on Mousehold Heath in the afternoon; as soon as the firemen managed to contain it, they were called to a grass fire behind houses on Intwood Road in Cringleford, then to a fire in woodland at Cannell's farm in Costessey, then to a fire in a coal shed in Cambridge Street and finally to a fire in a field near Boundary Road.

1944 saw a huge fire in Diss, when the workshops of G.N. Rackham & Sons (builder and funeral furnishers) caught light, resulting in several thousand pounds' worth of damage. Local residents brought water in pails and baths from nearby wells and pumps until the fire brigade could get there. It was three hours before the blaze was under control and six workshops and stores were gutted; however, they managed to save a donkey, a hearse, a cycle and office equipment.

1960 saw a downpour over Norfolk. Shops in Cromer were flooded; an inch of rain fell in Norwich in one and a half hours, and drivers found that their car windscreen wipers couldn't cope with the deluge. There was a landslip between Trowse and Swainsthorpe which blocked the rail line, and Swaffham flooded with the deluge forcing up manhole covers.

19 August

1796 saw a riot at Great Yarmouth – or not, depending on whose version you believe! The story goes that Mr Thelwall, a political lecturer, was declaiming in a room at Yarmouth, a party of armed sailors from the ships in the Roads broke in, and, in their attempt to seize the orator, knocked down every person who opposed them. Upwards of 40 persons were wounded in the scuffle; the orator escaped unhurt. However, a letter published in *The Times* said that the sailors wanted to hear Thelwall's 'patriotic Lectures' at Mr Hurry's malt-house, peaceably offered money for admission, and were refused entry. When they insisted, the keeper tried to hit one of the sailors, and there was a scuffle. Thelwall blew out the lights near him and 'effected his escape between two female democrats'. The sailors had a fight with the 300 citizens and won, then smashed Thelwall's pulpit, sang *God save the King* three times and were joined in this by citizens, then 'returned in the most orderly manner to their ships'. The following week, *The Times* said that a sailor had sung *God save the King* at the lecture, was thrown out, vowed revenge and came back two days later with a dozen and a half of his friends to start a fight, but only about a dozen people were involved in the fray and the disturbance was over before the constable managed to get there.

In 1815 there was a major fire in Norwich at Hubbard's cabinet makers, near St Lawrence's Church on St Benedict's Street. Mr Hubbard left at three in the afternoon, thinking everything on his premises was secure – but then fire broke out in a workroom on the upper floor. The roof, being thatched, was a sheet of flame by 5.30pm – and the fire spread to those of his neighbours: Mr Blake the pawnbroker, Mr Stannard the pork butcher, and Mr Taylor. The heat was so intense that houses on the opposite site of the road caught light, and the wood yards of merchants Mr Coleman and Mr Walker were threatened.

But then the wind dropped and the city's engines arrived – along with the West Norfolk Militia, commanded by Lieutenant-Colonel Nelthorpe. Thanks to their help, the fire was out by 7 o'clock in the evening. The *Norfolk Chronicle* was keen to praise 'the officers and privates who protected furniture taken to Mr Hitchin's yard and St Laurence's Church and kept communications with the engines as a big crowd gathered'. Six houses were destroyed; one private narrowly escaped being buried in the ruins but his 'eyes were much burnt', and another of his colleagues was injured during the fire. As well as the houses, Mr Hubbard lost four chests of tools and cabinet work, and Mr Lamb lost his furniture and bedding. A guard was placed overnight in case the fire started again, but, although he saw smoke and went to check, it didn't. Sadly, as the newspaper noted, while the guard was checking the ruins someone stole the leather pipe from the fire engine.

1977 saw flooding across the county after rain. It was described in the *Eastern Daily Press* as the highest rainfall for five years, when 1.17in fell in 24 hours. Parts of Hellesdon and Thorpe were a foot deep in water.

20 August

1773 saw a storm across the county which lasted for three hours at Norwich. There were fires in Great Yarmouth, where the counting house of Mr Chasterton was struck by a ball of fire, Mr

Dixon's horse was killed by lightning, and John Crisp was killed by lightning in the hold of a ship. William Adair's barn at Pulham was struck by lightning and gutted by fire; and at Dereham a carrier's horses were terrified by the thunder, stampeded, and trampled the driver.

22 August

In 1924 St Faith's abbey at Horsham was gutted. There was a thunderstorm at around 8.30pm and lightning struck the building, causing a huge blaze. The owner, 70-year-old Mr Warner Cook, and his friends Arthur Gowing and Mr Harvey had a lucky escape; they said they heard a noise 'like a salvo of big guns' and the wall in the breakfast room exploded. Mrs Cook was sitting by an upstairs window with her grandson when a huge flame entered the room and exploded; it blinded her temporarily, but she managed to grab her grandson and take him downstairs. The alarm was raised, but the firefighters had trouble dealing with the old building and it was gutted. The flames could be seen as far away as Norwich. The parishioners all came to help Mr Cook and they managed to take all the furniture from the building's ground floor; but many of the things that had come down from Mr Cook's family were lost.

1976 saw 10 fire brigades fighting a blaze on East Ruston common. They were called out at 7.30am and the fire was out six and a half hours later – but by then it had destroyed one square mile of the heath, and the fire brigades had to stay for a few hours longer to damp down.

23 August

1976 saw half a square mile of forest burned at Thetford when a USAF Phantom Jet crashed shortly after taking off on a training flight from RAF Lakenheath. The pilot and navigator parachuted to safety; 80 firemen from Norfolk and Suffolk and 100 US servicemen fought the blaze and had to spend the night there damping down the fire.

1977 saw a fire in a leather goods shop in Pottergate, Norwich, which ended up with six people evacuated from neighbouring properties. The alarm was raised at 3am when neighbours heard the roar of flames. Two months before, the shop had suffered severe damage when a runaway car crashed into it; the owners were planning to rebuild but were waiting for an insurance wrangle to be sorted out. However, after the fire the building had to be demolished – the entire inside and the roof were consumed by the flames. Part of the street was cordoned off to traffic for two days until the area was made safe.

24 August

In 1297 a huge row erupted between the men of Yarmouth and the men of the Cinque Ports, even though both had gone to the Swyn estuary with Edward I to reinforce the fleet of the Flemish allies against France. The Cinque Port ships attacked the Yarmouth ships in the English fleet: at least 17 and perhaps as many as 37 ships were lost, along with 200 men.

1961 saw a huge fire at the Jarrold printing works in Norwich. One onlooker described the blaze as like a torch – first smoke was seen, and then the highly-flammable material went up. Although the blaze was extinguished by the three attending engines, many valuable negatives were lost.

25 August

1794 saw a violent thunderstorm at King's Lynn; sadly, an eight-year-old girl was killed by lightning.

1988 saw a terrible disaster among the seal population in the North Sea – over 40 seal bodies were washed ashore, killed by a virus. It was finally identified as phocine distemper virus (PDV), spread by the migration of harp seals from the Arctic Ocean. The virus went on to wipe out half the seals in the county.

26 August

In 1780 there was a chimney fire at St Stephen's Street, Norwich; the thatch caught light and spread to the neighbouring properties, destroying four other houses and severely damaging the silversmith Bolingbroke & Yallop's.

1784 saw strong winds and heavy seas at Great Yarmouth; in Norwich, the steeple of St John Timberhill was blown down.

1898 saw a fire at Pinchen & Co, brewers and mineral water manufacturers at South Creake, causing £3,000 of damage – the brewery and all the stock was lost. Shortly before 1am it was discovered in the brewing area known as 'the tower'; Mr Pinchen and his son tried to check the flames with buckets of water, but the blaze was too strong. Mr Pinchen rode six miles to Fakenham to raise the alarm. By the time the fire brigade got there, the flames were huge, and it was feared that the Chequers pub next door might catch fire. The nearest water supply was 600 yards away, and the fire brigade had to use 2,000ft of hose to fight the blaze – but within an hour it was under control. The cause of the fire remained unknown.

There were major floods across the county in 1912 after a 30-hour deluge, although it was particularly bad in Norwich. Water rose 17ft above the water line, the river Yare broke its banks and the Wensum was a torrent. Four people died, 15,000 suffered damage to their homes and 2,000 were left homeless (and housed temporarily in seven schools). Fifty-two bridges and culverts were broken, the harvest was destroyed and roads and rail were blocked across the county. Norwich was cut off for two days, and the damage was estimated at around £100,000 (equivalent to around £6 million of today's money).

Read's mills in Heigham were flooded to a depth of 4½ft, Bullard's malthouse collapsed and the whole front of the *Norwich Mercury* offices was torn away and its boiler carried away by the river. There was a landslide at Carrow Abbey, and the starch cellar floor at Colman's was 3ft under water; to salvage as much as they could, holes were bored into the basement floors and the starch was handed up to a chain of workers by lamplight. Even so, 650 tons of starch were ruined; because the indigo in the 'blue bags' was involved, workers took their clothes off to stop them being ruined by the dye, and the local paper reported that 'naked men were a common sight on Tuesday'!

The rain started at 3am on the Monday morning and just kept going; the local paper reported that twice the amount of the water in Lake Windermere fell on the county during the rainstorm. Between 9am and 1pm 2½in of rain fell – nearly as much as the previous record of 2¼in in 24 hours! And it didn't let up – nearly two more inches of rain fell in the next hour.

Flood marker at New Mills Yard, Norwich. The road level has changed, although the marker has stayed in the same place. Half the marker is actually buried and the level of the 1912 floods would go two bricks above Christopher's head on the right. The other floods marked here (in descending order of depth) are those of 2 February 1570, 27 October 1614, 15 November 1646 and 27 October 1762. (See entries for those days for more details.) (Photograph by author)

At 3pm the rain was described as a 'blizzard' – it was raining so hard that it looked like clouds of smoke in the street. The Heigham and Coslany areas were the worst hit – by 6am the streets there were already filled with water, and overall 7.64in of rain fell on Norwich.

Many heroic rescues were performed. Volunteers from Norwich YMCA manned rowing boats to rescue people in Heigham, sailing through badly flooded streets where people were calling for help from their bedroom windows – distress calls from women and children moved the rescuers to tears. One of the boats capsized and dumped the rescued people in 10ft of water. Another volunteer had a narrow escape when the ladder gave way – luckily it crashed into the downstairs window frame, saving him and the blind 84-year-old woman he'd rescued from a ducking.

PC Horner and William Marrison (a labourer from Fox and Goose Yard) rescued over 100 people between them before their rowing boat sank. George Brodie, a fish porter from Sawmill Yard in Oak Street, spent four hours rescuing people despite suffering from asthma; his wife begged him to stop for a rest, but his reply (so typical of a Norfolk hero) was 'There are some more dear children to get out, and I shall not be long before I get home.' But at 11.30pm he lost his footing in the raging torrent and was swept away by the water. Five-month-old Edward Poll drowned when his family's rowing boat sank and his mother Florence fell unconscious and just couldn't hold on to him; Mrs Kemp of Goat Yard, Oak Street, was said to have died of 'fright and shock'. During the inquest, the foreman of the jury said that, in view of the flood, it was 'an extraordinary thing' that they didn't have inquests into more deaths.

An emergency council meeting was held on the Wednesday and a national flood relief was launched. A total of £24,000 was raised, including £150 from the King and Queen, £50 from the Prince of Wales and even the money collected for their annual summer treat by the Railway Mission Sunday School in Melton Constable – they felt the flood victims needed it more.

1959 saw a fire gutting the old mill at Burnham Overy. Four fire brigades were called out, but a whole range of the buildings, stretching more than 50 yards along the coast road, were ablaze. The roof collapsed, and despite the danger that the seaward-facing wall would collapse, firemen scaled it to douse the flames

1971 saw a six-acre barley field on fire at Silfield in Wymondham. While waiting for the fire brigade, two workers tried to put out the blaze by stamping on it, and saved some of the barley straw. Two engines managed to put out the blaze within half an hour and the combine harvester was also saved.

1990 saw three firemen having a narrow escape at a field fire in Scarning. Farmer Paul Howell had been combining wheat when the machine caught fire; he leapt off and ran half a mile for help as the fire spread to the stubble. Thirty-five firemen in engines arrived from four

Norwich, Fye Street Bridge, floods 1912. (Picture courtesy of Norfolk County Council Library and Information Service)

fire brigades in minutes, but the nearest hydrant was a mile away and the high winds meant that the fire kept changing direction. At one point, 10ft-high flames swept towards three firemen – but the wind changed direction again at the last moment. The fire was brought under control, but not until it had burned a swathe 800 yards through the field.

27 August

In 1549 Kett's Rebellion was suppressed. The city records state that the Earl of Warwick 'upon Mousehold Heath vanquished Robert Kett…from their most wicked rebellion, and did suppress them, and delivered this city from the great danger, trouble and peril.'

However, Kett's men were actually fighting for justice against the practice of enclosure (where rich men put fences round common land – which admittedly was their property but the lord of the manor was supposed to leave enough land unenclosed to meet the needs of his freehold tenants, as common grazing often meant the difference between starvation and survival for the poor). Unemployment had rocketed when arable land was switched to sheep production (meaning one shepherd was needed instead of 10 labourers to work the land), taxation increased to pay for the war against Scotland and France, and prices and rents soared. Droughts and a population boom added to the problem; food was scarce and riots began.

There had been other risings in Norfolk, but without a leader the uprisings failed. In the summer of 1549 people tore down the enclosure fences across the country, and in July rebels started tearing down fences around Wymondham. John Flowerdew, a lawyer from Stanfield Hall, paid people to rip down the fences of Robert Kett, a Wymondham landowner with whom he had a long-standing rivalry (involving Flowerdew's sharp practices during the Reformation) – but it backfired when Kett said 'Whatever lands I have enclosed shall be made common unto ye and all men, and my own hand shall first perform it.' Kett joined the rebels in tearing down his own enclosure fences (and then no doubt took great pleasure in ripping down Flowerdew's fences!); he gathered his followers under the oak tree on 9 July and led them to Norwich, where the army camped out at Mousehold. Although Kett allowed his followers to commandeer food for the troops, he forbade looting or abuses, stating that 'no violence or injury be done to any honest or pooreman'.

Kett and his followers sent the king a list of 29 requests – as well as stopping enclosure and rack renting, they wanted weights and measures standardised throughout the country, they wanted ineffective priests sacked and rich priests made to teach the poor children. In their own words, they wanted 'all bond men made free, for God made all free with his precious blood shedding'.

The royal herald offered a pardon provided the rebels dispersed, but didn't reply to the list of requests. Kett refused: 'Kings and princes are wont to pardon wicked persons, not innocent and just men. We… are guilty ourselves of no crime.' The royal herald retreated; Kett offered a truce, but Norwich refused, so Kett attacked Bishop's Bridge and Norwich fell to the rebels. A second royal pardon was offered and refused.

Kett's rebels held strong against the Earl of Northampton's 1,400-strong army, and there was a three-hour battle in Bishopgate, when 300 rebels died. The following day there was

The oak between Wymondham and Hethersett where Kett allegedly gathered his men on 9 July 1549 before they marched to Norwich. In 2002 the Tree Council listed it as one of the 50 greatest trees in Britain. (Photograph by author)

another battle, and the earl's deputy Lord Sheffield was killed. The rebels were finally beaten by the Earl of Warwick's 12,000 troops and a team of German mercenary knights. Three hundred rebels were executed, and Robert Kett and his brother William were taken to the Tower of London. The Ketts were found guilty of treason and were brought back to Norfolk to be hanged – William from the steeple at Wymondham Abbey, and Robert on 7 December from the walls of Norwich Castle. Robert's body was left in chains on the walls until the following summer, then buried in an unmarked grave.

However, in 1949 Norwich citizens recognised that Robert was fighting for social and economic justice and placed a tablet on the castle 'in reparation and honour to a notable and courageous leader in the long struggle of the common people of England to escape from a servile life into the freedom of just conditions.'

29 August

1973 saw a huge fire at Marham involving 600 tons of baled straw. A lorry burst in flames while it was carrying bales to the store, and the blaze threatened buildings nearby – though the driver was unhurt. Firemen from three brigades were joined by firemen from RAF Marham to fight the blaze; they used water from a private swimming pool at a rate of 3,000 gallons per minute to tackle the blaze, which was 13 bales high. Once the surrounding buildings were safe, the fire crews decided to let the straw burn itself out.

1976 finally saw an end to the dry spell. Over the previous two weeks, the fire brigade was called out 560 times to deal with fires caused by the drought. Finally the weather broke – over the Bank Holiday weekend – and the area had nearly the whole of the average August rainfall in just two days! Nearly 3in of rain fell at Great Yarmouth, and Wisbech had 4¾in – which was more rain than they'd had in the previous eight months.

1996 saw the county in the grip of gales and torrential rain. A thousand holidaymakers were evacuated from Wells for a second night in a row, and the Pleasure Beach at Great Yarmouth closed on the grounds of safety. Cley's shingle bank was breached, trees came down, roads were flooded and villagers were evacuated from Snettisham. There was a daring rescue by the Gorlestone lifeboat in 50 knot winds; the German yacht *Olline* was taking in water and one crewman had broken his collar bone. An RAF helicopter was able to fly a doctor to the spot but couldn't winch him down on a line because the wind made it too dangerous. The yacht was rocking violently, so Steve Bertram from the lifeboat crew made a 6ft leap above the 30ft waves to tend the injured man before the *Olline* was towed in. Mr Bertram said afterwards, with typical Norfolk modesty, 'I've done jumps before. It's all in the course of duty.'

31 August

Hurricanes don't just hit Norfolk in the winter months – in 1816 there was a hurricane that lasted for five hours, from 7 o'clock in the evening until midnight, which the *Norfolk Chronicle* described as 'such a tremendous Hurricane as was never remembered'. The brig *Messenger* was grounded and its sails torn to pieces, but the crew were saved. The brig *Ranger* was wrecked and only one saved out of its crew of 11, because the night was so dark that the lifeboat couldn't help. At Trimingham, an oyster smack was wrecked but its crew of three were saved. At Walcot, a Dutch smack – part of a fleet of 300 colliers – was wrecked in 15 minutes and the whole crew was lost. Several other colliers were wrecked between Blakeney and Mundesley.

A similar storm hit in 1833. Fifteen ships were forced ashore between Cromer and Blakeney, and three barks were lost with all hands. The *Norfolk Chronicle* reported that the oldest seaman in Kings Lynn said it was the worst gale he could remember. One ship there was lost with all hands, leaving wives and 22 children; although a fishing boat went out 12 miles in a raging sea to rescue the crew of the *Waterloo,* they were unsuccessful. Cley was flooded, and by 8 o'clock in the evening it was reported that 'the sea ran mountains high, rolling completely over our beach in every direction'. There were several ships wrecked at Cley but fortunately all hands were saved. The sluice at Blakeney failed and the marshland was inundated; the wind was so strong that the apple crop was torn off the trees. At Wells, all the fishing smacks broke loose in the harbour, and several were wrecked. On the following Monday, wrecks and bodies were washed up all along the coastline.

September

September 1075 saw Norwich at the centre of a rebellion against William the Conqueror, and the castle was besieged for three months. Ralph de Guader married Emma – the daughter of William Osborn, the 1st Earl of Hereford – without the permission of the king. The king refused to sanction the marriage, and at the bride-ale in September Ralph plotted a rebellion with his new brother-in-law Roger de Breueil (the 2nd Earl of Hereford) and Waltheof (the 1st Earl of Northumberland); the idea was that one of them would rule as king and the other two as earls.

Waltheof decided not to carry on with the revolt (but was later executed by William anyway), and Ralph found that his forces were not strong enough to fight the troops of Bishop Odo of Bayeux and Geoffrey de Montbray, so he retreated back to Norwich castle. He left Emma to defend the castle while he went to Denmark to get help from Cnut and Hakon. Emma withstood a siege for three months, but eventually negotiated terms with Archbishop Lanfranc – she and Ralph's followers lost their lands, but were allowed 40 days to leave England. Ralph died in the first crusade in 1096. Norwich was also punished for its part in the rebellion; the Domesday book says 32 burgesses fled the town and others were ruined by confiscation of their property, and the yearly 'farm' (lease of the revenues from tolls and court fines) that the burgesses had to pay to the king was tripled to £90.

The castle at Norwich – scene of one of the longest rebellions against William the Conqueror. (Photograph by author)

Cley, with its windmill. (Photograph by author)

1 September

Cley was badly hit by fire in 1612; 117 houses in the village centre were destroyed. As a result, the villagers migrated to the north of the town and a new harbour was built by the windmill.

1800 saw food riots in Norwich, when women at the New Mills served out flour at cheap rates, selling it at two shillings per stone. Magistrates arrived and stopped it.

There was a major gale in 1833, causing over 60 ships to be driven on to the Norfolk coast, and hundreds of ships were wrecked in the North Sea – including the 200-tonne prison ship *Amphitrate,* with the loss of the 108 female convicts and 12 children on board. Land wasn't safe, either, as the spires of both St Nicholas' and St Margaret's Church in King's Lynn were blown down. Forty wagon-loads of wreckage were removed from the beaches at Snettisham and Hunstanton.

Brancaster Church, where Susanna Roche, one of the victims of the Earl of Wemyss disaster, is buried. (Photograph by author)

Grave of Susanna Roche in Brancaster churchyard. The inscription is weathered, but reads 'Sacred to the memory of Susanna Roche aged 32 years and also to her nephew Alexander David Roche aged 4 years, who were unfortunately drowned with many others in the cabin of the Earl of Wemyss, Leith Packet, which was stranded on this coast during the dreadful gale on September 1st 1833 on its passage from London. Which melancholy affair has been doubly afflicting for the relatives of the deceased from the fact that no attempt was ever made to rescue them from their situation, and in continuation of such inhuman conduct their persons were stripped of every valuable and their property plundered.' (Photograph by author)

But the saddest story was that of the Leith Packet, the *Earl of Wemyss*, which was stranded at Brancaster. Six women, a man and four children drowned – and the inquiry at the Hare Arms in Docking, later that month, revealed a tale of negligence and tragedy, along with accusations that no attempt was made to rescue them and the bodies were then looted – an accusation still visible today in a gravestone in Brancaster Churchyard.

Captain Nesbit, the master of the ship, said he left London on 29 August with 19 passengers. Two days later, the gale started – and turned into a hurricane. He said the ship was grounded; there was no water in her, but then the keel gave way and the ship filled with water, the sea broke over her and the ship sank.

Mr Logan, a surgeon who was a passenger on the *Wemyss*, said the captain told them they could walk to safety when the tide ebbed. He thought the tide was flowing; and when a skylight broke no tarpaulin was put over it and water filled the ship. Mr Logan had no idea what happened next, but thought he must have been pulled through the skylight; his belongings were never found, and in his view the crew were negligent.

The Reverend Mr Holloway of Brancaster testified that the captain told him the ladies were already drowned in the cabin and there was no point in rescuing them as they'd been there for four hours. When the bodies were recovered, they were taken to the church; Mr Holloway believed that if the skylight had been battened the women would have been saved, and if they'd been rescued earlier their goods might have been saved, too.

John Large, a mariner of Brancaster, helped retrieve the bodies and saw Mr Newman Reeve – the son-in-law of the Lord of the Manor – taking jewellery from the ladies. William Green, the chief boatman of the preventive coastguard, said he'd called the ship to send the passengers to shore on a boat – they had no boat on the shore or would have sent it out. The crew claimed that the weather was too bad for them to secure the skylight – and even if the ladies had been out of the cabin they wouldn't have survived the weather.

Joseph Newman Reeve said he asked people to help get the bodies out of the ship and took the jewellery 'to protect them from revolting indignities – such as having their fingers cut off to get the rings off them' – though Reverend Holloway disputed this, saying that earrings had been torn out of ears and bruises caused, and the bodies were still warm. Newman Reeve claimed he'd kept everything safely (although others claimed he'd refused to give things back and said they belonged to the Lord of the Manor, who was entitled to everything cast up on the shore). He admitted he'd unwisely opened one bag, belonging to Mrs Pyne, without witnesses, but said that others gave him jewellery to look after. Mrs Pyne's husband, however, wanted to prosecute Newman Reeve for taking things and ripping out earrings – and Mr Pyne and three other surviving relatives of the deceased supplied a list of property and cash that was missing.

Newman Reeve stood trial in Norwich in March 1834, after a spell in the castle. He was allowed out on bail in November for £1,000 plus four £250 sureties. He was charged with stealing property of two of the drowned women – a bag, nine five-pound notes, four exchequer bills of £100 each, 100 sovereigns and a box. But he was represented by Sir James Scarlett, known for his success in court – much was made of Reeve's good name, and the fact that 100 sovereigns were found in his house was not seen as proof that he'd stolen them because they could have belonged to his father-in-law, the lord of the manor. He'd written to Mrs Pyne's husband, but as Mr Pyne had moved the letter never reached him. The verdict was 'not guilty'. A further trial at the Norwich summer assizes in July, of the ship's steward and cook and a local farmer who'd been put in charge of the wreck, included some very damning evidence about people who'd offered to lie to protect Reeve – but the evidence was dismissed and the jury of the second trial also gave a 'not guilty' verdict.

There was another storm in 1837, this time around Stibbard and Guist. Barley and wheat were beaten out by hailstones which lay 6in deep in places on the following morning; damage was estimated at £3,000.

1856 saw a flood after a huge storm in Yarmouth; one house was undermined by the water and collapsed.

1962 saw half a million paper sacks destroyed at a Gorleston factory, worth over £25,000. The fire broke out just after work had finished for the weekend on Saturday afternoon. Bystanders saw smoke then suddenly heard a whoosh and flames were licking out of the roof. By the time the fire brigade arrived, the building was well alight, and the asbestos walls and roof burst in the heat of the flames. The fire brigade stopped the blaze reaching a tank of oil but couldn't stop it reaching machinery.

1975 saw a huge field fire at Binham which burnt out the Wells fire engine. The crew saved some of the equipment and nobody was hurt, but they needed four other pumps to fight the 200-acre blaze of stubble and hedgerows. At one point there was a big explosion and the fire leapt from one field across the road to another, but the fire crews managed to contain the blaze and stop it damaging standing corn.

2 September

1780 saw two barns and a stable belonging to Mr Francis destroyed by fire at Shrimpling, when a haystack caught fire at noon.

1887 saw a huge gale. Twenty-five miles off the shore of Great Yarmouth, the 1,742-tonne ship *Falls of Bruar*, with its cargo of salt, was in trouble when its mast snapped and fell into the sea while men were working on the sails. The crew tried to cut away the masts so the ship could right itself, but it was impossible because the masts were cased in iron. Two of the ship's boats were under water; one smacked into the boat's side and was wrecked and one capsized. Three of the crew clung to the upturned boat, and two held on to the wreckage. The five survivors out of the original 29 crew were rescued by Great Yarmouth smack *Cygnet*. Afterwards, survivor William Hoghund said that the sea was so high, the smack couldn't help them at first, but it kept coming back. The sailors had been in the water for six hours; in Hoghund's view, they wouldn't have survived for more than another 15 minutes.

1975 saw a warehouse gutted at School Lane, Norwich. The warehouse, belonging to Thorn's ironmongers, was used for storing shelving racks and drain covers. The roof caved in and the wall collapsed, and there were fears for neighbours; 86-year-old Ada Olley, who was bedridden, was helped from her house. Luckily nobody was hurt and the fire crews managed to contain the blaze.

3 September

There was a serious fire at Swaffham in 1928 at Richard Deer's garage and motor works, which destroyed the premises and the neighbouring cottage. The building was formerly Fisher's Theatre and had also been used as a Roman Catholic church. The cause of the fire was unknown, but it started in the vulcanising shop. At 2.45pm Mr Drake, the clerk, heard a crackling noise. When he went to investigate, he saw flames and raised the alarm. The fire was under control by 4pm, but the poor occupant of the cottage, Mr Butters, was only able to save one couch and chair from the cottage.

4 September

In 1934 fire broke out on Hunstanton Pier just after 5pm; the alarm was raised and the fire brigade realised that the floor of the concert hall and the beams underneath were on fire. The timbers were tarred so they burned easily, and the hoses were not long enough to reach the fire, so the firemen cut up the flooring and threw it into the sea, then raised buckets of seawater on long ropes to extinguish the flames.

1974 saw a £40,000 blaze at Great Yarmouth, which started six hours after the building was locked up. Thirty men and five engines fought the blaze at a toy warehouse, but the building was already alight from end to end when they arrived. Thousands of teddies and toys were burned. Firemen stayed at the site overnight, despite torrential rain, to stop the blaze flaring up again.

5 September

1892 saw what *The Times* described as 'fire of great magnitude' at the premises of R.A. Cooper, biscuit manufacturer and sweet boiler at the corner of Bank Street and Queen Street in Norwich. At around 9pm a passer-by saw light from a skylight in the upper part of the factory;

within 15 minutes the whole interior was alight. Flames towered above roofs, 'illuminating with intense brilliancy the cathedral spire and the churches and houses in the neighbourhood'. The fire brigade managed to confined the fire to the premises, but they were gutted; the factory's contents, machinery and stock were all lost within an hour of the fire's discovery, at an estimated loss of £3,000. During the rescue operation, Police Constable Hook was struck by falling masonry when one of the chimneys fell; it fractured his spine and sadly he died five days later.

1896 saw a fire at Chantry Opening in Chapelfield, Norwich. Despite heavy rain, the fire broke out in the builder's workshops. The fire brigade and 50 men of the Dragoon Guards had the blaze under control in an hour, to the enjoyment of thousands of spectators.

1925 saw spectators watching a ship sinking in 30ft of water, 35 yards off the shore near Sandown Road at Great Yarmouth. The *Boadicea* was on its way to Hull to be broken up when Captain Fines realised that the ship was leaking at a rate of a foot of water per hour. He had no idea what caused the leak, but realised he was not going to make it to Hull, so he decided to beach the ship – but then it turned over. He and his crewmate were rescued by Mr Leach in his boat *Rose*, and spectators watched as the ship listed to port and just the funnel, deck rail and companion showed above water.

Late in the evening, in 1928, Norwich Guildhall had a narrow escape from fire, which started in a small store room near the Council Chamber and Sword Room on the first floor. The police, who occupied part of the ground floor, used their hand extinguishers as soon as they realised the fire had started, which stopped the fire spreading to the landing. Although the columns were blistered and blackened, they were able to be restored.

6 September

1971 saw a huge blaze at East Rudham, which gutted a Dutch barn and its contents – 250 tons of feed for 300 cattle – and was visible from the road. The farm workers were baling and carting straw when the fire started, and the blaze spread quickly to the 11,000 bales of hay and straw. Two men inside had to slide down the stacks to escape, but luckily they were unhurt. The fire brigade had to spread a third of a mile of hose across the fields to pump water from a hydrant in the village. There was no hope for the barn, so the fire fighters let it burn itself out, once contained; they managed to stop it spreading to 16 tons of fertiliser stacked nearby.

7 September

In 1670 there was a major flood in King's Lynn during high tide. Haystacks 'swam about the fields', many thousands of sheep and cattle were lost, and boats were rowed in the street from Eastgate to Gaywood.

Rough weather hit the county in 1805 – Mackie's *Annals* reports that there was a whirlwind at Rockland St Mary. A rowing boat on the bank of the broad was lifted into the air and thrown 70 yards; the young man inside it was lifted three or four yards into the air.

1896 saw a fire a Cullingford's marine store near Whitefriars Bridge in Norwich. The building, used for storing rags and waste, caught light at 11pm and the blaze spread quickly. The roof fell in, but by midnight the fire brigade had the flames under control.

1974 saw a blaze causing several thousands of pounds' worth of damage at F & G Smith's maltings in Dereham. The alarm was raised by a neighbour who heard popping noises at 6am; 12 fire engines attended and concentrated on stopping the fire spreading. The blaze damaged hundreds of tons of barley and destroyed a third of the rear part of the premises; however, in March 1970 there had been an even more serious fire which wiped out half the firm's production capacity and ruined malt to the tune of £30,000.

8 September

An earthquake was felt at Norwich in 1692, although the 18th-century historian Francis Blomefield added that it was felt more strongly at London.

In 1741 there was a huge storm at King's Lynn. The notes of clergyman Thomas Peirson at King's Lynn refer to 'about 20 mins after 12 at noon, there was a most violent storm of wind and rain'. It blew down the tall spire and central lantern tower of St Margaret's Church and the spire of St Nicolas's Church. Custom House was flooded, and the west gable end and its chimneys at Middleton Hall were blown down, as were barns at Tilney and Outwell. The gale also caused much damage to trees.

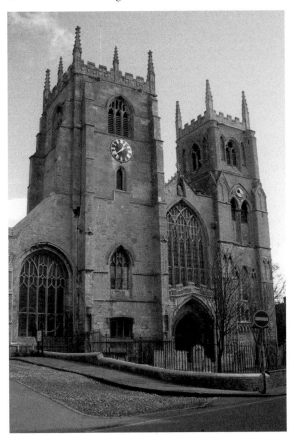

In 1915 there was a Zeppelin raid in Dereham; the airship dropped bombs on Church Street, killing five and causing much damage.

1975 saw firemen rushing to Costessey to stop a hedge blaze setting light to the Round Well Sawmill on Dereham Road. The fire started at a tip and spread from there to stubble in the field that backed on to the sawmill. Firemen arrived as the hedgerow went up in flames; the wind blew the fire towards piles of timber in the yard, and some started to smoulder. Although there were lots of hydrants nearby, there wasn't

The twin-towered west front of St Margaret's Church, King's Lynn. The porch has flood markers (see 11 March) and the clock on the right is the 'tide clock', which shows when high and low tides are due. (Photograph by author)

enough water. The flames started licking tree trunks that were waiting to be sawn, and neighbours had to throw water on to their fences to stop them going up. Dogs in the nearby kennels were evacuated and the traffic was diverted, but firemen managed to contain the blaze.

9 September

1888 saw a serious fire at the Orchard Street Saw Mills in Norwich, owned by the Cunnington Bros timber merchants. The alarm was raised at 1.40am when the 72ft by 20ft building was on fire. The fire brigade managed to contain it; with the help of the employees, the fire was under control by 2.15am, but the turning and sawing mills were destroyed and other saws were lost. Eight horses in the stables were very scared – but they were rescued.

In 1915 there was another Zeppelin raid at Great Yarmouth, killing two and causing much damage at St Peter's Plain.

In 1917 there was an enormous fire in Norwich, when the factory of Norwich Components Ltd was destroyed at Foundry Bridge. The fire started at midnight and the building quickly became five storeys of flames. The night shift there – including 150 women – managed to escape without injury, although a soldier who helped had to go to hospital for treatment. The factory was gutted in 20 minutes, causing damage estimated at £100,000 (the equivalent of over £3.8 million in today's money) and putting 600 women out of work.

10 September

1874 saw the biggest rail disaster in Norfolk, when two trains on the Great Eastern Railway crashed head-on just outside Norwich. The mail train left Yarmouth at 8.40pm, was joined at Reedham by a train from Lowestoft, then travelled three stations further on to Brundall and waited until the express train from Norwich to Yarmouth had gone. Recently, the Norwich train had been running late, so the station master at Brundall had been told he could send the mail train down. The procedure had happened before, but there was a routine that had to be followed: the station master had to write the telegram down and enter it in a book, then put the instructions in writing and give them to the guard, who in turn had to give them to the driver. That night, Brundall received a telegram saying they could send the mail train. Station Master Platford did so – but two minutes later, when it was too late, a second telegram came telling him to stop the train. He'd broken the rules by giving verbal instructions instead of written, because he was anxious to get the train going.

But Inspector Cooper at Thorpe had broken the rules even more – he'd allowed his clerk Robson to send a telegram without his signature. And when Robson received the Brundall telegram saying that the mail train was on its way, he didn't ring the bell for Cooper because he was afraid Cooper would 'make a row' about being called away from other business.

The trains crashed on a bend, where neither could see each other's lights until it was too late; there was also torrential rain and the line was slippery. The crash took place at low speeds in modern terms – 20mph – but it pushed the mail train almost vertical so that it landed on the top of the express engine. The carriages were piled up to a height of 15 or 20ft, and then the train rolled over, taking the carriages with them. A piece of iron was hurled from the train and knocked a huge hole in the back of an outbuilding 30 yards from the line. Over 20 people were killed – including both train drivers and their firemen – and around 40 were injured.

The noise of the crash was so loud that the residents of Thorpe rushed out to see what was going on – one witness described the noise as 'sharp, like a thunderclap' followed by two thuds. Dr Eade of Lowestoft was travelling on the train; he had minor injuries so was able to start treating people. He was joined by city doctors who'd been gathered by the station master at Thorpe and sent to the crash site by a special train. The doctors set fractures and temporarily dressed wounds, then sent the injured back to Norwich by the special train, while most of the dead bodies were placed in a boat house near the accident site.

The rescue teams lit huge bonfires on either sides of the crash to help them see what they were doing, and used bits of the wreck to fuel the flames. Local people – both rich and poor – gave up pillows and blankets to help sufferers, and tore sheets into strips to make bandages.

There were some amazing escapes. Horace Booty, master of the Presbyterian School in Norwich's Calvert Street, had objected to the rough conversation of a fellow traveller in their third-class carriage and moved his wife and family to another carriage. Their original carriage was smashed to pieces, and if they hadn't moved they would all have died. One drunken fisherman was found lying insensible across a seat – when he woke, he was shocked to find he'd slept through the lot! Miss Woolasten had been sitting next to two soldiers, who both died in the crash; she was thrown out of the door and nearly all the clothes were torn from her body, but she was alive. At first she didn't think she'd been injured, but when she tried to sit up she discovered that her knee was fractured and her 'foot and leg reversed'.

The quiet beach at Mundesley. (Photograph by author)

Others were not so lucky. The injuries included fractured ribs, internal injuries, a smashed arm that had to be amputated, fractured skulls, fractured legs, scalp wounds and five people had cuts that were severe enough to require hospitalisation. One 19-year-old girl had to have her foot taken off – horribly, the surgeons needed to amputate twice.

1924 saw a truly terrifying event when a tidal wave hit the beach at Mundesley at 5am. There had been a storm and heavy rain the previous day, but high tide wasn't expected for another couple of days. When the enormous wave hit, it cleared the beach, and bathing huts and tents were lost – luckily, nobody was hurt.

1933 saw a series of disastrous fires. There was a major fire at Mousehold Heath at lunchtime, which was beaten out; this was followed by a fire near Harvey Lane in Norwich, and then another at Ringland hills, where the water had to be carried through 20 lengths of hose (each 100ft long) to the top of the hills. For the first time in living memory there was a fire in the boggy land at Fritton Warren near Yarmouth; volunteers fought the blaze for five hours with sand, wet sphagnum moss and bunches of wet grass, but 50 acres were still burned.

1964 saw the biggest forest fire of the year in Thetford. Three fire brigades and two forestry commission firefighting lorries (each carrying 600 gallons of water) and 32 troops helped to tackle the blaze. It started in a young plantation near West Tofts; flames leapt 10ft in the air, and most of the destroyed trees were between three and six years old and 3–5ft high.

11 September

In 1794 a fire broke out at the Phoenix Foundry in King Street, Norwich; within an hour, the foundry, account books and tools were destroyed. The *Norfolk Chronicle* said that because it was a windless night, the fire didn't spread. They also mentioned an unnamed hero 'who, at the hazard of his life, climbed up to the top of a house, knocked down the flew-board, and extinguished the fire, which had collected under it, and thereby prevented any further mischief'.

1968 saw chaos as floods swept the county; it went down in records as Norfolk's wettest ever September day. In three hours there was 1.89in of rain in Norwich. Carrow Road was the worst affected area, up to 9in deep in water, and the A47 at Costessey was 6in deep in water. Norwich Corporation said that nearly half an inch fell in just nine minutes, and added that it was the sort of storm you get once every 10 years.

12 September

1859 saw a fire in the outhouse belonging to confectioner and soda water manufacturer Mr Ives in Howard Street, Great Yarmouth – in a densely populated area. A lad saw the flames and smoke from windows and raised the alarm. The fire brigade were delayed slightly because they were told that the fire was at his premises in Church Plain. They spent two and a half hours fighting the blaze and managed to confine it to the outhouse so the joinery shops on either side didn't go up; however, the stable and warehouse were destroyed, including a tonne of hay and a quantity of 'show glass'.

1972 saw a huge fire at Banham – in the same barn where fire crews had spent 48 hours tackling the blaze two months before. Hundreds of tons of baled hay and straw were affected, and five crews worked though the night to damp down the fire.

1977 saw 30 firemen with four engines fighting a blaze at the British Sugar factory in Cantley. The crews stopped the fire spreading from the store room to the manufacturing plant by pumping water on to the flames from the River Yare. They had to evacuate the employees, then cut holes in the roof to draw out the intense heat and let the smoke escape. The fire was under control in an hour.

13 September

Boat repairman Arthur Walker had an amazing escape at Yarmouth in 1927. He was repairing a shrimp boat in his yard near the suspension bridge and had made a fire to heat up a bolt; a piece of rope caught fire and went on to one of the metal cylinders he used as ballast. The cylinder exploded; Arthur escaped with cuts to his head, but his 18-year-old son Joseph was blown into the river. Vivian Searson, who lived in a caravan on the river bank, escaped with cuts to his arm and head. Everyone thought the eight metal cylinders were old mill rollers – but it turned out they were actually bombs! It was thought that they were incendiaries dropped by German aircraft during World War One; several of the bombs, which the *Eastern Daily Press* described as 'resembling thermos flasks', were still on some of the shrimp boats. They were collected up and moved to a safe place – and, considering that they'd been used as ballast for the previous five years, Arthur was very lucky indeed.

1959 saw the end of the driest summer for over 200 years – unsurprisingly, there was one of the worst ever heath fires in North Norfolk at Salthouse.

1974 saw a £60,000 blaze at a farm in Necton which destroyed a farm building and 1,500 tons of fresh barley straw. The alarm was given at 1am, when the blaze lit up the night sky. It took two fire brigades 12 hours to fight the inferno and damp down, but the fire was confined to the building. Coincidentally, on 5 November three years earlier a fire hit exactly the same spot and burned down the building – this one had replaced it.

14 September

1933 saw a burning wreck at Great Yarmouth when the cargo of 4,100 tons of esparto grass (used for paper making) caught light on the steamer *Porthcawl*. The 24 crew fought the blaze for three hours, but then were taken off by the Yarmouth lifeboat rescue. Thousands of spectators watched; children called out 'The sea is on fire', as oil spilled on the top of the sea and caught light. The ship was still blazing the following day; the reflection of the flames could be seen miles away at sea, and the Yarmouth coastguard could hear the roar of the fire at their station one and a half miles away.

15 September

1973 saw a huge fire at Saham Hall at Saham Toney, causing £100,000 of damage. Fifty firemen from seven fire brigades fought the blaze for two hours and ferried out valuable antiques, silver and china worth £50,000. The fire was spotted after a lunch party at 2.40pm, but because the phone was out of action the owner had to call from the nearest phone box. Water was pumped from the tenders, then the swimming pool, then from a hydrant 400 yards away. The fire got between the lath and plaster on the ceiling and spread quickly. After five hours the blaze was out, but the roof and 10 rooms on the first floor were destroyed completely, and half the ground floor was severely damaged. The fire crews stayed for a further 24 hours to damp down.

16 September

In 1968 torrential rains caused flooding in the Tas Valley, and Saxlingham Thorpe water mill was damaged to the tune of £10,000. The bad weather seemed to hit south of a line between Norwich and Thetford. People were evacuated at Lakenham, and in Trowse a farmer had to save his 300 pigs from the floods. At Kenninghall, the floods were 9ft deep and at New Buckenham the Dam Brig burst overnight, causing a 6ft flood in parts of the village. Families were rescued at Newton Flotman by a dinghy from the upper floors of their houses; Duffield's mill in the village suffered £6,000 of damage, with tons of fertiliser being wrecked.

1974 saw seven fire engines fighting blazing silage and straw in a barn at Hempstead near Holt. The barn, a cattle lean-to, 200 tons of straw and 350 tons of silage were lost, but the fire crews saved nearby buildings containing 500 tons of hay and 200 pigs. The 45-strong herd of pedigree Friesians were also saved, as was the stud bull – who reportedly was not very happy about his farm being invaded...

17 September

There was a shocking accident at St Giles' Hill, Norwich, in 1853 when the kitchen floor of Mr Bunting's house gave way – apparently, a water pipe had leaked and weakened the soil above one of the chalk mines honeycombing that area of the city. Mr Bunting's wife, daughter and their furniture went straight down a 27ft hole – they fainted with the shock, but amazingly they were unhurt.

The rescue proceedings sound incredible to modern ears. A lit candle was lowered down to Mrs Bunting, and then Mr Stamp, a nearby tailor, had a rope round his middle and went down to rescue her. A crowd had gathered to watch – and Mr Stamp noticed that there was a huge hole beneath the area where the spectators were standing, and warned them to move out of the way. He fastened the rope around Mrs Bunting's waist, but while she was being hauled up the rope gave way and she fell; again, luckily, she was unhurt. The second time was more successful, and then Mr Stamp stood aside so he could fasten a rope to Miss Bunting's waist – and promptly sank into the soil down to his waist. Even so, he fastened the rope round her so she could be hauled to safety. Finally, he fastened another rope around his own waist and was pulled out of the hole.

In 1906 there was a dramatic fire at Roughton, a strong north-easterly gale making the sails of the mill revolve backwards at speed. The heat from the friction set the mill on fire, and despite the best attempts of the Cromer Fire Brigade the mill was destroyed, leaving only the shell of the tower.

1935 saw a major gale across the county. Between 60 and 80 tons of pears and apples, valued at £1,000 (the equivalent of nearly £48,000 in today's money), were blown from trees belonging to Westwick Fruit Farms near North Walsham and lay strewn on the floor in their thousands; orchards were also damaged at Lynn and Wisbech. At Yarmouth, the wind reached 55mph.

18 September

There was a major fire in St Giles' Gate, Norwich, in 1820 at Mr Neale the coachmaker's, causing £2,000 worth of damage (the equivalent of over £124,000 in today's money). At midnight the fire was discovered at the workshops; because the building was a timber building, the fire spread rapidly, and the whole lot was destroyed in an hour and a half. Four engines arrived to help, and the fire was contained to two shops. The *Norfolk Chronicle* says that Captain d'Este of the Fifth Lancers 'distinguished himself by his personal exertions'; he was also helped by the West Norfolk Militia. By 12.30am, flames extended several yards above the roof and 'an immense column of fire issued forth and covered the neighbouring houses'. Basketmaker Mr Gay had 2,000 osiers in the workshops, which were uninsured; he lost all his property, but his friends started a subscription for him. The *Norfolk Chronicle* added sadly that much property was stolen, including a watch, silver spoons, furniture and a four-poster from Mr Flint. The same evening, someone tried to set fire to the property of Mr Gurney in Bowling Green Inn in Chapelfield; lit charcoal was placed near wood in an old building that was due to be taken down, and there was a blaze but luckily no damage.

1972 saw a huge blaze in the store for the market under the memorial gardens in Norwich. A quarter of the 200ft by 50ft store was affected, but hundreds of pounds' worth of damage was caused to dresses, linen and fruit.

1992 saw huge storms across the county. Thousands of homes were without power, especially in Wymondham, Swaffham, Watton and Wells. Fakenham had 2.5in of rain in two and a half hours – its heaviest rainfall since 1953 – and the Lord Nelson pub was flooded to a depth of 3in. The Cathedral in Norwich was struck by lightning, but luckily was not damaged; homes in the city were also struck.

19 September

1970 saw a huge fire at the Kitfix Hobbies Ltd factory in Swaffham. The alarm was raised at 10pm, and shortly afterwards fire ripped through the building. The flames could be seen all over town and explosions were heard as tins of paint burst; then a 40-gallon drum of paraffin burst and spread the fire even further. Volunteers bravely broke down the office door and rescued all the records and furniture. The fire was out just after midnight, but the factory was gutted and fire crews spent the next nine hours damping down.

20 September

In 1778 the paper mill at Lyng burned down at 4am, although the house next to the mill survived. Parson Woodforde wrote about it in his diary, and mentioned that the damage was

£3–4,000 (the equivalent of £283–377,000 in today's money), including £1,000 worth of paper lost. The rotting rags used to make paper were very combustible, so paper mills were very much at risk in the 18th century.

1782 saw a violent storm off the coast which started at 2am; there were several wrecks at Blakeney and Sheringham, and many sailors died.

1796 saw a major fire in Guildhall Street at Thetford; four houses, five shops, a cow and two sheep were lost, resulting in around £583 of damage (the equivalent of nearly £42,000 in today's money).

21 September

There was a fire at the Pleasure Beach in Great Yarmouth, which ended with the Noah's Ark ride being consumed by fire. The constable in the police box opposite the Pleasure Beach saw the flames just after 11.30pm and raised the alarm; the fire brigade put out the blaze and managed to save the ghost train next door, but the diving saloon and high diving board opposite were also destroyed.

22 September

In 1859 there was a major storm and miller George Goddard had an amazing escape when Billingford Mill was blown over and ruined in the space of a few seconds. He fell 25ft into the mill, but the mill post saved him from being crushed in the debris; the *Norfolk News* said that he was found 'standing wedged in between the mill stones & a large cog wheel close by', without a single scratch. Sadly, an elderly man who worked for him was fatally injured because he fell into the wreckage and several bags of meal fell on him, fracturing his ribs and causing internal injuries.

In 1935 there was a severe flood at Cromer, just six weeks after the last one. One and a third inches of rain fell in 45 minutes, and 300 houses and shops were flooded – some up to 7ft deep. The hole in the cliff from the August inundation had been repaired, but the torrential rain wrecked the repairs and caused another huge hole to open. Hail was also a problem this time round; the *Eastern Daily Press* described them as being 'as big as walnuts' at North Walsham (one measured an inch wide, half an inch long and ⅝ of an inch deep), and the hail broke greenhouses at Bawdeswell.

1940 saw an air raid over Sheringham which left one person dead.

There was a huge fire in Norwich in 1947 when Firmin & Co's sack and bag factory caught fire. The roof fell in just after midnight, and 70 men from the Britannia Barracks were on standby to help the firefighters. Although the fire brigade was worried that Gertrude Road might need to be cleared, the fire didn't spread to neighbouring houses. The factory itself was gutted.

1971 saw four fire brigades fighting a fire for a day and a night in a huge hangar at Egmere. There was more smoke than fire, they said afterwards, but the blaze in the feedstuff unit of British Field Products Ltd took some subduing.

23 September

There was a huge blaze at F. W. Waters' steam flour mills in Westwick Street, Norwich, in 1855, which resulted in the loss of the building, 200 sacks of flour, 400 coombs of wheat (a coomb is a measure equivalent to four bushels or a little under 8,900cu in) and 'much valuable machinery'. Damage was estimated at £4,000 (the equivalent of over a quarter of a million pounds in today's money). Three of the firefighters – Mr English, Sergeant Ireland and Mr Neale – were nearly killed by flames spreading while they tried to save the granary, but John Rix put a ladder against tiles so they were able to escape. The fire engines managed to stop the fire spreading to neighbouring buildings, but the flames were fierce enough to melt tar on a roof and to roast all the apples on one side of a nearby apple tree. The fire was discovered at 2.30 in the morning, and a couple of hours later the roof fell in, wrecking the machinery. The fire was subdued by six and was thought to have started by some of the machinery overheating.

The same day saw a disastrous fire at Wymondham in 1924, when the saw mills of Briton Brush were completely gutted by fire. The fire was seen a few minutes after men left work at 6pm that evening; there was dense smoke and sparks over the Church Meadows, and flames were leaping through the roof of the 150ft long building. The fire was well under control by 8pm, but the fire brigade spent several more hours damping it down. Luckily, the factory 50 yards away in Damgate Street was undamaged.

24 September

In 1774 there was a major fire at Mr Hines the cord spinner's in St Stephen's Street, Norwich. It was caused by someone taking a candle to the hemp room to look for something they'd lost, and the entire stock was destroyed.

In 1845 Henry Teasdel's warehouses in Southtown, Great Yarmouth, were destroyed by fire. At 9.30pm a fire was seen in a ship chandler's store which contained very flammable material – tar, turps, canvas, and rope. Three sides of the chandler's store were surrounded by Teasdel's warehouses, which included corn and general merchants' goods. The top of the building was in flames, but when the owner unlocked the door to get to the counting house and rescue the cash box, the fire went up rapidly. The *Norwich Mercury* commented that the three town engines were 'in a bad state' but 'the one from the factory [i.e. Grout's silk mills] was well managed'. Although they were unable to save the chandler's or Teasdel's warehouses, the fire was contained and didn't reach Lacon's beer stores next door. The fire was out by 4am and the damage was estimated at £1–4,000 (equivalent to between about £75,000 and £300,000 in today's money).

25 September

There was a major storm on the east coast in 1692. Around 140 colliers going to Newcastle to fetch coals to take to London were driven on to the shore and lost, with few of the crew saved. Ships from Lynn and Wells bound for Holland had just left the Roads and were also caught up in the gale. Overall, that night, around 200 ships and 1,000 people perished.

In 1866 the boiler at Stark & Co's dye and chemical works in Duke Street exploded; luckily, 30 of the workmen were having their midday break or the loss to human life would have been much greater. As it was, Daniel Taylor and James Breeze, both aged 63, and Henry Clarke, aged

50, died on the spot, and three others died later of their injuries. The boiler was 21ft long and 6ft in diameter; it was only six months old. The inner boiler ring gave way and blew up all the internal walls, killing the men doing odd jobs. All the force of the explosion clearly went into damage rather than noise, because a man driving on Duke Street a few yards away didn't even hear the explosion; he was shocked when tiles started raining down on him. The building was raised into the air by the force of the explosion, and Pitt Street and St George's Middle Street were covered in slates and brick.

1962 saw a large timber blaze at King's Lynn, which wrecked a shed of planed timber and battens and did much damage to another store at Pattrick & Thompsons Ltd. Thirty firemen fought the blaze; although several thousands of pounds' worth of damage was caused, the crew managed to contain the fire to those sheds and it didn't spread to the rest of the four-acre site containing mills and yards.

1976 saw torrential rain at Great Yarmouth; nearly an inch of rain fell during the day, mostly over lunchtime, and the flood water was 8ft deep in the cellars of the cinema and the Star & Garter Club on the seafront.

26 September

A violent hurricane in 1853 halved the apple crop in the county, and much shipping was lost. The schooner *Mary Ann* of Stockton was driven on to the shore at Blakeney, but happily the crew were saved. One man had a lucky escape; as Mr Conley was driving his carriage, he saw a tree starting to fall, which could have crushed his carriage and the four passengers. The *Norfolk Chronicle* reported that 'with great presence of mind he whipped the horses on' – the tree just missed them. The noise caused the horses to bolt, but he managed to get everything under control.

There was another bad storm in 1924. The *Eastern Daily Press* reported that the streets of Norwich were deserted by 7pm; the courts and yard by the river were flooded, and water lay a foot deep from Duke Street to Museum Court. Cellars of the shops in Davey Place were flooded to 4ft, and St Andrew's Church was flooded too – vicar Revd Baumer stayed until late in the night to bale out the water and save the church organ from damage.

2006 saw flash floods in Great Yarmouth. Eleven schools in the area were closed by lunchtime and over 90 properties were affected – some under 5ft of water. The railway station had to be closed, and a pump at the Great Yarmouth pumping station couldn't cope with the deluge and failed for two hours.

28 September

In 1014 the *Anglo-Saxon Chronicles* refer to the great sea-flood of St Michael's Eve; apparently many settlements and people were drowned.

1960 saw a major fire in Great Yarmouth when the amusement arcade and fish bar near the Hippodrome, together with stores and offices, caught fire. A policeman walking past at 3am raised the alarm; the arcade was saved, although it was badly damaged by water.

29 September

1969 saw the worst storm since 1953. A high tide, combined with heavy seas and a severe wind, meant that Great Yarmouth was awash up to the sea wall, and cars on the South Denes had to be pushed to safety so they were not taken away by the river, which was 4ft above its normal level and flowed on to the quay. Wells was also flooded and beach huts were washed away, and at Hunstanton the sea came over the wall on to the promenade, causing damage.

1990 saw a huge blaze at Hoveton; the owner of the Exel shop discovered the fire while putting out rubbish at the back of the shop and raised the alarm. Nobody was hurt, but the flames shot 40ft into the air, spreading through the video shop, electrical shop and saddlery shop. It took 50 firemen to subdue the blaze, and luckily they were able to stop it spreading to a workshop at the back where gas canisters were stored.

30 September

In 1740 the Shire House on Castle Hill in Norwich (built in 1578) was destroyed by fire; it was rebuilt in 1749. It was subsequently replaced by a new Shire Hall in 1822, which started to sink 24 years later and needed to be propped up on a raft of concrete 10ft thick.

1959 saw a mile-wide belt of fire on the heath at Marsham, involving 400 acres. The flames were visible 18 miles away at Holt, and the firemen were forced back by the heat and dense smoke. The blaze broke out at 2pm – and despite having eight fire brigades attending it was still burning six hours later. By 8.45pm it was under control; there were also other heath fires that afternoon at Horsford and Felthorpe.

October

October is chiefly remembered for the floods and gales – particularly the 'it's not going to happen' hurricane of 1987, which will no doubt haunt weather forecasters for years to come, and the hurricane of 2002.

October has also been a month of sickness; 1665 saw the beginning of the last serious epidemic of bubonic plague in Norwich, which lasted for about a year. According to the 18th-century historian Francis Blomefield, there were 2,251 deaths from plague in the period, and 203 people died in just one month. When the plague was finally over, 9 September 1667 was declared a public holiday. But plague was not the only epidemic: typhoid was also prevalent in the county in the late 1800s.

1 October

In 1250 there was a major storm in the North Sea and the English channel, resulting in severe flooding. The chronicler Holinshed said 'the moon appeared red and swelled and great damage was done by wind to sea and land'.

In 1973, in heavy seas, the 45ft fishing boat *My Doris* started to sink while being towed in after its engine had failed. The two crew were forced to jump overboard and were in the sea for 10 minutes before the Gorleston lifeboat managed to snatch them to safety. Both had lifejackets and held on to each other for support, but it was difficult for the lifeboat searchlight to find them in the huge waves. Afterwards, the rescued men said it was the longest 10 minutes of their lives.

1976 saw a huge flood at Weybourne when the beck burst its banks; a dozen houses were flooded to a depth of 4ft. There was also flooding at Blakeney after torrential rain.

2 October

In 1570, according to the 19th-century historian William Richards, Marshland and the town of Wigenhale overflowed, so 'from Old Lynn to Magdalen-bridge there were not left 10 roods of the bank whole and firm'.

1972 saw a £10,000 fire at the dress shop Camelot on Castle Meadow, Norwich, which ruined clothes, jewellery and perfume. The fire started half an hour after the close of business. A passer-by saw smoke in the front of the shop and raised the alarm. Four engines had the fire under control in five minutes; there were not many flames, but the heat and smoke were problematic. The damage was confined to the ground floor.

3 October

The last serious epidemic of the plague started in Norwich in 1665; in July the following year the market was transferred outside the city walls in the hope of preventing people bringing plague into the city on market day. In one week in August, 203 people died from the plague.

In 1713, according to the *Norwich Remembrancer*, the Yarmouth ferry was overturned on Breydon Water and drowned 20 people.

1872 saw a serious fire at the oil merchants Leach Bros in the Market Place at Great Yarmouth. The shop contained many lamps with paraffin and oil; turpentine was stored in the back room, and matting and rope in the warehouse. When the fire broke out at 7pm, it spread rapidly. The residents escaped, and three fire engines came to deal with the blaze. By 7.30pm the *Norfolk Chronicle* described the house as 'exhibiting the appearance of a volcano'. Thousands of spectators watched the blaze and heard the explosions. Luckily, the wind wasn't strong so the fire was under control within two hours, although the roof had fallen in and the top three floors were destroyed. The *Norfolk Chronicle* reported that Mr Evans from the 50th Regiment of Foot was a hero; he 'gallantly mounted a ladder', despite the choking fumes, and smashed a window with a sledgehammer so the fire brigade could get access to fight the fire. The blaze was due to a careless assistant who upset a lit Benzoline lamp. The shop, its contents and the house were gutted, and the neighbouring properties were damaged by water.

4 October

In 1737, according to the 18th-century historian Francis Blomefield, rain fell almost continually in Norwich from the night of 4 October (except for a couple of hours on the 6th) until noon on 10 October. The lower part of the city was badly flooded and the water broke down the bridges at Trowse and Harford.

1883 had seen a week of heavy rain, with floods at Fakenham more than a foot deep. That afternoon there were tumultuous seas; the Cromer lifeboat was called out at 3.30pm and managed to launch but couldn't get out to the ship. Rockets with lifelines were fired, but either they were blown wide of the mark or the ropes broke. Finally lifeboatman Mr Davies managed to swim out with a line and the crew of five were rescued and taken to the Red Lion and the Hotel de Paris. The rescue took until 7pm, watched by a large crowd who even lit a tar barrel on the Marrams above the wreck so everyone could see!

1958 saw a whirlwind descending on Dereham, moving from south to north. It burst open a 15ft sliding door and blew the front of the building out, smashing a plate glass window; it also flung copper cowling from a roof 100 yards away into a garden, uprooted trees and ripped off shed roofs.

5 October

In 1811 there was a tragic accident when the ferry boat at King's Lynn overturned and drowned 11 people.

6 October

1696 saw 'St Faith's flood' in Norwich.

In 1835 a Spanish ship was in trouble about 12 miles off the coast of Great Yarmouth. The beachmen went off in the yawl *Increase* to rescue them – but on the way back, the yawl was capsized in a squall. Seven men were drowned (and one of them, Mr Rishmer, left a wife and nine children); Samuel Brock and Mr Emmerson survived the capsizing and started swimming back to shore. Emmerson couldn't make it; Brock spent seven hours battling the waves. He was safely taken aboard the brig *Betsy* at 1 o'clock, the next morning – where they worked out he'd swum 14 miles in a rough sea. They put him ashore at Lowestoft, and despite his ordeal he survived and lived until he was 69, in December 1873.

9 October

1926 saw a huge gale at Yarmouth, which left Southtown and North Quay flooded; fortunately, nobody was hurt.

1930 saw a huge fire at Cromer, when a cake, grain and hay store caught fire early in the morning. The top storey of the building was wood and corrugated iron; the iron became red hot and the fire brigade couldn't get near it at first. Carriages in the LNER goods shed were blistered by the fire and had to be moved to a safer place. After three hours of pumping, the fire was finally extinguished, but much of the stock was damaged by fire or water.

1939 saw another daring rescue by Henry Blogg and the Cromer lifeboat crew. The captain of the Greek steamer *Mount Ida* said they had been at sea for 50 days, with no lights to guide them, when the boat sprang a leak and the engine room flooded. There was a major gale and the ship listed to starboard; the lifeboat reached them at noon, but heavy seas prevented the rescue for three hours. Finally, the 29 crew managed to scramble down ropes and jump on to the lifeboat; Blogg said afterwards that it was a more difficult rescue than the *Monte Nevoso*. (See 16 October.)

10 October

1926 saw a huge fire in Prince of Wales Road, Norwich, when the furniture showrooms of Wallace King caught fire. The alarm was raised just after 8pm, and although firefighters managed to confine the blaze to the showrooms and Mr King's house the roof fell in and the chimney stack came down at 9.40pm. Fortunately, only one injury was reported – PC John Wright's hand was lacerated by falling glass.

1978 saw a huge fire at the Overstrand Court Hotel. Twenty people fled the blaze, which was believed to have started at 10pm when the lights suddenly went out. Fifty firemen from six brigades managed to extinguish the fire, which was in the roof void.

11 October

There was a major storm in 1838 and 2,000 ships sought refuge at Yarmouth – luckily, the wind didn't change direction or there would have been many wrecks. Even so, boats lost their anchors and chains, and fishing boats lost their nets and buoys. The *Norfolk Chronicle* reported that while the ships were there, £3,000 was spent (the equivalent of over £200,000 in today's money). The butchers had to kill every bullock and sheep – and every spare anchor sold within the space of two days!

1974 saw a £30,000 blaze at a farm in Mundford, when two Dutch barns containing 120 tons of baled straw went up. Six fire brigades were called but the fire had already taken hold and the roofs caved in. The straw was singed, burned or ruined by water, but nearby pigs were saved. The fire broke out at 11.15am, but by mid-afternoon the fire crews were able to damp down.

OCTOBER

12 October

1993 saw major floods across Norfolk. The rainfall that month was twice the monthly norm, and on 12 October an inch of rain fell over Norwich in just three hours. The villages south of the city suffered most; Framlingham Pigot, Mulbarton, Bramerton and Saxlingham Nethergate were washed out. At Bungay, the river burst its banks; some people had to be rescued by boat at Utilux Components Ltd as there were floods 4ft deep outside; 100 children at Bungay High School couldn't get home and had to stay the night with friends. Two days later, hundreds more homes were flooded. The floods were 4ft deep at Stalham, and Saham Toney was cut off. The railway from Sheringham to Holt was closed after a landslip, and there were 250 999 calls in just one hour at Swaffham.

13 October

In 1822 there was a serious gale; five brigs and a sloop were lost near Winterton, 10 of the Cromer herring boatmen were lost and the revenue cutter *Ranger* was lost off Happisburgh. The beach at Great Yarmouth 'and for many miles' were 'covered in pieces of wrecks and bodies washed ashore'. All bad enough, but there was a severe storm in the local papers afterwards, with accusations of plunder and refusal to help on the part of Happisburgh inhabitants.

The cutter had a crew of 40; one was off sick, and seven were at Cromer in another boat, on the lookout for some expected smugglers. When the ship went down, the remaining crew, including Captain John Sayers, were drowned. The *Norfolk Chronicle* reported allegations that people plundered instead of helping the distressed seamen – and that although 'the shrieks of the unfortunate men were heard distinctly on the shore' they were ignored by the people from Happisburgh.

It provoked an outrage – there was a furious letter in the following week's newspaper saying that they'd already rescued 18 fishing boats and their crews before the *Ranger* arrived; on the beach, they got Manby's gun out but the distance of a mile and a quarter was too far for them to be able to help.

1891 saw severe gales, which brought many trees down. At Norwich, a large garden wall was blown over and the sign of W. Hanworth in the Arcade (30ft by 9ft) was carried off on to a roof. The following day, there was a severe thunderstorm at Norwich. Two thatched cottages at Little Melton were hit by lightning and wrecked; fortunately, their occupants, the elderly widows Mrs Bunn and Mrs Bishop, were rescued.

14 October

In 1824 there was a serious fire in Norwich, at the upholsterer and cabinet maker's Mr Ling in Bridewell Alley. At 8.30 in the evening, the bells of St Andrew's rang what the *Norfolk Chronicle* described as an 'awk or jangling peal' to raise the alarm – and then hundreds of people rushed to the scene and impeded the work of the firemen.

For the first couple of hours, the fire was confined to the workshop but there simply was not enough water to deal with it. By 10pm the dwelling house was on fire. People could hear rafters falling; fire burst through windows and the roof, illuminating the smoke. Heavy rain stopped sparks setting fire to the neighbouring buildings, and Mr Parsons the bookseller's on the corner escaped damage.

The cells in the Bridewell were filled with smoke, so the prisoners were moved to the city jail for safety. Mr Culley, whose house was at the top of St Andrew's Steps, opened his house as a repository for his neighbours' goods – the newspaper reports describe him as 'a hero', and he was probably instrumental in establishing the human chain of buckets between the engines and the water supply.

 The conflagration was at its at height around 11pm, and the flames lit an area of several miles. Women ran out with their children in their arms, wanting to save them. When Mr Culley's house was full, property was put in St Andrew's Church – and there was so much that the vicar was unable to hold a service there on the Sunday after the fire.

The fire was finally put out at 4 o'clock in the morning, with the help of the Second Dragoon guards, but the shop and house were gutted. The firefighters managed to save the manufactured goods, but Ling's workmen lost all their tools. Although there was no serious injury or human life lost, two dogs were burned to death and there was £3,400 of damage (the equivalent of over a quarter of a million pounds in today's money).

1875 saw a huge gale at Great Yarmouth; the schooner *Meta* from Truro was dashed to pieces on the north pier, but the crew were saved.

1884 saw a severe storm over the coast. At Great Yarmouth, people found it hard to walk – particularly women in crinolines – and the new wood covering on Britannia Pier was demolished. One boy had a lucky escape when he was blown away with his pony and cart; they slipped on the fishnets and were thrown into the river between the quay and the luggers. Luckily, they were seen and pulled out in time. Many trees were lost, and in the parish of Hunstanton around £2,000 of damage was caused by the storm. There were many rescues at sea; Caister lifeboat rescued four from the schooner *Time* of Hull, which was carrying wheat when it was in distress off Winterton. The Italian coal barque *Unione* was lost, but four of the crew were rescued by Lowestoft fishermen, and eight by the Great Yarmouth smack *Sunflower,* whose crew were simply amazing: they left their ship in a small boat to rescue the sailors and persuaded the men to jump into the sea, where the *Sunflower's* crew pulled them to safety.

There was a serious fire in 1928, when Ranson's timber mills in Mountergate, Norwich, caught fire; it spread to Harrison & Sons' marine store yard and Mountergate Saw Mill, and the Georgian House in Spring Gardens was also burned down. The Eastern Counties Joinery Company was affected, as were the furnishings businesses of A. S. Howard and Wallace King, general merchants Harrison and son, general contractors T.C.R. King and son, engineers Morris and son and the Ordnance Survey office. The fire was brought under control with the help of troops as well as the fire brigade, but not before the yard and sawmills were gutted. *The Times* noted that 'for many years there has not been such a big fire in the city and but for the splendid work of the fire brigades one of the oldest parts of Norwich might have been swept away'. As it was, the damage ran into tens of thousands of pounds. The *Eastern Daily Press* said that the roaring furnace could be seen over the whole city. The United

Automobile Company lost motor coaches and omnibuses worth £8,000 (the equivalent of over £330,000 in today's money), but amazingly the only living casualties were a horse and a dog.

1963 saw millions of crackers worth hundreds of thousands of pounds go up in flames in just a few minutes. A former aircraft hangar used as a store for crackers caught light at around 10.40pm the fire brigade was called, but five minutes later the roof crashed in and flames leapt hundreds of feet into the air. The blaze could be seen for miles around; although a nearby printing shop suffered cracked glass from the heat, the fire crews contained the blaze. The city fire chief said it was the biggest blaze he'd seen since coming to Norwich, and he thought it would burn for 24 hours longer. A representative from Caley's, which owned the crackers, said that a year's work had gone up in just five minutes. The factory, which produced 20 million crackers a year, was back in business 10 months later.

16 October

1784 saw a bad fire at Stanfield Hall, when a woman threw out hot ashes and set straw alight. The fire burned the stables, a barn, outhouses and tenements, as well as 14 lasts of wheat and eight lasts of barley (a last is equivalent to 640 gallons).

In 1914 Gressenhall mill burned down, and the fire lasted for four hours; 200 sacks of flour and 1,500 sacks of wheat were destroyed, and the building was gutted. The glow from the fire could be seen 18 miles away in Norwich.

1925 saw a fire in Kett's Hill, Norwich, which was visible from the whole of the city. The fire started at the premises of fish merchant Mr Roberts; the people who discovered the flames got three cars out of the garage so they were not burnt, but Mr Roberts lost everything else. The fires was extinguished within an hour and a half.

Henry Blogg was awarded the RNLI's silver medal – as well as a silver medal from the Canine Defence League – for rescuing 30 men and a dog from the Italian cargo steamer *Monte Nevoso*. The steamer became stranded on 14 October on the Haisborough Sands in fine weather, and the Cromer lifeboat stood by; during the night, a gale and heavy seas hampered the rescue attempts. The steamer was at the point of breaking up on 16 October when Blogg drove the lifeboat next to it and encouraged the seamen to jump across when the sea lifted the lifeboat to the top of the steamer's rails. In between, the boat plunged 20ft and its buffers were ripped to shreds, but during the next hour 30 crew were rescued. The captain, captain's mate, chief engineer and wireless operator refused to leave the boat; the lifeboat crew took the rescued men to safety then returned to persuade the remaining four men to leave, despite having had nothing to eat since the previous morning. The lifeboat crew had spent 60 hours on the rescue – 16 of them in a howling gale – and when they got back to Cromer, they were 'greeted with cheers by large crowds and a peal of the church bells', according to *The Times*. The dog decided he wanted to stay with Blogg – who named him Monte, after the ship.

In 1963 an explosion wrecked Tony's Place, a snack bar in Norwich's Exchange Street, at 3am and also damaged Thorns' Ironmongers and Sutton's Piano Showrooms next door. Two men were taken to hospital with burns to their face and hands.

1972 saw a major fire in the chip store of chipboard manufacturer Airscrew Weyroc Ltd at Thetford, destroying its contents. Three fire brigades fought the blaze with four engines; water had to be pumped from the other side of the A11, causing traffic hold-ups – the smoke also affected the A11. The blaze was soon under control, but the asbestos roof was badly damaged and 150 tons of chips were ruined.

1987 saw people reassured when the weathermen said we didn't need to worry about the weather... and then the storm hit. Villages in the Glaven valley – Langham, Letheringsett, Holt, High Kelling and Hempstead – were hit by hurricane-force gusts just before 9am. The wind was measured at over 100mph. Thousands of trees were blown down (including 25 oaks along the drive at Felbrigg Hall, and much devastation at Thetford Chase and Tyrrel's Wood at Pulham Market – fallen trees also blocked Castle Meadow in the centre of Norwich), and the overall damage was estimated at £1,000 million.

There were some narrow escapes: at Diss a lorry driver jumped from his cab as power lines came down, and seconds later a tree fell and crushed his cab, and at Tydd St Mary a tree came down just in front of a Wisbech fire engine. A falling chimney crashed into a Great Yarmouth guesthouse kitchen just after the owner had walked out of the room, and a three-year-old boy was rescued in Bradwell when a chimney collapsed, burying his bed in rubble. Caravans were damaged at Cromer and Runton – one was swept over the edge of the cliff. Waxham's mediaeval barn was blown down, and 40 oil rig workers were airlifted from a gas rig at Cromer when a diving vessel got too close. Roads were blocked and power lines came down.

As always in Norfolk, people mucked in to help. Breakdown truck drivers, farmers and people owning chainsaws rang the police to offer help clearing fallen trees.

17 October

In 1822, according to the 19th-century historian Charles Palmer, there was a bad storm and the revenue cutter *Ranger* was lost off Happisburgh along with its captain and crew.

1971 saw a family's lucky escape when their weekend cottage at Waxham – which had been in the family for more than 40 years – caught fire. Mr Bradshaw and his son heard a noise, saw smoke and realised that the thatched roof had caught fire. They tried to contain it with buckets while waiting for the fire brigade, but it spread too quickly. The chimney stack crashed down and fireman Jack Brackenbury managed to push Mrs Val Bradshaw clear of the debris; he was hit on the leg but only had minor injuries. Fireman Paul Brown was about to leave for his honeymoon when the warning sirens went – his honeymoon was a little delayed until the blaze was under control. The roof was destroyed and the bedrooms were damaged, but it was hoped the family could repair it.

19 October

Norwich Cathedral records refer to high winds in 1343, which sank the boat from Yarmouth near Cantley. The 18th-century historian Blomefield adds that 38 out of the 40 passengers drowned.

1858 saw a terrible tragedy when the sloop *Queen* was lost at Yarmouth. The ship beached at 2 o'clock in the morning, but no attempt was made to rescue the crew for a further five hours, despite them shrieking for help and showing red lights. Skipper John Watkinson was washed overboard with his three-year-old son George. Although his wife Mary Ann managed to keep hold of five-year-old John and 14-month-old baby Mary Elizabeth, John died from exposure. At the inquest, Mary Ann said that she'd been to sea for the previous 10 years; the *Queen* had less than 7ft of water in it and a boat could have been launched to save them. She was backed up by Robert Martin, the landlord of the Northumberland Arms pub, who said that a boat could have been sent but the beachmen refused to do it.

In their defence, Henry Hutchins, the coastguard chief, said that he'd fired lines to the ship but there was no response, and when they did finally get a line over to the ship, the *Queen*'s crew didn't fasten the ropes properly. The *Norfolk Chronicle* added that the water was too shallow for the lifeboats to travel over to the stricken ship – they'd needed flatter boats. The coroner's observation was that the beachmen showed 'an uncommon want of sympathy'.

The sloop *Kingston* was grounded the same night at Horsey, and *The Times* reported that the master and two crew were swept away. The master's wife was lashed to the rigging for safety, but when the beachmen finally managed to get to the ship she'd died from exposure.

1862 saw a major fire at Tillyard & Howlett's boot and shoe factory in Water Lane, St George's Colegate. The fire was thought to have originated in a defective drying store, and the alarm was raised when the fire was seen in the upper floors at 6.30am. The fire brigade used water from the river to fight the flames; £2,000 of hides were saved, but there was also £2,000 worth of damage (equivalent to nearly £130,000 in today's money).

20 October
1875 saw the 391-tonne barque *Young England* wrecked on the Cockle Sand at Great Yarmouth. Thirteen of the crew got into the ship's boat, but the holding rope snapped before the other four could get in. The boat capsized; the sole survivor of the boat managed to get to Caister, who sent the lifeboat out and rescued the captain and the remaining three crew clinging to the wreck.

21 October
1922 saw the 24-strong crew of a Newcastle steamer in a dramatic rescue off Scroby Sands. The crew were trapped for three days on the *Hopelyn*; for the first 24 hours, flooding in the ship cut off the crew from drinking water and food supplies. At low tide, they managed to get to the galley to rescue baked potatoes, onions and the water supply, but the Gorleston lifeboat was unable to rescue them. The crew took shelter in the wireless room on the boat deck, and finally the Lowestoft lifeboat managed to rescue them. Amazingly, *The Times* reported that the rescue 'took only 8 minutes in a strong wind and nasty sea'. The following month, the RNLI awarded its gold medal to Coxswain Swan of Lowestoft and Coxswain Fleming of Gorleston for the rescue of the 24 crew and the ship's cat.

1971 saw a fire in the paint dipping pit at Sprowston Ironworks. Employees were dipping a gate when the fire started; they tried to fight it with extinguishers, but the smoke was too much for them. Most of the damage was caused by smoke from the thinners in the paint.

22 October

In 1751 fire started at a lumberer's in Bridewell Alley, Norwich, at 1 o'clock in the morning; the flames were so bad that the prisoners were released from the Bridewell for their safety (including Peter the Wild Man). The fire destroyed everything in the Bridewell except the crypts and the flint wall, although the building was rebuilt by Thomas Dove in 1786.

1857 was a night of storms. The brig *Ontario* founded off Yarmouth with the loss of the captain, his wife and son, and 24 of the crew – only the chief mate, William Coates Robinson, escaped. The *Zillah* was lost at Winterton, with five out of the eight crew drowned. The *Norfolk Chronicle* estimated that 40–50 lives were lost on the coast that night – and they thought that more would have been saved 'had the lifeboats and apparatus been in an ordinarily effective condition'.

Gales also sank a ship in 1924; the nine-man crew of the Great Yarmouth steamer *Clansman* held on to the last moment before abandoning ship in their lifeboats. They battled for four hours to get to shore, and were rescued by Cromer lifeboat. Captain Thomas Spurling said the gale started near the Dudgeon lightship; the kegs of paint on the deck cargo broke loose and were swept overboard by the sea, and then the hatches came off and water poured into the ship. Some of the wreckage landed at Overstrand, including barrels of grapes, starch boxes and the ship's clock.

1940 saw a huge fire at the Back of the Inns in Norwich. The *Eastern Daily Press* reported that 'scores of shops and businesses were completely or partly destroyed by fire', which was discovered at 4am. Four large engines attended and water was pumped from the river at Duke's Palace bridge into a tank on the market place, but it was difficult to work in such a tight area. The flames were out by seven, but the area had to be cooled down for hours afterwards. The damage stretched from the Castle Hotel to the Haymarket pub, and then as far down as the Royal Arcade, where three shops were completely burnt out. Amazingly, there were no major casualties, although firemen and policemen suffered cuts from falling glass.

23 October

1967 saw the centre of King's Lynn evacuated when a flame suddenly shot up on Chapel Street at 9 o'clock in the morning. The flame was 10ft high at one point and burned for 45 minutes. Although workmen dug around the area later, they couldn't find the source. There was no leak from the gas mains, and it was thought that they must have hit a pocket of gas when they drove piles into the street.

24 October

In 1934 there was a huge fire at the silk factory of Fras. Hinde & Hardy on Botolph Street in Norwich. The alarm was given just before 2am and within half an hour the three-storey building was just a shell. Firemen managed to contain the blaze to the building; luckily, there was no wind, or the neighbouring dairy would have burned to the ground, too.

Flint wall of the Bridewell in Norwich, which survived the 1751 fire and was described by travel writer Celia Fiennes in 1698 as 'the finest piece of flintwork in England'.

25 October

1859 saw a violent gale. At Winterton two ships were wrecked and 13 lives lost. A sloop, the *James & Jessie,* was driven through the Britannia Pier at Great Yarmouth and severed it in two. Thirty shipwrecked seamen were lodged at the Sailors' Home in Great Yarmouth, and the remains of cargoes and ships spread across the coastline for miles.

1891 saw yet more severe gales. The schooner *Royal George* of Shoreham was driven on to the shore at Great Yarmouth opposite Nelson's Monument; lines were sent out by rockets, but the seamen on the ship apparently didn't know how to use them, so lifeboatman William Waugh went out to fasten a cradle line to the ship. On the outbound journey, the whip line gave way and he ended up in the sea. He managed to get to the shore and his colleagues pulled him out; fortunately, he was not hurt apart from some bruising. The lifeboat was launched and even though it kept filling with water in heavy seas they managed to rescue the four crew. However, there were several wrecks on the coast that night.

26 October

1772 saw a major storm at Blakeney. The hailstones were 4in in circumference and weighed 2oz; unsurprisingly, they broke most of the glass on the east side of the street.

In 1812, according to the 19th-century historian Charles Palmer, there was a major storm. Five ships were beached between Great Yarmouth and Lowestoft and a further three between Great Yarmouth and Caister; others foundered at sea.

1897 saw typhoid at King's Lynn; by 18 December there were 440 cases and 43 deaths. At least three quarters of the cases were traced to people drinking unboiled water from an impure supply. *The Times* said that 'conditions leading to the present enteric fever in that town are substantially the same as those responsible for the epidemic of 1892. Dr Bruce Low made a report for the local government board and thought that the typhoid cases were related to the public water service. The water came from chalk springs in Gaywood and were pumped into a tower in King's Lynn. He noted that two of the springs rose directly below Grimstone Churchyard (so, as with the parish pump in the Maddermarket, Norwich, the water went through a graveyard first), and that the river in King's Lynn 'receives slop-water, the soakage from privy pits and refuse heaps, the overflow from cesspools, and the contents of drains leading from water closets'. Nearer the town, gardens backed on to the stream – and people emptied the contents of their 'privy pit' on to them as manure. Frost, followed by melting snowfall and heavy rain, meant that all the effluent went into the water supply. The town council of King's Lynn applied to the local government board to amend its existing Waterworks Acts and improve the water supply to the town; in the meantime, the local government board suggested that they should supply boiled water or bring in clean water in carts and visit infected homes to disinfect them. Meanwhile, King's Lynn Sanitary Committee 'expressed great indignation' that it was reported in the London papers!

1930 saw a tragic accident, when a Great Yarmouth lodging house was gutted by fire and four of the nine men sleeping there were suffocated. Scots labourer Robert McLeman had been staying at the house in Row 47 for the previous five weeks during the fishing season; he woke around 5.30am, smelled smoke and roused the other men in his room. He also woke the men in the room above his, then smashed the window and threw his clothes and shoes out, jumped out after them, and put his clothes on while he was yelling for help. It was too hot for the firemen to enter the building, but as soon as they'd started to douse the flames the firemen got a ladder up to the first storey. They found one man face down and gave him artificial respiration before getting him to hospital. The fire brigade managed to stop the fire spreading, but it was too late for pensioners Chas Garwood, John Wilson and George Barrell and 45-year-old Herbert Hampling. At the inquest, the origin of the fire remained a mystery – nobody was allowed to smoke in the bedrooms, so a lit cigarette wasn't thought to be the cause.

27 October

Floods hit Norwich in 1614; 300 houses and eight parish churches were inundated. (See photograph on 9 August.)

Floods hit Norwich again in 1762, and the water rose 12ft in 24 hours – it was 15in higher than the 1691 flood (though also 15in lower than the 1614 flood). Three hundred houses and eight parish churches were inundated – St Mary's Coslany was flooded to a depth of 3ft. Houses and bridges were washed away; cattle and linen on the bleaching grounds fell victim to the water, and according to the *Annual Register* several people died. (See photograph on 26 August.)

In 1941 the Cromer lifeboat managed to rescue 44 men from a British freighter in heavy seas, but then the seas rocked the lifeboat, which nearly capsized. Five men were washed overboard, including Henry Blogg; four were pulled to safety, but Signalman Walter Allen died – the first and only death in the history of the Cromer lifeboat.

2002 saw storms hitting the county, with winds at gale force 8 to 10. RAF Marham recorded gusts of 76mph, and the Breydon Bridge at Great Yarmouth was closed. Hundreds of trees were blown down and over 50,000 houses were left without power for up to 15 hours – some unlucky families were without power for five days. Sadly, there were two deaths in the region; 12-year-old Christopher Vince pushed his brother out of the way of a falling tree at Costessey but tragically was hit by the tree, and 50-year-old lorry driver Eric White was also killed by a falling tree.

28 October
1882 saw a gale across the county; the River Yare overflowed and the whole marsh from Norwich to Great Yarmouth was under water. The brig *Light and Sign* of Whitby got into trouble just off Eccles; rockets with lifelines were sent out but were blown off course. Before the lifeboat could reach the ship, it had broken in two and the six or seven crew were lost.

29 October
There was a tragic accident in Norwich in 1774, when a fire broke out in a house near the pit in Ber Street; according to the *Norwich Mercury*, some children had set fire to dried bean stalks under the stairs during their mother's absence.

1880 saw a terrible disaster at Wells when the lifeboat *Eliza Adams* was lost, and only two of the 13 crew survived. The crew had gone to rescue the brig *Sharon's Rose*, which had been beached at Hunstanton and the crew of seven were in danger of drowning. They returned from the rescue to find the brig *Ocean Queen* riding anchor in a heavy sea. Although the crew were wet, hungry and tired, they were not prepared to ignore a ship in trouble; some of them agreed to change places with a fresh crew, but the majority insisted on going out. The Ocean Queen's anchor parted and the ship was driven on to the sands; because it was aground, the lifeboat couldn't get near enough to help, so the coxswain ordered the men to go back to shore.

But then the lifeboat was capsized in the heavy sea; although the boat was self-righting, the mast had been driven into the sand so it couldn't turn the right way up again. Twelve of the crew were washed out of the boat and 11 of them drowned. The man on the boat was tangled in the boat's lines until the mast snapped and the boat righted itself; the other survivor lay on the boat's rudder until washed ashore.

The *Ocean Queen* survived the storm; when the tide ebbed the crew was able to walk to the shore. The lost men of the Eliza Adams left 10 widows and 28 children, and they were interred on the 2 November apart from one, whose body was never found. At the inquest Captain Thomas Kew, one of the two survivors, said they all had cork lifebelts on; he explained that the heavy boots and lifeboat gear, when saturated with water, made it impossible for a lifeboatman to get into the boat without help.

A monument was built at Wells to commemorate the crew: Coxswain Robert Elsdon, Frank Abel, John Elsdon, William Field, William Green, Charles Hinds, George Jay, Charles Smith, Samuel Smith, John Stacey and William Wordingham.

1974 saw a huge blaze at the 18th-century Ingoldisthorpe Manor Hotel. Two guests climbed down knotted bedclothes to safety. Fifty firemen and eight pumps fought the blaze in high winds and managed to contain it to half the building. The roof caved in and one fireman was taken to hospital with a head injury and burns to his face, but he was later allowed home.

30 October

According to the 19th-century historian Charles Palmer, 1789 saw a severe storm, in which 80 fishing boats were lost between Yarmouth and Cromer and 120 bodies were washed ashore. A further 40 ships had been grounded between Great Yarmouth and Southwold, and there were wrecks everywhere along the coast. The severity of the losses persuaded the authorities to build two new lighthouses at Happisburgh.

Monument to the lifeboat crew lost in the *Eliza Adams* disaster. The inscription at the base reads 'In memory of eleven of the crew of the lifeboat "Eliza Adams" who lost their lives on duty in the disaster at Wells, October 29th 1880.' (Photograph by author)

In 1829 there was a serious fire in Norwich at Squire, Hills & Son's distillery in St Faith's Lane. The fire was discovered around 9 o'clock in the evening in the vinegar yard; it was thought that it started in the spirit room, under the mustard room and barley chamber; then it extended to the cask house and carpenter's shop. The *Norfolk Chronicle* described the first as 'most awfully grand in its appearance; when the flames burst forth the Cathedral, the Castle, the bridges and the river were illuminated in the most brilliant manner'.

Twelve to 14 pipes of vinegar were thrown on to the flames, and this stopped the vat shed (containing 21 large vats) catching fire. Squire, Hills and Son used their own engine and were joined by Captain Hodges and Seventh Dragoons. By 11pm, the fire was out, and all the stock in the mustard and barley rooms were burnt. It was estimated that the total damage cost £2,000 (the equivalent of over £135,000 in today's money).

1956 saw a major gale and a ship sinking off the Norfolk coast. The steam collier *Wimbledon* sprang a leak; Captain Arthur Hill, while trying to save the ship by plugging a ventilator, was washed overboard, and although he was rescued by the ship *Eleanor Brooke* and RAF Coltishall flew a doctor out to him, he didn't respond to artificial respiration. Mr Drummond, the first officer, took command; six crew remained on board while the others were taken off by the ship *Sydenham*. The *Wimbledon* sank at 2pm and the remaining crew were rescued by the Sheringham lifeboat.

1960 saw enormous rainfall across the county. Over the previous 24 hours, Taverham had 1.48in of rain, making the total for the month nearly 4in – the average was usually just over half that. A bridge also collapsed at West Bradenham, due to the heavy rain.

1965 saw a whirlwind at Heacham which wrecked a caravan, ripped off a garage roof and blew over several beach huts. The caravan site manager Mr Dix saw a dark sky, heard a loud wind and saw hail before the whirlwind struck.

31 October

In 1822 the chandling office of Staff & Chamberlin in St Martin at Palace, Norwich, was destroyed by fire. At 2 o'clock in the morning, the watchman discovered the fire and raised the alarm; several engines arrived but only one was well supplied with water. With lots of tallow and cotton in the building, the fire raged. The firemen and neighbours managed to contain it so that no buildings around were set on fire. One thatched roof on Quayside caught light and the thatch was pulled off before any more damage could be done. Several hogsheads of tallow and a large quantity of candles melted, and the wax and tallow ran down the street to the river 50 yards away. At daylight, people in boats managed to skim off more than a tonne of wax! It was thought that the cause was spark from a candle in the room where the cotton candle wicks were prepared, and the loss was estimated at £700 (the equivalent of over £50,000 in today's money).

The following year saw a major storm – which *The Times* said was the worst storm since 1696 – when '200 sail of colliers and others' were wrecked and all hands were lost in the bay of Cromer. At two in the afternoon, the coal brig *Duchess of Cumberland* came ashore near Cromer lighthouse; the lifeboat went out to rescue the crew of 16 but couldn't reach the brig. At four, the vessel split into two 'with a dreadful crash'; two men were found in the timbers and rescued from 'waters which washed the cliff with great violence', according to the *Norfolk Chronicle*. Land wasn't safe, either; at Corpusty, Robert Faircloth and two women felt the house move, got out, and saw it sink into the earth, 'leaving a vacuum of several feet deep above it which presently filled with water'.

November

November appears to be a month of storms and floods. The period before 1600 appears particularly bad in terms of damage, and the Great Storm of 1703 was probably the most damaging storm the UK has ever known – even more so than the October 1987 hurricane. And it's also the month when one of the saddest tragedies in lifeboat history occurred: the loss of the *Beauchamp*. James Haylett's words apply as much to the lifeboat crews in other stations around the county as to Caister: they never turn back.

1 November

In 1570 the 'All-Saints' Day storm' hit the east coast, and it was recorded as the worst storm known since that of 1 October 1250. There was much flooding and many people were killed in Europe as well as the UK.

According to the 19th-century historian William Richards, there was a 'dreadful inundation of the sea in 1613', which left all of Marshland and Wisbech under water.

In 1755 there was a violent earthquake followed by a tidal wave that wrecked 12,000 houses and left Lisbon in burning ruins for six days. The effects of the earthquake were also felt in Norfolk; according to the *Norwich Remembrancer*, people observed water in fishponds at Bracon and throughout the county became 'violently agitated' – some to the point of throwing out all the water, so the fish died.

There was a severe gale on the coast in 1855. *The Times* reported that the gunboat *Hind* was driven ashore at Cley; the *Norfolk Chronicle* added that many colliers in the Yarmouth Roads lost their anchors, resulting in several collisions.

1891 saw a serious fire at Sandringham House – the residence of the Prince of Wales. It started in a nursery bedroom near the top of the house; at 7.30am letter-carrier Mr Emmerson was walking across the park when he saw smoke. He told Police Constable Middleton and raised the alarm. Twenty years before, the house was pulled down and rebuilt; according to *The Times*, the second floor was deliberately built 'on iron girders and concrete' to make it fireproof. Men rode through Sandringham on horseback, shouting 'Sandringham House is on fire!' Sandringham fire brigade were joined by King's Lynn fire brigade; an hour after the alarm was raised the entire top floor was ablaze, and it could be seen for miles around. Meanwhile, men took valuables from the lower rooms on to the lawn and from there to a place of safety. The fire was under control by 11.30, but the roof had crashed in; the upper part and the second and third floors were gutted, with the contents destroyed, and the lower rooms were damaged by water. The damage was estimated at £10–15,000 – equivalent to between three-quarters of a million pounds and £1.25 million in today's money. One fireman was hurt by falling debris, but Dr Plowright of Lynn reassured everyone that the injury was minor.

In 1930 there was a huge explosion in Goldsmith Street, Norwich. Gas fitters had been making repairs to 73-year-old George Dawes's house. One of the neighbours was chatting to another, worrying about the smell of gas, when suddenly there was an explosion. The front wall of the ground floor was blown out, the party wall was demolished and the ground floor of Mr Dawes's house and his neighbour's was wrecked; windows in the Heigham area cracked as a result of the blast. One of the gas fitters rescued Mr Dawes, who was in bed on the ground floor and partly buried in debris; he and his 80-year-old wife were taken to hospital to be treated for shock. The gas fitters were also taken to hospital; William Gooch was suffering from concussion and abrasions, and Charles Coman had a broken arm.

1960 saw major storms across the county. At Mundford 1.56in of rain fell before teatime – most of this was in just half an hour! At Fakenham, lightning was counted at 15 flashes per minute over lunchtime; at King's Lynn, an inch of rain fell and the drains couldn't cope; the A47 was 9in deep in water at Little Fransham.

2006 saw one of the worst incidents of fish dying from natural causes, when strong north-westerly winds drove salt water into the Broads. Because of the warm weather, many fish stayed lower down the rivers, closer to the sea – so they were caught out when the sea water rushed in. The strong wind prevented the salt water going back out to sea, so salt levers in the river rose dramatically – just as they did on 2 March 1988. The Environment Agency estimated that tens of thousands of fish died; however, the fish barrier was raised at Potter Heigham in time to save thousands of fish that were over-wintering at the boatyard. Birds were also affected, as an RSPB reserve in the fens at Strumpshaw was under 3ft of salt water after the tidal surge sent salt water up the River Yare and it went over the banks – it was the third highest surge since January 1953.

2 November

A severe gale started in 1810 which lasted several days and several ships were wrecked; Manby's Mortar (see 18 February) was responsible for saving 18 lives. The *Norfolk Chronicle* reported that a 'shallop' laden with coals came ashore at Trimingham, but the crew of four were saved. Sadly, the brig *Anna* from North Shields was not so lucky when it came ashore at Mundesley, as it was a complete wreck within an hour and eight crew, along with a female passenger and several children, were lost. The *Trafalgar* of Cromer was also lost, with 15 crew, although the *Anna* of Sunderland, together with 14 crew and a female passenger, was saved at Cromer while 'buffetting the billows of a tremendous sea'. The *Norfolk Chronicle* reported that the 'beach from Wells to Yarmouth was covered with wrecks and strewed with the bodies of unfortunates' – but the crew of the *Eliot* was rescued at Yarmouth, again thanks to Manby's Mortar. *The Times* reported that he had 'a new construction' on his mortar, with a three-inch rope that held.

In 1922 there was a storm on the coast and the Peterhead herring boat *Cordelia*, which had been working from Great Yarmouth, started leaking. The crew knew they couldn't reach the shore, and although they tried to pump out the boat for four hours the bilge pumps couldn't cope. The engine room was flooded and it was too rough to launch their own lifeboat, which would have capsized or been stoved in. They hoisted a distress flag and the steamer *Mayberry* of Wick came to their rescue; despite the rough seas, they steered alongside so half the crew of the *Cordelia* were able to jump across, then came back to save the nine remaining members of the crew. The same day, the Leith motor drifter *Flourish* had a terrifying event; they were making for Great Yarmouth with herrings when their paraffin tank burst and sprayed on to the stove, which ignited. The crew of eight managed to put the fire out with buckets but were stranded; the Montrose drifter *North Esk* came to the rescue and towed them to Great Yarmouth.

1930 saw a tragedy in Thetford, when 42-year-old caddy William Noah Hewitt was struck by lightning on the golf links. The rest of his party were driven to the clubhouse by rain, but Mr Hewitt decided to stay outside until he found the ball. Sadly, he was struck on the top of his head by lightning and was killed instantly.

1938 saw the Spanish merchant ship *Cantabria* shelled in the North Sea by orders of General Franco; the shop sank 10 miles off Cromer, and 11 of the crew were taken to Great Yarmouth by the British steamship *Pattersonian*, while Captain Manuel Ardulles, his wife Trinidad, their two children and the ship's steward were rescued by the Cromer lifeboat.

1968 saw a major storm across the county. 30 yards of the sea defences were swept away at Overstrand, causing £15,000 of damage, and part of the beach subsided by 8ft.

3 November

1860 saw an explosion in the boiler of the steamship *Tonning* off Great Yarmouth, just after the captain had exchanged goods with another ship. The ship was carrying bullocks, sheep and lambs; the steamship's funnel hurled itself into the sea, and the main and spar decks were sliced open. Between 50 and 60 bullocks were scalded to death; eight people were blown off the ship and were never seen again, six died and several were injured.

1875 saw the iron Schooner *Harmston* stranded on the Middle Cross Sands at Yarmouth. It keeled over and the sea smashed the ship's boats and bulwarks. The crew took to the rigging; although surf was breaking all around them and they were nearly washed out, they survived the night. Caister lifeboatmen saw the ship's masts at daybreak and launched a rescue boat; they had to cross heavy surf over Scroby Sand. Although they couldn't board the ship, they managed to throw a line to them and dragged the crew one by one through the surf to the lifeboat, saving all seven.

1914 saw German ships bombard Great Yarmouth and Gorleston.

1969 saw a 200-acre blaze on the heath at Hevingham, which started at 10.30pm. The 40ft-high flames could be seen six miles away; at one point they were only 20 yards away from bungalows in Hevingham. However, the crews from nine stations had the blaze under control by 1am.

4 November

There were major storms in 1821 which saw 10 ships stranded, but all the crews were rescued. There was also a bad storm in 1836; 14 ships were lost in the harbour at King's Lynn and all the crews were drowned.

1902 saw a dramatic rescue when the 176-tonne schooner *Maggie Williams* crashed into the pier at Gorleston. The evening saw a tremendous sea with squalling winds; the ship's captain tried to sail into the harbour, but the wind and sea drove the ship on to the breakwater, then on to the pier, wrecking the three-masted iron schooner. The coastguards climbed on to the breakwater of the pier, even though there was a lot of spray, and threw lifelines to the crew, who each fastened one end of the rope round their waist. The seven crew were landed safely on the pier, although the boat was not insured and the crew lost all their possessions. Captain Tyrrell was the last to leave the ship; he went below decks to get some papers, but Gorleston boatman Charles Burgess saw the state of the ship, jumped aboard – regardless to the risk of his own life – and persuaded Tyrrell to leave. The damage to the pier was estimated at £250 (the equivalent of nearly £20,000 in today's money).

5 November

In 1795 there was a high wind across the county. Cranworth mill was blown down, and miller John Greef was killed; the mills at Aldeby and Bressingham were also blown down, although nobody was hurt. Sails were ripped off other mills in the county, including those at Cringleford, Mulbarton, New Buckenham and Poringland.

King's Lynn saw a lucky escape in 1928 when Neal's Restaurant at the Tuesday Market Place was gutted by fire. At 3.30am Mrs Neal smelled smoke; Mr Neal thought it was probably from the neighbour's chimney, but then he saw flames under the door of the drawing room. He helped his wife and daughter Winifred out of the house; his son Sidney had to jump from an upstairs window. The family dog sadly perished in the flames, despite attempts to rescue it, and Mrs and Miss Neal suffered burns to their feet. The fire gutted the building, and although it spread to the neighbouring roofs of Lloyds bank and Clarkson's solicitors the buildings were saved – albeit flooded with water.

In 1933 the Spring Gardens ballroom in Norwich was destroyed by fire. A ball had ended at midnight; an hour later, the place was locked and all was well. However, an hour after that the building was in flames. The fire brigade managed to confine the blaze so it didn't spread to Ranson's timber yard, but the flames lit the whole neighbourhood and all the band instruments were destroyed – only the iron frame of the piano was left.

1934 saw a major fire at the saw mill of Mann Egerton's school furniture factory on Aylsham Road, Norwich. The night watchman switched off the lights just after midnight, and all seemed well; an hour later, flames were seen and the alarm was raised. The fire brigade extinguished the blaze, but the damage was estimated at £10,000 (the equivalent of nearly half a million pounds in today's money).

1971 saw two big fires in the Swaffham area. A Dutch barn full of fodder and produce went up 'like a firebomb' at 7pm in Necton, and the blaze was visible for miles. A thousand tons of silage was lost, together with tons of hay, straw and potatoes – enough bedding for the herd of 160 cattle for the whole winter. The owner thought it was started deliberately as the silage had been there too long to have heated by itself. Two brigades fought to contain the blaze and stop it spreading to a huge steel and asbestos building only 20ft away, which was filled with grain and beans. Heat splintered the walls of the building, but the wind blew the flames in the opposite direction; just in case, two firemen stayed inside on top of 8ft of grain, ready with hoses.

Nearly an hour after the blaze started, there was another blaze in Swaffham, at the Downham Tyre Distributors. The Swaffham fire engine was already fighting the Necton fire, so the Watton and Dereham brigades attended. However, they couldn't save the two-storey building as the flames were fierce, fanned by the wind; the roof collapsed quickly, the building was gutted, and showers of sparks were blown all over the town. What really worried the firefighters were the oxygen and acetylene cylinders in the centre of the blaze; however, they managed to keep water playing on them until the fire was out and the cylinders cooled.

1976 saw a fire break out in baled straw that had been stored at the disused Regal Cinema in Watton. Five brigades turned out to fight the blaze; it was hard to reach the source of the fire as the building was smoke-logged. The fire was under control within two hours, but the fire crews had to spend another four hours damping down.

6 November

St Leonard's Day in 1519 saw a great flood in Norwich, which broke the bridge at Cringleford.

In 1794 rainfall caused the River Wensum to overflow in Norwich. The floods were 2–3ft deep in the streets; as usual, Heigham was the worst-affected area, and boats were rowed in the streets. The *Norfolk Chronicle* commented that it was the worst flood since 1762.

In 1942 Heacham Hall burned down. The alarm was given just after 8am and the fire brigade was there 10 minutes later, but the back of the hall was already blazing fiercely. Fifteen pumps from different fire brigades were there, using water at a rate of 2,500 gallons per minute from the lake. The fire was under control by noon, but the hall was gutted. It was thought that the fire started in the kitchen.

1922 saw a serious fire at Wramplingham; the owner woke at 5.30am to discover that his two-storey wooden workshops were ablaze. Neighbours helped fight the fire with buckets of water until the fire brigade arrived; they concentrated on the house, as the doors and windows had already caught fire. Wymondham fire brigade concentrated on the drying shed with timbers, but the workshops were gutted along with their contents – the top floor had contained benches and carpentry tools, and the ground floor had contained a car, van and carts. The cause of the fire was unknown.

7 November

1863 had seen major gales for the previous week, and several shipwrecks were reported in the weekend's newspaper.

1896 saw the steamer *Commodore* driven ashore at Sheringham in a gale. The local fishermen went to offer help, but the wind increased and stopped them reaching the ship, so they had to return to shore for the lifeboat, leaving the 14 crew on board. The lifeboat brought them back to safety; the gale became worse over the next day and the steamer became a total wreck. The wreck stayed on the beach for the next seven years, until Trinity House decided it was a danger to shipping and blew it up.

1971 saw a huge fire in a King's Lynn sawmill; there was a strong wind and the building was already well alight when the fire brigade was called at 4.50pm. Six pumps from four brigades fought the blaze and stopped it spreading to a timber store near the mill; by 9.30pm the flames were out, but three quarters of the building had burned down.

11 November

In 1099 there were high tides, causing major floods along the east coast. The *Anglo-Saxon Chronicles* mention that the flood occurred on the Feast of St Martin 'to such a height, and did so much harm, as no man remembered that it ever did before'.

Armistice Day 1927 held a shock for Norwich – just before the two-minute silence, the surface of Merton Road started sinking. The gulf deepened until there was a hole 30ft wide and 16ft deep; it spanned the whole road and went up to the garden gate on one path. The gas and water mains were broken, but luckily nobody was hurt. It was thought that the road was built over an old lime and gravel workings – and 1,500 loads of material were needed to fill the hole.

1932 saw a major fire at Maidment's shoe factory fire in Westwick Street, Norwich. The fire started at 9pm on the Friday evening and the *Eastern Daily Press* reported that 'the whole skyline of Norwich was silhouetted against a red glow deeper than a sunset' – it was even visible from Christchurch Road! Thousands of people came to see the spectacle, which included clouds of sparks and red smoke. Firemen were worried that Cushion's timber yards in Barn Road would be involved, but luckily they'd fireproofed their roof and the fire was contained by midnight.

1949 saw one of the fiercest fires in Great Yarmouth for years, which gutted the North Quay warehouse of Messrs Norton Bros, a wholesale tobacconist and confectioner. The warehouse was huge – 99ft by 40ft – and contained a full stock of tobacco, 50 cases of matches, two motor vans, a car, petrol and oil stores; aided by a strong wind, the fire gutted the place and lit up the riverside. People at Yarmouth saw a red glow in the sky and the *Eastern Daily Press* reported that some mistook it for the Northern Lights! The alarm was given just before midnight; although the fire brigade couldn't save the warehouse, they stopped it spreading to neighbouring houses and the nearby timber yard and corn merchant.

1966 saw a fire in the packing store at the Hartmann Fibre Factory in Great Yarmouth, which was full of egg trays and moulded pulp products. Flames burst through the roof and sides of the building and lit up the sky for miles. The fire crew were called out just after midnight; an hour later, the other buildings were out of danger and much was saved from the packing store.

12 November

According to the chronicler Holinshed, there were major floods in the county on 'the day after St Martin's Day' in 1236, coupled with a gale; many people in the east of England drowned. Chronicler Matthew Paris said that it 'deprived all ports of ships, tearing away their anchors, drowned a multitude of men, destroyed flocks of sheep and herds of cattle, plucked out trees by the roots, overturned dwellings [and] dispersed beaches'. The Elizabethan historian Henry Manship added that there were major floods around King's Lynn and Marshland 'the day after Martinmas day and for eight after'. The wind whipped up the tides so under the pressure of water the banks broke and water rushed in, 'so that of small craft, cattle and men great multitudes were destroyed'. The same thing happened again 19 years later, and in 1437 there was a breach in the bank near Wisbech, causing a flood over 4,400 acres of land.

There was a major fire in Thetford at the Bell Inn in 1845. Thirteen horses in the stables were lost, but the post boys in the hay loft escaped.

1904 saw St James' Hall in King's Lynn destroyed by fire. A ball had been held there the previous night, and there seemed to be no problem when the building was locked up. However, at 4am PC Jarvis saw a glow through the windows and raised the alarm. By the time the fire brigade got there, flames were licking through the roof; then a pipe in the steam fire engine burst, hampering efforts to fight the blaze. It couldn't be saved, but the fire was finally under control at 6am.

In 1962 Audrey Weeds had a lucky escape when she went outside to see why her TV set was not working – the power cable had been damaged by a fire, which started in a corrugated iron outhouse containing paint and spread to her kitchen. She snatched her four-year-old daughter to safety from 30ft-high flames, and a neighbour helped to rescue furniture. The fire brigade arrived swiftly and were able to save the bungalow, though the outhouse was gutted.

1972 saw a major storm across the county, with wind gusting up to 70mph. Many trees were brought down, and at Great Yarmouth two 28ft caravans were blown 20 yards away.

13 November

1775 saw a huge storm over the county. Somewhere between 2 and 4pm a fireball fell on Happisburgh church and the steeple cracked from top to bottom; large stones were thrown 80 yards. The storm lasted for 20 hours, and several ships were lost at Great Yarmouth.

1904 saw Porter's Sawmills in Fishergate, Norwich, gutted. It was thought that a bearing overheated on the Saturday, was overlooked, and the fire smouldered until the Sunday. Extensive damage of £3–4,000 was caused in just 45 minutes, and the glow was seen as far away as Earlham Road and Aylsham Road.

1977 saw a huge fire at Duffy & Son's haulage contractor depot at Fakenham. The alarm was raised at 3.46am, and the fire could be seen from great distances. Despite explosions from the asbestos roof, six crews contained the blaze and damped it down over the course of a few hours; however, 500 tons of hay and the building itself were destroyed.

14 November

1775 saw a major fire at Swaffham, when a servant left a window open in a room where the fire had just been lit. The Blue Bell pub and 30 houses were destroyed.

1783 saw a windmill blown down on the Denes at Great Yarmouth; the damage was estimated at £700 (the equivalent of over £62,000 in today's money).

In 1835 the extensive flour mills of Taylor & Tingay at Hardingham were destroyed by fire, with a total loss of £2,000 (the equivalent of nearly £160,000 in today's money).

1901 saw an absolute tragedy for the Caister lifeboat team, when their ship the *Beauchamp* tried to rescue a ship in a howling gale. It took 2¾ hours to get the lifeboat afloat; they were heading for Barber Sands when a heavy cross-sea hit the lifeboat and threw it back to the beach. Coxswain Aaron Haylett ordered the mizzen sail taken down; then the sea hit the lifeboat on starboard and it overturned. James Haylett Snr, aged 78, and his grandson Frederick heard cries. They rushed to the beach and James rescued his son-in-law Charles Knights, while Frederick rescued John Hubbard. They both managed to drag Walter Haylett to safety, but the

The market cross in Swaffham, built in 1781. (Photograph by author)

remaining eight crew died. They searched for bodies and found five; when the boat righted itself at ebb tide the following day they found the other three.

At the inquest, James Haylett – who had lost two sons and a grandson – said that, 'Caister Lifeboatmen never turn back and would have kept there if necessary till now to save men in distress. It was against the rule to go back when distress signals were shown.' Newspapers across the country reported this as 'Caister men never turn back'. James added that the boat was not at fault, though it 'would be helpful to have a stronger light on shore'. None of the crew had worn lifebelts, but James pointed out that if they had they still would have died because the

HEREUNDER LIE
THE BODIES OF NINE MEN OF CAISTER
WHO LOST THEIR LIVES IN THE LIFEBOAT BEAUCHAMP
ON THE MORNING OF NOVEMBER 14TH 1901
WHILST GALLANTLY RESPONDING TO
SIGNALS OF DISTRESS.
THIS MONUMENT
HAS BEEN ERECTED TO THEIR MEMORY
BY A LARGE NUMBER OF THEIR FELLOW COUNTRYMEN
WHO HONOURED THEIR BRAVERY AND PRESERVED THOSE
DEPENDENT UPON THEM FROM WANT.

Memorial to the crew of the *Beauchamp* at Caister. The inscription reads 'Hereunder lie the bodies of nine men of Caister who lost their lives in the lifeboat Beauchamp on the morning of November 14th 1901 whilst gallantly responding to signals of distress. This monument has been erected to their memory by a large number of their fellow countrymen who honoured their bravery and preserved those dependent upon them from want.' (Photograph by author)

lifebelts were cumbersome. In 1903 a memorial to the crew of the *Beauchamp* was erected in the cemetery of the Holy Trinity Church at Caister.

1943 saw a violent storm over Norwich; 15 barrage balloons were struck by lightning and burst into flames.

1974 saw a whirlwind hit Norwich, causing £5,000 of damage to goods at Comet's electrical warehouse when water came through a hole in the roof and 'ran down the walls like a waterfall'; the warehouse had to be pumped out. Fences were blown down, a caravan overturned, and the A47 at Thorpe was closed temporarily due to a dangerous building; reportedly, the pavements in the Long John Hill area were completely covered in tiles that had been ripped off roofs.

1993 saw Cromer Pier cut in half by a runaway rig in 60mph winds. The 100-tonne rig was ripped from its moorings, went through the pier, and severed power cables. The landward third of the pier was swept away, leaving a 30 metre gap, and the rig remains ended up in Overstrand. The winds were estimated at gale force 10, with gusts of gale force 12; in addition, there was heavy rain, and almost 2in fell at Norwich. Dozens of minor roads were flooded or blocked by trees; Breydon Bridge at Great Yarmouth was closed to traffic due to the high winds; and part of the roof at Norwich station was torn off. There were flood alerts across the region, and at Wells the flood barrier was used; 100,000 homes were left without power.

Cromer Pier on a calm spring day, 2007. (Photograph by author)

Cromer Pier facing the sea on a much rougher day, December 2003. (Photograph by author)

15 November

In 1646 there was a major flood in Norwich, and boats were rowed in many of the streets – including Magdalen Street, according to 18th-century historian Francis Blomefield. A flood at Itteringham destroyed the bridge. (See photograph on 9 August.)

1868 saw the Britannia Pier at Great Yarmouth damaged by a storm for the second time. The pier was originally 750ft long, but a sloop crashed into it during a storm in 1859 (see 25 October) and it was decided not to rebuild the last 80ft. Again, there was a huge storm; the collier *Sea Gull* of King's Lynn was parted from its anchor and the sea pushed it into the north side of the pier, ripping away 105ft of the centre portion. The crew of six escaped by climbing on to the pier.

1969 saw a double disaster in a force 8 gale when there was a blowout at a drilling rig and the supply ship *Hector Gannet*, which came to help evacuate the drilling rig workers, was blown against the platform. The ship holed and sank within five minutes, and two of the crew died. The ship *Boston Hornet* rescued the remaining five crew and 11 men from the rig, and a search and rescue helicopter from RAF Coltishall winched the survivors from the *Boston Hornet* on to the rig next door. Texan expert Paul 'Red' Adair was called out to cap the blown well.

16 November

1878 saw a huge flood across the county – Norwich was particularly badly hit. Heavy snow on 12 November was followed by a high tide, continuous rain and a rapid thaw. At 2pm on 16 November the river rose a foot in an hour. And then the river burst its banks at New Mills and flooded the streets. Heigham was under water to waist height and boats were rowed in St Martin's Street; carts and boats were used to rescue people from top floors. The floor and wheels

Norwich, Heigham Street, floods 1878. (Picture courtesy of Norfolk County Council Library and Information Service.)

were broken at the New Mills and there was much damage to machinery. Grout's silk mill was flooded, with several thousands of pounds' worth of silk lost, and the gasometer in Barn Road was surrounded by 3ft of water. The *Norfolk Chronicle* reported that Bullards' store room (aka Anchor Brewery on Westwick Street) was flooded, and the casks (which had been plugged) floated and were 'a seat of refuge for a great number of washed out rats'. Barnard & Bishop's iron works were flooded, which meant people were out of work for a time. St Mary's Churchyard was completely flooded; Cunnington's Saw Mills and Orchard Gardens were flooded to a depth of 4–5ft, wrecking new machinery that had only just been put in at a cost of £600 (equivalent to about £40,000 in today's money). Nearly 300 people had to leave their homes, and the Guildhall was opened as a storehouse, with 2,600 loaves of bread and hundreds of blankets lent by the barracks, jail and workhouses. Various schools were set up as places for flooded-out people to get food and drink, and 200 refugees were housed overnight in the governor's house at the jail.

It rained all the following day, but the *Norfolk Chronicle* reported 'the whole of Norwich turned out to look upon the great calamity and to render aid. From the Mayor to the humblest citizen, the one prevailing desire was to afford relief and comfort'. People and businesses gave money, food, clothing and coal to help those affected, and later that day the waters subsided by 2ft. Four days later, the water level had dropped by 5ft.

Sadly, four people died: 17-year-old George Churchyard, who was found in the warehouse of Wills the fellmonger in Heigham Street; Robert Rudrum from Carrow Works; 'carman' Thomas Arnup, who'd been out delivering coal and hadn't known about the city floods when he tried to come home – his horse was also drowned and his cart was smashed; and a bedridden woman named Barber in St Martin's, who died of shock when the water rose to the edge of the bed she'd lain on for the previous 12 months.

17 November

In 1783 the postmill on the South Denes at Great Yarmouth was destroyed by fire. The damage was estimated at £700 (the equivalent of over £62,000 in today's money).

1965 saw a major blaze at the gas works on Palace Plain in Norwich. Fire broke out in a retort house where the gas was made; the top 20ft of the building quickly caught light. The fire was caused by a blockage in the gas main by tar and liquid, which restricted the gas flow and so the gas caught fire. Two engines fought the blaze in the pouring rain; luckily not much damage was done.

18 November

In 1925 there were lucky escapes in the busy thoroughfare of King Street, Great Yarmouth, when the top of an electric sub-station was thrown off. A woman and two girls were treated for shock and minor wounds. The cause of the explosion was not known, though the experts' theory was that sewer gas had accumulated and was lit by a spark. Witnesses saw a flash, and then concrete around the area was forced up; afterwards, they could also smell gas.

1962 saw a big fire in the three-storey storage block at Johnson & Sons Ltd's clothing factory in Great Yarmouth. The alarm was raised at 5.30am and four engines made their way there. The fire started out on the ground floor, which contained oilskins, finished material and linseed oil in drums; much oil had soaked into the floor so the room was quickly ablaze. Fireman Bert Bentley fell through a fanlight in the roof and was taken to hospital; the fire crews were successful in containing the blaze.

1974 saw severe flooding at Sporle; some homes were marooned and the A47 was flooded. Heavy rain also broke water tanks at a trout farm, and a quarter of a million rainbow trout worth £15–20,000 were washed into the River Glaven and lost.

19 November

In 1770 there was a flood in Norwich, 4in deeper than the flood of 27 October 1762. St Mary's Coslany was flooded to a depth of 3ft, despite the precautions taken of banking up the churchyard after the 1762 flood, and a house near the churchyard was washed away. Other houses were flooded up to a depth of 9ft.

In 1775 there was a major fire in Swaffham; between 22 and 24 houses were burned.

1971 saw a big blaze in the sack cleansing room at Reckitt & Colman in Norwich. It started at 5am and 20 men fought the blaze with four engines; nobody was hurt, though much stock was damaged.

21 November

1971 saw a gale across the county which lasted for two days; Wells had a force 8 gale, gusting to force 9, which scoured the beach and brought many trees down, as well as taking 3ft of the sand dunes. Gorleston beach was also eroded, leaving behind a mini cliff of sand 6ft high. Oulton Broad caravan park was flooded to a depth of 18in. The following day, villages were blacked out as power lines were blown down; over 1,000 people were without a phone in the Norwich area.

22 November

1927 saw a dramatic rescue after a weekend of storms, with winds of 42mph and gusts of 50mph followed by heavy rain. A large steamer was spotted sinking three miles off Cromer; it struck Haisbro Sands, split in two and the two halves drifted apart during the morning. The Cromer lifeboat went out and discovered that the ship was the Dutch oil tanker *Georgia* of Rotterdam. Nobody was on board and the small boat was missing.

Eventually it was discovered that the 16 crew on the stern were picked up by the Dutch steamer *Trent*; the 15 men left on the fore of the ship took refuge in the wheelhouse, where they were crammed together like sardines. It was nearly 40 hours until they were rescued – and they had no food or drink because the mess room was amidships and went with the stern of the ship. According to *The Times*, the men spent their time 'chatting, smoking and sleeping as best they could'.

The Gorleston lifeboat crew tried a rescue but couldn't do anything in the heavy seas; it took five attempts before they could get a rope across the ship, and then a huge wave dropped the lifeboat into a trough and the rope snapped. Also, the lifeboat's engine was not working properly, and they'd been out for 21 hours when the exhausted crew returned to Gorleston to get oil to pour on the waters around the *Georgia*.

At 4.30 that afternoon, as the light was fading, the Cromer lifeboat got near enough to try a rescue – and then one of the *Georgia's* cargo tanks burst open and the crude oil calmed the waves. Henry Blogg, the coxswain, decided that the job had to be done before dark; he manoeuvred the lifeboat as close as he could, and then the sea slammed the lifeboat against the wreck. The lifeboat was damaged but seaworthy, so Blogg and his men threw ropes which the *Georgia's* crew secured on the deck to keep the lifeboat steady. The stranded crew then jumped 10ft down into the lifeboat, one at a time in order of age (though Captain Henry Kissing insisted on being last). The lifeboat crew were able to give the exhausted sailors bread and cheese, and brought them in safely to Cromer.

But while the Cromer lifeboat rescued the men, the Gorleston weren't aware of this and went back to find them – and were nearly injured themselves. Coxswain James Stubbs said that at 3am they were nearly run down by a large boat: 'This boat seemed to come from over the sands. We could see the line of the broken water and could hear the surf. When we saw the big boat approaching slightly to the north of the wreck we burnt six or seven blue flares and did our best to attract her attention but apparently without success. Ultimately we had to start up the engine and run for it. I cannot understand how she managed to get across the sands without grounding.'

Compass on the promenade at Cromer in front of the pier, showing the direction in which the lifeboat had to travel on major rescue missions. The *Georgia* is represented by the seventh line anticlockwise from the far right. (Photograph by author)

The RNLI awarded Cromer's coxswain Henry Blogg his second gold medal, and a bronze medal to William Fleming of the Gorleston crew.

23 November

In 1829 Cromer Hall caught fire. It had cost £12,000 to build, and had just been finished but not furnished – and George Wyndham had only insured it for £2,500. The only occupants were the gamekeeper and his wife, who were in the north wing of the hall; at midnight, they discovered the fire in the centre and south wing, which formed a sheet of flame. The engine came from Felbrigg and the townspeople of Cromer came to help – but sadly the roof fell in and the place was gutted. The cause remained unknown.

24 November

The day after the Cromer Hall fire, there was a severe gale at Great Yarmouth. Five ships were blown ashore; one was blown on to the north sand and was wrecked. Eight people died, although one was saved; another three died on a fishing smack.

1976 saw a fishing boat sink and two others were swept from their moorings when the 144-tonne coaster *Spithead Trader* was caught on a flood tide and carried up the river to Great Yarmouth bridge. It was stuck there for 20 minutes until it was taken away by a tug.

25 November

1774 saw a major storm along the coast from Yarmouth to Leith. It was the most severe wind for 30 years, and there was much snow. A dozen ships were lost, and a wherry sank in Breydon Water, drowning two.

26 November

The 'Great Storm' of 1703 was the worst ever experienced in England, lasting for four days, and Daniel Defoe described it in his work *The Storm 1703*. He said it blew with such fury on 30 November that people were afraid to go to bed. They were also afraid to leave their houses in the day, because so many bricks, tiles and stones were being smashed about by the wind. Church steeples were blown down, windmills caught fire, there was a bad fire in Loddon and up to 500 ships sheltered at Yarmouth. After the storm, the price of tiles trebled.

27 November

In 1932 a gale hit the Norfolk coast. Winds at Cromer were measured at 70mph, and the ketch *Matilda Upton* got into major difficulties when the topmast was blown away. The lifeboat went to the rescue, despite the fact that water swept over its bows, and towed the ketch to Great Yarmouth. The gale also smashed 100 yards of promenade at Hunstanton, where slabs weighing a quarter of a tonne were thrown into the sea. The cliff path was washed away at Bacton, and the beach scoured at Mundesley.

1965 saw half the tower at Wighton church come down in a gale. The vicar thought that the tower had been hit by a thunderbolt, a few weeks before, as he'd seen some cracks in the masonry. The gale finished the thunderbolt's work and hundreds of tons of masonry fell; the bell and belfry were hanging precariously, and there was a danger of more stone falling, so a demolition crew was brought in to deal with it. A new tower was built within the ruins of the old one in 1975–76.

28 November

1883 saw a fire in the boiler shop at Burrell & Sons in Thetford. Men who'd been working late that night noted the fire at 4am; it had started when the furnace used for heating rivets lit some combustible material stored nearby and spread to dry timber. Men climbed on the rooftops to take off roof coverings in an attempt to stop it spreading; although the fire brigade managed to contain the fire, the wood store was destroyed and several

The church at Wighton with its restored tower. (Photograph by author)

thousands of pounds' worth of damage was caused.

In 1897 there was a huge storm on the coast, which some newspapers called the 'Great Rage'. At high tide, the Marine Parade at Great Yarmouth was badly hit; several seats and shelters on the sea wall were carried away, and the new beach gardens – which had only been opened the previous summer – and the south gardens were flooded and ruined. The fishing stage at Britannia Pier was partially demolished; the north side of the jetty sustained considerable damage. The river burst its banks to flood offices, houses and warehouses on the quay to a depth of 3ft, and the railway lines were under 2–3ft of water.

The storm also breached sandhills at Horsey, and the sea poured on to the marshes. Between Haisborough and Bacton, five ships were wrecked and all the crews were drowned. The ketch *Lord Wolseley* from Shields collided with the Cockle Lightship on its way to Yarmouth and was lost with its three crew; the brig *Pennine* sank at Hemsby with all hands; and the *Vedra* of Sunderland went ashore at Bacton, losing the master, the mate and one seaman. Miller David Jarvis spent the night on the top floor of Salthouse tower mill – partly to escape the rats that had come into the mill for shelter!

29 November

According to the Elizabethan historian Henry Manship, in 1530 there was a storm 'as if from hell' over England, which was very destructive on the Norfolk coast; it started the day Cardinal

Wolsey was seized with a fatal illness (the last week of November 1530) and remained until his death a few days later.

In 1836 there was a severe gale, which blew down the circus building at the De Caux Gardens in Norwich. An oak tree at Necton – for which the owner had been offered 120 guineas, back in 1812 – had two branches each the size of trees blown off it; barns were blown down in Necton, Ashill and Bradenham. Sadly, the windmill at Carbrooke belonging to Robert Homes was wrecked and his son was killed during the gale. The tower mill at Bressingham lost its cap and sails and the friction caused by the wind set the mill on fire, but luckily workmen were able to put the blaze out. The mill at Acle also lost its cap and the shaft was displaced, but luckily it didn't catch fire and it was repaired at a cost of £100 (the equivalent of over £7,000 in today's money).

1965 saw huge gales across the region, which were measured at 60mph inland and 95mph in the North Sea. At Sheringham, a chimneystack weighing several hundredweight blew down and just missed a woman. At Cromer a 12ft chimneystack smashed into the roof of the Grand Hotel and 1.2 tonnes of rubble landed in one room; luckily it was unoccupied at the time. The decking at Cromer Pier was also damaged.

30 November

1614 saw the 'St Andrew's Flood' in Norwich; although it wasn't as bad as the flood of 2 February 1570, it was the deepest flood in the city until the 1912 floods, which were 15in higher. (See photograph on 26 August.) According to the 18th-century historian Frances Blomefield, the sea came 12 miles inland; nobody was killed but there was much damage to churches, cellars, houses and tannery yards.

Spectators at the equestrian performance in the Orchard Gardens, Norwich, got more than they bargained for in 1857, when the supports of the gallery gave way and the structure containing 300–400 people fell down. People were thrown out of their seats but amazingly nobody died or had any serious injury.

1866 saw a violent downpour and a huge storm. At Great Yarmouth, the fishing smack *The Friends* was blown off its anchor; two of the eight crew got into a boat, but it capsized. Their comrades managed to get a lifeline to them; then the smack was grounded on the sands. All eight of the crew were rescued by rocket line. At Caister, the schooner *Coronation* sank; the lifeboat crew managed to rescue the three crew members.

December

December will be remembered as the month of the tornado that hit Long Stratton.

It was also a tough month for Norwich in 1266, when the Disinherited Barons sacked Norwich. The barons had fought with Simon de Montfort against Henry III to set up the first parliament and have an active role in running the country, but when de Montfort was killed in 1265 his supporters were forced back to Kenilworth Castle and then to the Isle of Ely. They used it as their base and sacked the surrounding areas; they reached Norwich in the middle of December 1266 and sacked it for a day and a night, carrying off 140 carts and wagons full of loot.

The county as a whole saw the 'great winter' of 1607, where three rivers around Yarmouth were frozen for 40 days; the big freeze started in December and didn't thaw until February.

1 December

In 1557 Great Yarmouth was flooded to the depth where people were able to row boats on the streets.

1860 saw an explosion at Marrison's gunmaker shop in Little Orford Street in Norwich. There were 40lb of gunpowder as well as fireworks and ball cartridges in stock that day because there was more demand on Saturdays. Mr Marrison went next door to see his neighbour, and three minutes later all the gunpowder exploded. Charles Hill, Marrison's shop boy, was killed instantly, and the shop front was wrecked. Franklin's photographic shop next door was wrecked, and the photographer's sister sitting above the shop was badly injured. Boston the pawnbroker's party wall was damaged and lots of glass was broken; the windows of the Bell Hotel were shattered, as were the windows of the Napier tavern on the other side of Marrison's, and Kemp the saddler's opposite had its shop front blown in. Neighbour Mrs Dady was in her house with her children at the time of the explosion; sailor Robert Crabtree rescued them and threw them into street, where bystanders caught them.

1866 saw the storm of the previous day turn to hurricane proportions. The *Norfolk Chronicle* described it as 'a hoarse sustained roar that was awful to listen to'. At 9pm the brig *Arnon* collided with the brig *Oregon*, and the crews were rescued by the Gorleston lifeboat. The crew of five got off the French schooner *Ameline* before it went down, but Captain Trevernie went down with the ship – crew members confided that he'd been 'very unfortunate' in his time and had lost several other ships, and this time he just couldn't face the owners to tell them he'd lost yet another ship. A new gasholder containing 100,000cu ft of gas and surrounded by massive iron columns was blown over at Yarmouth Gas Works; the gas tank burst and the gas escaped. Luckily there were no buildings with lights nearby so the gas didn't catch light. The *Norfolk Chronicle* reported that after the explosion the gas tank looked like 'an immense piece of crumpled brown paper'.

1867 saw a major storm; the wind was at hurricane level and blew the sea on to the shore many feet above its normal level. There was much flooding in Great Yarmouth, along with sharp falls of snow and hail. The tide came up and inundated low-lying land from the harbour mouth to the north river as far as Reedham. Floods were at depths of 1–3ft in houses, and boats were rowed in the high road. At the North and South Quays, it was impossible to tell where the river ended and the street began, and the marshes were badly flooded. That night, the *George Kendall* from Liverpool and 23 crew (including the captain and one of the owners) became stuck on the Cross Sand at Great Yarmouth. They took to the ship's boats, and the Gorleston lifeboat was launched. The lifeboat picked up all the crew bar the pilot Mr Bass, who was towed behind them; it was a tight fit, with 38 people in the boat. Then the boat collided with the lugger *James and Ellen*; the lifeboat capsized, and all bar four of the *George Kendall* crew were drowned, along with six of the lifeboat crew. By horrible coincidence, the accident happened in almost exactly the same spot as the January 1866 tragedy.

2 December

In 1763, according to the 19th-century historian William Richards, there was a high wind and a high tide; many ships were wrecked near King's Lynn, and cattle and sheep were drowned in Marshland and near Snettisham. Mr Barrel and Mr Corfe of Snettisham lost 800 sheep each.

1863 saw a gale which lasted for two days; more than 20 ships were wrecked and 144 men drowned at Great Yarmouth. There was also much damage inland; in Norwich, a 45ft-tall chimney at Mr Burrell's horse-hair manufactory (known as Havelock Steam Mills) in Havelock Street crashed down. Foreman Mr Betts had a narrow escape, as he was standing under a beam when the chimney brickwork smashed on to it; the beam held and saved him. The *Norfolk Chronicle* reported that many other chimneys and gable ends of houses were blown down.

1940 saw an air raid over Norwich with high explosive bombs dropped. People were killed in St John Street. A family at Orchard Tavern in Mountergate Street had an incredibly lucky escape when a bomb exploded as they ran into the cellar; a beam over them held, and they came out unhurt.

3 December

Trowse mills burned down in 1762, resulting in £2,000 of damage (the equivalent of over a quarter of a million pounds in today's money).

1977 saw a building in Pottergate, Norwich, badly damaged by fire. A printer, dentist and a record shop were affected; thousands of pounds' worth of stock was ruined at the record shop, which had just bought in extra stock ready for the Christmas rush. The fire was fought by two Green Goddess army machines.

1990 saw a huge fire in Thetford, where 30 firemen from four crews spent an hour fighting the 20ft-high flames. The alarm was raised at 6.30am when a motorist saw flames coming from the roof of a building that housed a Chinese restaurant, a charity shop and the Bury Free Press. The fire started in the kitchen of the takeaway; the cook tried to put out the blaze but the flames were too strong, and the fire spread through extraction ducts. A neighbour 100 yards away heard crackling fire but thought it was rain against a window. The firemen were able to save the building, which dated back to the 17th century and stood on a 12th-century crypt.

1999 saw storms across the county, with gales up to 60mph. The power was out at Diss, and Breydon Bridge at Great Yarmouth was closed to high-sided vehicles. Schoolchildren had a lucky escape when a tree fell on to their bus on the A143 between Haddiscoe and Beccles; amazingly, the driver and children all walked away unhurt.

4 December

In 1950 the Ostend trawler *Yarmouth* was wrecked on Scroby Sands – and years later was actually swallowed by it! When the distress flares showed, the Gorleston lifeboat turned out; the sea was so rough that the first rescue attempt was abandoned, but at the second attempt the lifeboat got there. Despite the fact there was a snow squall and visibility was nil, and the sea was breaking over the trawler, the crew jumped one by one to safety. Coxwain Bert Beavers called it a 'tricky job' – a typical understatement from a brave Norfolk lifeboatman. They managed to take the 2,000-stone cargo of fish off the trawler, but it was stuck fast and nobody could shift it. The January 1953 storms made the sands shift and sucked the trawler into the middle. By 1986 just the top of the cabin and part of its mast was visible, but nowadays nothing at all can be seen of the wreck.

1958 saw a major fire at the three-storey warehouse of H. Thompson & Sons Ltd in Rosary Road, Norwich. The *Eastern Daily Press* called it the biggest city blaze in months; the flames rose 50ft high and the heat could be felt 100 yards away, but luckily there was no wind or the carbide and petrol store or cellulose shop might have caught fire – or the petrol station 50 yards away, or the gas-holder 80 yards away. The fire in the wholesale factories began in a basement just after 11am, but the fire brigade managed to confine it to the warehouse.

1960 saw a weekend of floods – there were 20 continuous hours of rain in Fakenham alone. The Caister lifeboat managed a difficult rescue when the engine of the 18-tonne fishing boat *Gloamin' N* broke down in high seas and gale force winds. Journalist Robert Rodwell bought the boat and converted it into a home for his wife and baby; he was sailing it from Hull to Thames with two others when they got into difficulty. Despite the fact that the boat was bigger than the lifeboat, the lifeboat managed to tow it safely in.

5 December

1766 saw a fire at the fish-house of William Boult in Great Yarmouth; although the fire was extinguished, there was much damage.

1929 saw the worst gale of the year at Great Yarmouth; the wooden steam drifter *Tryphena* was wrecked on the North Sands 100 yards from shore when it returned to port with its catch. It took rescuers six attempts with rockets before they could get a line to the boat and haul the 10 crew, one at a time, across the rough seas. The captain later said that the boiler tubes gave out so they couldn't raise steam; they were being towed by another Yarmouth drifter, the *Oswy*, but the rough seas and 90mph winds snapped the rope. There were more severe gales the following day, and winds of 60mph were recorded at Cromer.

2002 saw an environmental disaster on the east coast; more than 600 birds covered in oil were collected on the Norfolk and Suffolk coast between Great Yarmouth and Lowestoft. The slick mainly affected guillemots, razorbills, great crested grebes and red-throated divers. Shipping minister David Jamieson thought that the oil might be from a wreck dating back to World War Two, as the oil in the sea was heavily weathered.

6 December

There was a midnight fire at Diss in 1828 which gutted the garage shed containing several cars and lorries belonging to W.D. Obitty & Co., motor engineers. The 90ft by 40ft structure of corrugated iron and wood contained 16 lorries. All was well when the building was locked at 7.30pm, but four hours later a passer-by saw flames and raised the alarm. By the time the fire brigade reached the building, it was a raging furnace and they just couldn't get in. The windows of the United Methodist Church were broken in the heat and the School Hall windows were burned out, but luckily no other neighbouring properties caught fire and nobody was injured. The fire was out by 4am, though the fire brigade stood by until 7.30am; there was no clue as to what had started the fire.

1965 saw £3,500 damage to Happisburgh sea defences, after a week of gales; 150ft of the revetments were torn up.

7 December

1706 saw a bad flood in Norwich, according to the *Norwich Remembrancer*.

Norwich had its sixth flood in two months in 1841, after 24 hours of solid rain; the marshes were completely flooded.

1935 saw fog and ice across the county; there had been 12 degrees of frost the previous night, and the ice was thick enough for skaters to take to the Westwick Pond in North Walsham. The drifter *Young Sam* ran aground on the Barber Sands at Great Yarmouth at 9am, but the Cockle lightship didn't notice it until 11.30am because of the fog. Caister lifeboat was summoned and almost landed on top of the ship because the crew couldn't see the drifter in the fog until they were within 15 yards of it; they stood by until the ship managed to refloat until 3.30pm.

8 December

1872 saw a storm which turned into a hurricane. Chimney stacks came tumbling down – sometimes, as in the case of one home in Pottergate, Norwich, the chimney brought the roof down with it. Two elderly women in an apartment had a lucky escape when the chimney from Chamberlin's in the Market Place fell on their building. Trees were uprooted and there was much damage to buildings, although no lives were lost inland. Great Yarmouth reported blinding snow along with the wind, and the *Norfolk Chronicle* listed a huge number of ships as lost.

In 1931 there was a dramatic rescue at Great Yarmouth; the ketch *Harwich* from Hull was taking tiles to Norwich when it was wrecked, and the crew of three were rescued in heavy seas. As the mate, Tom Wilson, was jumping into the lifeboat, he fell into the sea; however, he caught the lifebuoy and lines thrown to him and the rescuers managed to pull him to safety.

1937 saw subsidence in Ber Street, Norwich. The foundations of the three-storey shop and house belonging to butcher W.D. Waldrich broke down, leaving a 9ft-deep hole, and there were cracks on the front and back walls; Mr Waldrich and his family left the building and managed to save their downstairs furniture and goods, but the building was demolished by the end of the month.

10 December

There was a huge fire in Colegate, Norwich, in 1925, at the Flextoe Company (toe puff manufacturers) and the Bacon House garage at the corner of Calvert and Colegate Streets. Customers in the Black Boys pub opposite saw the flames around 8.45pm and phoned the fire brigade; the firefighters managed to get the cars out of the garage before they exploded, and the neighbours in St George's Street were evacuated for safety's sake. Luckily, the fire brigade managed to contain the fire and save the ancient Bacon's House, although the garage and the toe puff manufacturers were both gutted. But they had a narrow escape – if the fire had reached the celluloid (used in the manufacturing of shoes) contained in 10 gallon drums at the Flextoe Company's premises, the resulting explosions would have spread the fire to the other shoe manufacturers in the area.

11 December

There was a major flood in the west of the county in 1852. According to *The Times*, around 8,000 acres around the area of Southery and Feltwell were flooded to a depth of between 4 and 6ft, and 100 families had to leave their homes. Losses were estimated at £25–30,000 – the equivalent of between £1.9 and £2.4 million in today's money – and it was thought that it would take four months to drain the land.

1923 saw dense fog on the coast – and a disaster at Happisburgh. At around 11am, the crew of the Haisbro Light Vessel crew of LV heard three blasts in warning from a steamer, an answering blast, then the sound of a collision: the *Livorno* of Grimsby had collided with steamer *Rose Marie*. The *Rose Marie* sank, but luckily the crew was rescued and taken to safety by the *Livorno*.

In 1940 Carrow Hill in Norwich saw another air raid. Eighty-three-year-old William Warnes was blown out into the street while he was still in bed; he was not badly hurt, but sadly his granddaughter was killed in the raid.

12 December

In 1762 a bad high tide resulted in many ships being wrecked, and many cattle and sheep drowned.

1990 saw the whole village of Eccles evacuated, and at one point the villagers feared it might be a repeat of events 400 years before, when the original village was washed away by the sea. It was the biggest flood alert since the 1950s, and the flood sirens sounded at Great Yarmouth. The tide advanced until there were only inches of protection left – and then, to everyone's relief, it turned.

13 December

In 1933 the Cromer lifeboat crew were involved in a very daring rescue. The barge *Sepoy* sent up a distress call shortly after dawn at Overstrand; because the motor lifeboat was out on another call, a rowing lifeboat was launched. However, the seas were so heavy that the boat kept being thrown back to the beach. Hundreds of people watching from the cliffs saw two men climb into the rigging – and over 100 men and women helped to drag the lifeboat along the beach. Meanwhile the rocket brigade got a line over the ship. The lifeboat was finally launched, but was swept over the breakwater; and when it reached the *Sepoy* it was driven back on to the shore and broke the line to the ship.

The barge was grounded about 150 yards from Cromer beach, and despite the severe weather Coxswain Henry Blogg went to the rescue. The lifeboat was driven back from the barge twice, and Blogg realised that the boat had a hole in it, so he simply drove the lifeboat over the wreck and grabbed the mate from the rigging, then performed the same risky manoeuvre to grab Captain Hemstead. Blogg was awarded a gold medal for his work, and there's also a stained-glass window in St Peter's Church, Cromer, commemorating the rescue.

The memorial window in St Peter's Church, Cromer, commemorating the rescue of the *Sepoy*. (Photograph by author)

1957 saw Brandon Parva school burned down. Flames were noticed at 3.30am and the Wymondham fire brigade arrived 20 minutes later – but the school was already a roofless shell.

In 1974 Friday 13th saw storms hit the county. Two ships sank – including the London coaster *Biscaya,* which sank after colliding with a barge – and one caught fire.

14 December
1990 saw a million pounds' worth of damage caused in Long Stratton in the space of 10 seconds when the tornado hit. Incredibly, only one person was injured as chimneys and roof tiles were ripped off buildings and car windows were smashed by the 60mph wind. One Stratton man described it as everything 'going white then whoosh'. The A140 was blocked, one car was rolled over, signs were blown 100 yards off a building and the florist's stock was blown down the street. The Swan pub lost five windows and 90 percent of its roof; a chimney smashed through the roof of the Angel pub, and manageress Jackie Unwin's living quarters were wrecked.

15 December
1866 saw the old lighthouse at Cromer topple over the edge of the cliff; the lighthouse was immediately buried by a large cliff fall.

16 December
1964 saw a huge blaze at Dereham, where flames leapt 40ft above the five-storey flour mill of H.C. Stammers & Co. at Dereham. The alarm was raised at 7.30pm and the fire was under control one and a half hours later; six engines from five brigades attended, and the combination of fire barrier walls and good firefighting meant the blaze was confined to a mere fifth of the building.

17 December
In 1942 there was a huge fire at Beaton's furniture store on Farmer's Avenue, Norwich, causing several thousands of pounds' worth of damage. All was well when the managers locked up for the day, but then the fire started on the first floor and spread. The building was steel-framed with much glass, which was smashed by the heat.

In 1973 the five-man crew of the salvage ship *Deep Venture* had to abandon ship when their boom came adrift and sent the mast crashing into the ship. The *Deep Venture* took on water incredibly fast, and the crew ended up in their dinghy. They managed to stay afloat for an hour in 60mph winds and 30ft waves as rescuers headed towards them; finally a Dutch rig came near enough to reach them, and as a wave took the dinghy up they jumped from the dinghy on to the ship.

19 December
1770 saw a major storm that went on for two days. Trees were blown down and made roads impassable. In Norwich, part of the city wall fell down between the Brazen Doors and Ber

Street and crushed a new house. A stable in Bishopsgate belonging to farmer John Chase was blown down; four horses were buried alive in it, but luckily they were rescued. Two brick sheds were blown down outside St Stephen's gate. Two cottages were wrecked at Easton, and the storm across the county smashed windows – including windows in churches – and tore lead from church roofs. At Yarmouth, a mare was killed by lightning at the Bear public house. At Happisburgh, Postwick and Strumpshaw windmills were blown down. Ships were wrecked at Happisburgh, Sea Palling and Caister, and one collier was lost with all 20 hands.

1927 saw a fiery spectacle at Yarmouth. The steamship *Oscar*, laden with timber bound for Jewson's in Yarmouth, caught light at 2am; the fire spread up to the deck cargo, and it was too hot for the crew to reach the rocket flares. The steamer anchored on Yarmouth Roads, then the 23-strong crew took to the boats. It was so hot that even tugs couldn't go alongside, and the *Eastern Daily Press* described the burning boat as being 'like a huge torch'. The steamer burned for five days and nights, and finally was sunk by a controlled explosion.

1971 saw a huge fire at the engineering workshop and boat building sheds of Porter & Haylett in Wroxham. The fire was noticed just after midnight from the other side of river, but nobody could get across to free the boats. The fire spread from the workshop to the boats, including two that were due to go to the London Boat Show the following week. Half the stores were also lost in the blaze, including paint and chandlery stores; two engines fought the blaze for three hours until it was under control.

1990 saw 60 firemen fighting a blaze on a cruise liner in Great Yarmouth. The 1,400-tonne cruiser was having its annual refurbishment when fire broke out in a laundry room at 1.20pm, possibly from a spark on a welder's torch. Nobody was hurt and firemen managed to contain the blaze, although the fire gutted the laundry room and there was smoke damage to the deck.

20 December

In 1770, on the second day of a storm, the 141-tonne sloop-of-war HMS *Peggy* was caught up in the gale and snow and was driven towards the shore. Although Captain Richard Toby gave orders to throw casks of beer and water overboard, cut away the mainmast and let the sheet anchor go, it was too late – the ship was grounded at Happisburgh and waves swept over the decks. It was another five hours before the villagers at Happisburgh were able to bring wagons to the beach and take the 59 surviving crew to shelter. Thirty-two of the crew died and were buried in Happisburgh Churchyard.

1960 saw flooding across West Norfolk, when 24 hours of rain coincided with a high tide. Lynn had 0.84in in a day, but Wells had nearly twice that much, at 1.55in. A bungalow in Dersingham was flooded to a depth of 18in.

1980 saw a Drayton couple having a narrow escape at Shotesham ford. Alan and Brenda Miller had dropped their daughter at a party in Woodton and were on their way to deliver Christmas presents when they reached the ford. Suddenly the water swept over the bonnet and the car corkscrewed down the swollen River Tas. Luckily the car became wedged as the water reached waist-height, and they were able to climb out to safety – and at that point the car sank up to its roof.

21 December

In 1487, according to the 18th-century historian Francis Blomefield, there was an earthquake in Norwich on 'St Thomas's Day'.

1862 saw major flooding along the coast. The sea broke over sandhills at Wells and flooded 700 acres of reclaimed land; damage was estimated at £10,000 (equivalent to nearly £650,000 in today's money). The gale lasted for three days, and on the final day the tide was the highest it had been for 26 years. The bank at Salthouse, which had had £1,000 spent on it (the equivalent of nearly £65,000 in today's money), had a breach nearly 100 yards long, and the road from Salthouse to Cley was flooded to a depth of 8ft. Water was 4ft deep in houses in Cley, and 400 acres of marshland were flooded.

1894 saw a major gale across the county. Great Yarmouth saw its worst flood since 1867; from Southtown to the North Quay the roads were 3ft deep in water, and the floods rose so rapidly that people couldn't prepare for them. Much damage was caused to contents of the the granaries in the quayside area. It was equally bad at Gorleston, where the slipway was blown out and marl was washed away from the quay, leaving huge holes 14ft square and 4ft deep – and water in the the William IV pub actually rose above the level of the bar. The Yare burst its bank, causing floods on the railways, and tracks between Reedham and Breydon were washed away. At Mundesley, there was the highest tide ever known, which ravaged the cliffs. Throughout the county, haystacks were damaged (particularly at Acle), trees came down, chimneys fell and tiles and slates were ripped from roofs. The *Norfolk Chronicle* reported that the 'passage in the narrower Norwich streets was dangerous due to tiles falling' – and a cab driver in London Street had a narrow escape when the chimney of Miss Langford's confectionery establishment smashed on to the road next to him. At South Walsham there was much damage to stacks and thatched houses, and at Attleborough Mr Arnup had a narrow escape when the back of his house was wrecked by a fallen tree. His wife had minor injuries.

22 December

In 1933 there was a disastrous fire at the Norwich shoemakers Barker & Ramsbottom in Pitt Street. The alarm was raised at 9pm and nearby residents had to leave their homes for safety. Neighbour Mr Ladbroke and his wife took their 10 children, aged between two and 13, to safety; Mr Ladbroke reported afterwards that 'the baby asked if it was Father Christmas'. The fire was under control by midnight, but the four-storey factory was gutted, at an estimated cost of several thousands of pounds, and 70 people were thrown out of work.

23 December

1909 saw a huge fire when Jewson's mills in Norwich caught light; it was thought at one point that the whole area from the mill to Wensum Street would burn down. The fire broke out at midnight, and due to tidal difficulties it was hard to get water from the river. Many spectators ended up with burns to their hands because of the sparks. However, the fire crew managed to contain the blaze and had it under control by 1.15am.

A year later saw the biggest fire ever known in Downham Market, when Augustus Pope's Clothing Factory and Army Surplus Stores near the Castle Hotel caught light. The owner of the hotel raised the alarm; horses were led to safety, two cars with full tanks of petrol were moved, and the straw from the stables was removed. Even so, the stables were damaged and the glass roof covering the yard was cracked. The window frames of the Wesleyan church were burned and the schoolroom was flooded. The roof of the clothing store fell in at 4.30am, and the building was still smouldering four and a half hours later. The *Downham Market Gazette* estimated the damage at thousands of pounds, and notes that even though the fire brigade didn't have proper equipment – such as helmets, Wellington boots or axes – they worked without complaint.

1977 saw gales across the county. The wind tore the roof off a bungalow at Snetterton, but the family were unhurt. Power lines were brought down and at one point 12,000 people were without electricity. The wind speed was measured at 80mph. The fair at Norwich was completely wrecked, including a shooting range worth £1,000 and a stall that had been in the family for 40 years. Many of the fairground stallholders simply packed up and went home.

24 December

According to the Elizabethan historian Henry Manship, in 1251 there was 'a great tempest throughout Norfolk and Suffolk, to the great wonder and astonishment of the people'. In 1739 there was also a huge gale; according to the 19th-century historian Charles Palmer, 16 ships were stranded between Great Yarmouth and Lowestoft, and sadly all the crews were lost.

Christmas Eve in 1830 was so cold that the rivers froze between Yarmouth and Norwich. The thermometer was still at zero degrees Fahrenheit on Boxing Day, but then it thawed rapidly until it was 48 degrees on New Year's Eve.

Six years later, there was a huge gale and snowstorm across the country, which left many roads impassable and drifts of up to 50ft. The snow in Norfolk was 10–12ft deep – the mail coach couldn't get through and one passenger actually walked 28 miles from Thwaite (where the coach was held up) to Norwich. When the thaw came, a couple of weeks later, there were major floods across the county.

1909 saw a huge fire in Great Yarmouth when the pavilion on the Britannia Pier caught light. Someone saw smoke coming out of the shops at 9am; the fire brigade arrived in minutes, but couldn't use sea water to fight the blaze as it would have blocked the pumps with sand. The fire was seen 20 miles out to sea, and black smoke drifted as far as Caister. Within half an hour of the smoke being seen, the pavilion was an inferno; the tower collapsed 30 minutes later, and the pier was gutted by 11am. People who'd walked on the pier beyond the pavilion were unable to return and had to be rescued by the Great Yarmouth lifeboat.

Fire struck again in 1926, this time in Tombland, Norwich; the previous evening, the caretaker had tidied up and all seemed well. Then, late in the evening, van driver Francis

Jolly saw a glow in the windows as he was passing and raised the alarm. There was dense smoke as far as Prince of Wales Road and London Street, and the fire brigade had been working on the building for a while when they had quite a shock – the caretaker Albert Kerrison, his wife and niece appeared. They had been asleep on the premises when Albert's wife smelled smoke and they left the building – amazingly, they had no idea that the fire brigade was even present! It seemed that the joists beneath a new fireplace in the solicitors' office had ignited; the office, including many documents, was gutted but the strong room had no damage. Afterwards, the police insisted that all city businesses should let them know if they had a caretaker on the premises overnight, in case of future fires. Albert and his family were lucky to escape unhurt.

1937 saw further subsidence in the Ber Street area of Norwich; a house in Flecked Bull Yard sank, and occupants of neighbouring houses were unable to shut doors and windows. There were cracks in the walls and pavements, and 21 families had to leave and find other accommodation. A builder demolishing Mr Waldrich's house said that seven old wells were discovered on the opposite side of the street during the last couple of months and were filled in, which may have affected the ground.

25 December

Christmas Day in 1281 saw a major cold snap; the 18th-century historian Blomefield says that bridges in Norwich were damaged by snow and frost.

According to the 19th-century historian P. Browne, the whole of Norwich felt an earthquake on Christmas Day 1601; the 19th-century historian William Richards dates it to 1602 and says the earthquake was felt at King's Lynn, but no damage was recorded.

There was a tragedy in 1766 at Ber Street, Norwich, when butcher Mr Ward's house burned down. Mrs Ward, her mother, two children, one grandchild and a maidservant were killed.

26 December

Boxing Day 1251 saw a 'very great tempest throughout all Norfolk and Suffolk', according to the 18th-century historian Blomefield.

27 December

1791 saw a high tide; the sea breached defences at Winterton, Horsey and Waxham, and threatened the marshes from there to Great Yarmouth.

There was a major gale in 1849 – combined with heavy snow and a high tide, it virtually cut Norwich off. The trains to London were delayed by snowdrifts, and the railway between Norwich and Great Yarmouth was under water.

1897 saw a major fire at King's Lynn which resulted in 13 businesses being destroyed and £150,000 of damage (equivalent to nearly £11.7 million in today's money) was caused. The fire started at 7am in the draper's shop of Jermyn & Perry. The shop lad, Benton, went to start his usual task of 'sweeping out'; it was dark, so he used a wax taper to light the gas. Either the match or the taper came into contact with flammable stuff, and according to *The Times* the fire spread 'at an alarming rate'. There was plenty of water available to fight the flames, but the firemen's steamer broke down. Within an hour, 1,500 square yards of the shop, including its contents, had been destroyed. Also gutted were the shops of Jermyn & Sons, furnishers; Mr Trenowarth, butcher; Messrs Lipton, provision merchants; Mr Howard, confectioner; Mr Taylor, stationer; and Messrs Eastman & Co, butchers. Then the flames crossed Union Lane and destroyed the shops of Mr F.W. Count, chemist; Mrs Pegg, milliner; Mr B. Curson, clothier; and Messrs Cash and co, boot manufacturers. The firemen couldn't check the fire until it had reached Messrs Kendrick and son, boot manufacturers – but the flames still did much damage to Kendrick's. Other shops suffered damage by water; three cottages were destroyed, and one fireman was so seriously injured that he was taken to hospital. By painful coincidence, there had been a fire in the same area in 1884, and a similar thing happened – the fire engine broke down then, too.

1925 saw another storm – and the Cromer lifeboat was directed to rescues by a Norwich wireless operator, Mr Newby. He picked up a morse code message saying that a boat, the SS *Gleneden*, was stuck at Winterton Ledge. The other boats in the area were already out on rescues so the Cromer lifeboat launched; the crew struggled with the gale until they had a message from Mr Newby saying that the ship had managed to float itself again. But on the return journey the lifeboat men saw distress signals – it was the South Noll lightship, whose cable had snapped so it was drifting helplessly, a danger to shipping. The Cromer lifeboat men managed to save the day.

1929 saw major floods around Norwich. The Yare valley was flooded from Trowse to Cringleford, and the Wensum valley around Costessey was several feet deep in water. The *Eastern Daily Press* described the sluice at Costessey mill as a 'foaming cataract'.

1968 saw a huge fire in the warehouse of Conran furniture makers in Thetford, causing £180–200,000 damage. The building was a write-off, as were raw materials and finished stock. Slates burst off the roof, narrowly missing passengers who were heading for the station, and the blaze was visible from the whole town.

28 December

According to the 18th-century historian Blomefield, there was an earthquake in 1480 which damaged many buildings in Norwich and Norfolk.

29 December

1930 saw a major fire in the boot factory of Adcock and Mitchell in Rose Yard, Norwich. Just after the factory closed for lunch, at 1pm, the fire broke out; an hour later, the roof fell in, and the premises were gutted by 3pm. The fire brigade managed to contain the fire so it didn't spread to a row of cottages next door, or to the silk factory of Fras. Hinde & Hardy Ltd., which contained much flammable material.

31 December

In 1287 there was a storm surge which caused major flooding in Hickling and the coast. The monastic chronicler John of Oxnead describes the flooding at Hickling and Horsey Gap as 'parts which no age in past times had recorded to have been covered by water'. The chroniclers Holinshed and Matthew of Westminster added that after heavy rain 'on the Feast of the Circumcision of our lord', the sea flowed over the land 'three or four leagues in breadth' from Yarmouth to the Humber and drowned cattle and knocked over buildings.

The *Norwich Remembrancer* remarks that 1734 saw the worst flood in Norwich since 1696 (the 'St Faith's flood').

Bibliography

A true report of certaine wonderfull overflowings of waters 1607 (no ISBN or author).

Baker, T.H. *Records of the Seasons, Prices of Agricultural Produce and Phenomena observed in the British Isles* Simpkins, Marshall & Co., London (no ISBN or date but approximately 1883).

Bayne, A.D. *A Comprehensive History of Norwich* Jarrold, 1869 (no ISBN).

Blomefield, Francis (and continued by Charles Parkin) *An Essay towards a Topographical History of the County of Norfolk* 11 volumes, 2nd edition 1807.

Browne, P. *The History of Norwich* Bacon, Kinnebrook & Co., 1813 (no ISBN).

Edghill, Jamie and Keith Entwistle *Cromer Fire Brigade 1881–2006* Poppyland, 2006, ISBN 0946148813.

Garner, Mary and John Wilson (eds) *Wymondham: History of a Market Town* Wymondham Heritage Society, 2006, ISBN 1901553035.

Leach, Nicholas and Paul Russell *Wells-Next-the-Sea Lifeboats* Tempus, 2006, ISBN 0752438751.

Mackerell, Benjamin *The history and antiquities of the flourishing corporation of King's Lynn in the county of Norfolk* 1738 (no ISBN).

Matchett, J. (ed.) *The Norfolk and Norwich Remembrancer and Vade-mecum* 1821 (no ISBN).

Norton, Ben *The Story of East Dereham* Phillimore, 1994, ISBN 0850339081.

Palmer, Charles John (ed.) *The History of Great Yarmouth by Henry Manship, Town Clerk, temp. Queen Elizabeth* Great Yarmouth, 1854.

Richards, William *The history of Lynn, civil, ecclesiastical, political, commercial, biographical, municipal, and military, from the earliest accounts to the present time* 1812.

Rye, Walter *Cromer, Past and Present* Jarrold & Sons, 1889 (no ISBN).

Savin, Alfred Collison *Cromer, a Modern History* Holt, 1937 (no ISBN).

Sayer, M.J. *Reepham's Three Churches* 1972 (pamphlet, no ISBN).

Archived issues of:
Downham Market Gazette
Eastern Daily Press
Norfolk Chronicle and Norwich Gazette
Norwich Mercury
The Times